Some Trails Never End

A creative non-fiction novel
By
Terrie Biggs

Blue Mountain Publishing
1105 N Avenue, La Grande, OR

Copyright © 2007 Terrie Biggs

(as *Earth, Wind & Fire*)

All rights reserved.

First printing October 20, 2014
Updates: November 24, 2014, September 27, 2016, December 19, 2018, April 10, 2020, September 10, 2021, December 2022 (revised Native American narrative from first-person to third-person)

Cover by Daniel Biggs
Http://www.DanielBiggsPhotography.com

ISBN: 10-149369989X
ISBN 13: 9781493699896

Table of Contents

Table of Contents..iii
Epiphany & Apology vii
Special Thanks viii
Introduction x
Map of the Route and Location of Missions and Forts....... 1
EARTH... 2
Stories of Tribal Life 3
The Season of the Valley of Peace 10
Sacred Waters & Fishing Grounds 17
The Noble People 23
The First Encounters with White Men............................... 27
WIND 37
The Call for Missionaries 38
The Proposal 47
Return from the Rendezvous... 54
The Spaldings Join the Mission Party 70
The Wedding 78
Journey to the Rendezvous.. 84
The Rocky Mountains to the Blues 94
The Arrival... 110
A New Life at Waiilatpu... 127
The First White Child in Oregon 130
Marcus & Stickus Meet.. 133
Civilizing, Evangelizing, & Doctoring 134

A Visit to Lapwai	139
Madame Dorion	141
Don't Bet on a Full House	149
Reinforcements Cause More Problems	155
A Tiny Angel	158
More Friends Lost	165
A Safe Haven	168
Signs of Trouble	174
Demand for Payment	178
Narcissa's Frightening Night	185
Two Cultures Conflict	191
Dr. White, a "Notorious Blockhead"	196
The High Chief	202
A Year's Absence	204
Family Visits	210
The Oregon Trail Established	212
Marcus Returns Home	215
FIRE	218
Introduction of the Sager Family	219
We're on Our Way	221
Seven Alone	227
Mother & Father	231
Our New Life	236
Legal Guardian	240
Good Times	247
Ominous Signs	249

Journey on the Oregon Trail 256
Lorinda & Crocket Stay at the Mission 267
Knocking at Death's Door 270
Father and the Catholics 272
Council of Death 275
The Tension Mounts 279
Accused of Poisoning 280
The Attack 282
Not Over Yet 294
A Few Escape 297
Henry Eludes Death 300
Life in Captivity 305
Five Crows Took Me for His Wife 311
Council at Saint Anne's 316
Peter Skene Ogden, the Negotiator 318
Christmas Pie 321
I am Free 324
Journey from Captivity 326
Alone Again 331
RETURN TO EARTH 336
War & the Militia 337
Hanged by the Neck 341
Life's Circle 346
REFERENCES 347
Significant People 347
Significant Places 353

People at the Mission When Attacked.................................355
Timeline..357
Bibliography & Reference Sources...358
Internet & Miscellaneous Sources...360
About the author 361
Other Books by Terrie 362

Epiphany & Apology

It hit me like a punch in the gut when I finally realized how offensive it was to the Umatilla tribes that I wrote many chapters about Istukus (Stickus) in first-person narrative. Bobbi (Roberta) Conner at Tamastslikt Cultural Institute in Pendleton had graciously allowed me to do research at the cultural center's archives. However, she turned down carrying this book at the cultural center because I, a current day white woman, wrote about a Cayuse/Nez Perce man in first-person. Recently I began reading <u>This is the Fire</u> by Don Lemon. He explained how reprehensible it has been for decades, primarily in movies, for white people to represent other ethnic groups. The light went on, and I realized my audacity of thinking I could "talk" as a Native American man. Blacks, Asians, Latinos, and Native Americans should and could speak their truths for themselves.

Therefore, I apologize for being so resistant to Bobbi's wise advice that I ignored.

I initially used Istukus' voice to describe the daily lives, culture, and some history of the Nez Perce and Cayuse, which I gathered from years of research. His involvement with the Whitmans was documented as authentic encounters in my sources. Was it Istukus' version? Probably not.

I present a revision of my book and humbly apologize for my ignorance and insensitivity.

Special Thanks

My first thank you goes to my son David for introducing me to this story, and second to Kevin Costner, who unknowingly inspired me to continue to research to provide all the tools he might need for a movie. I thank and love my friend Bettie Rector who encouraged me and accompanied me to Walla Walla and the mission and who is now lost to me as a friend due to brain damage who died too soon with dementia. Dan, my husband, has listened endlessly to my rambling about many of the tales I discovered. I am so grateful to Phillip Hunt, who generously allowed me to have a copy of his private family manuscript about Lorinda Bewley, which helped me complete the story.

My appreciation and admiration go to Clifford M. Drury for researching and producing two volumes called <u>Marcus and Narcissa Whitman and the Opening of the Old Oregon.</u> I turned to his vast knowledge and years of research in his volumes when I had questions. I used his books as my primary source of reference.

Narcissa Whitman contributed significantly through her incredible letters to her family, which they presented in the book, <u>The Letters of Narcissa Whitman.</u> Author Robert Lansing also contributed through his excellent work covering the trial in his novel <u>Juggernaut</u>.

To my neighbor/editor Mike Shearer, who aided me in punctuation and sentence structure I offer my appreciation.

Larry (Lawrence L.) Dodd, now retired from the Whitman College Library archives, was kind to me and my friend, Bettie, when we visited the archives at Whitman College in Walla Walla, Washington. I was able to photocopy newspaper articles from the Sager family's scrapbook. He was surprised that I knew that the Sager women had produced a quilt, presumably from Narcissa's dresses. Larry showed us this delicate quilt, but it was apparent that it could not have been made from her dresses, as evident from her history.

Thank you to my talented son, Daniel, who created beautiful covers for this book and others I have published.

And finally, and with my deepest love and appreciation, my dear friend Kathy Boyne rescued my book by taking the proof I sent her and editing, correcting, and making suggestions to the first proof and then again to the second one. I will be forever grateful for her expertise, honest input, and advice.

Terrie Biggs

Introduction

My initial introduction to this compelling true story began when my son David returned from a fifth-grade field trip to the Whitman Mission near Walla Walla, Washington. He was so captivated by the history that we went back as a family the following weekend. I bought a book, <u>Lorinda Bewley and the Whitman Massacre</u>, by Myra Sager Helm, which aroused my initial curiosity and began my discovery of the stories surrounding the Whitmans. At that time, I worked for the La Grande Police Department in Oregon, and we were hosting the first Oregon Chiefs of Police Association annual meeting. We invited the police chiefs' wives. I had purchased the book and wasn't aware that it was a romanticized version of a relationship between a young white woman living at the Whitman Mission and a Cayuse Chief.

  I turned the story into a reader-theater presentation to entertain the wives. Four of us, including a dispatcher, an officer, my husband, and I read our parts to tell this story. We also repeated it for the 150th celebration of the Oregon Trail, held at our local Riverside Park. Only four people attended, including a descendant of Myra Sager Helm by marriage, who wrote the book. I don't think he, Carl Helm, was impressed.

  I had a vision that Kevin Costner would do this story on the big screen after the dignity he gave Native Americans in *Dances with Wolves*. That inspired me to research more of the history and people surrounding the Whitman Mission to provide Costner with a synopsis and the tools to do the screenplay. The more I researched, the more trails I followed, discovering more realistic versions. I felt the Whitman Mission saga involved several chronicles. I studied the history and culture of the local Native Americans. I was fascinated by the Whitmans' and Spaldings' journey to Oregon's "country." Next, the tale of the Sager family and seven orphans brought to the mission was compelling and tragic; their experiences needed to be part of my book. I explored a more factual story of Lorinda Bewley and Chief Five Crows versus the romanticized version that I originally read. The rescue and aftermath of the killings at the mission were necessary. I added the men who surrendered and details of the sham of their trial. I had read many books, Narcissa's diary and letters, and historical documents, but none had combined the story from what I considered the beginning to the end. However, some trails never end. I walked in the footprints and discovered where they led and the mark they left in the past and present day.

Photo by Terrie Biggs of the quilt sewn by
the surviving Sager sisters

My goal was to make the book as factual as possible, and in doing so, I updated language and phrases from Narcissa and Marcus Whitman, and others. I left the words "heathen" and "savages" used in letters and other forms of communication to be true to the times, even though it makes me uncomfortable. I enjoyed writing about the Sager children in first-person because it felt as though I was right there, living through and telling the experiences.

I have incorporated music written by the members of the Trail Band, formed by Marv Ross in 1991, with the vision that if this story makes it to the "big screen," their music should be considered. They performed all over the Northwest, and their music embodies the hardships and sacrifices of people on the Oregon Trail.

The Band's website is http://www.trailband.com

Some Trails Never End

Map of the Route and Location of Missions and Forts

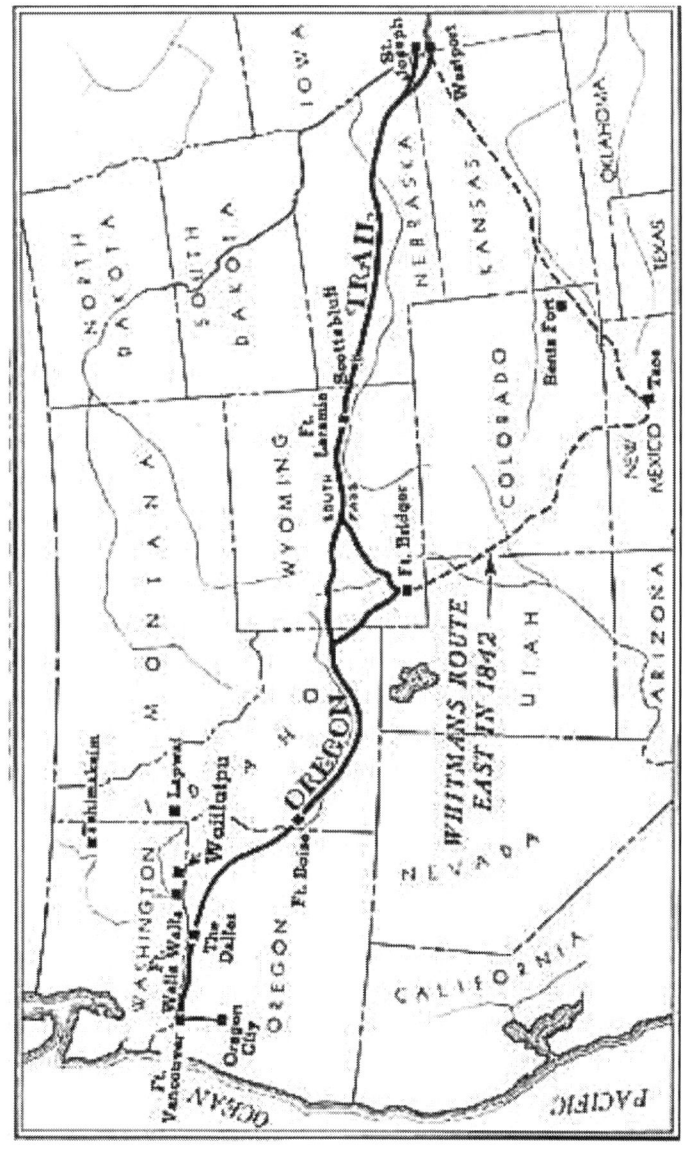

Terrie Biggs

They are like the EARTH

Istukus, half Nez Perce and half Cayuse, is the subject of tribal history and daily life.

"The earth was created by help from the sun and was made without lines of demarcation, and it is no man's business to divide it. The earth and myself are of one mind. The measure of the land and the measure of our bodies are the same.

Understand me fully with reference to my affection for the land. I never said the land was mine to do with as I choose. The one who has the right to dispose of it is the one who has created it. I claim a right to live on this land, and I accord you the privilege to live on it also."

Nez Perce Chief Joseph

Stories of Tribal Life

Cayuse mat lodge up to 200 feet long, housing many families

Istukus was half Cayuse and half Nez Perce. The white traders spoke his name as "Stickus." He came into this world at a time to witness catastrophic, irreversible changes for his people. His father was Cayuse, and his mother Nez Perce. When she was sixteen, his father brought his new wife and her parents to his Cayuse village overlooking the Great River, named the Columbia by white men. His mother gave birth to him, a younger brother, and a sister. His mother's father and mother lived in their lodge. Both were very wise, and each shared different stories, as they did not have a written language.

Behind every living thing is a story. Every storytelling is an occasion for learning. The oral traditions offered them guidance and a proper understanding of their world from childhood to adult life, teaching life principles, ecology, and survival. Each night the elders filled them with stories of their culture and bravery. He especially loved the stories of Coyote, the trickster.

His very wise grandmother told the children, "Since time began, we made a promise to take care of the land. The Earth Mother provides food. Her water provides our most precious resource--salmon. Our people, the Cayuse, sprang from Coyote blood. Coyote must not be harmed, for he was Creator; neither must camp dogs be harmed, because of their relationship with Coyote.

"There is a soul in all living things: people, animals, plants, and forces of nature. The presence of life implies intelligence, will, and consciousness. All living beings must respect one another. We live in harmony with nature. We have the ability to communicate with animals. Animals give us the answers.

"My children, you must ask the assistance of your spiritual powers. Listen to the wind. Listen to the water. Listen to the rain. They will guide you and sing songs to you and keep you from being lonely if you are ever lost and alone."

They said that "Earth Mother" raised the children, and their elders imparted wisdom. The male children were kept with the women for the first twelve years to learn patience and gentleness. The women nurtured the children and taught lessons and oral history. Girls were taught to clean and tan the animal hides and sew clothing decorated with delicate beadwork. The girls learned to forage for berries and edible offerings from the earth, clean and dry fish, and meat. The men taught bow making, hunting, and how to be cunning warriors.

"Tell us another story, Grandfather," the children pleaded. It had been a warm summer day, and their bellies were full of fresh salmon, gooseberries, wild celery, and a delicious root they baked called camas. The longhouse they called their lodge was too hot with all the families who stayed there, so as night approached, they sat council-style outside. The stars were so bright and close that Istukus felt that he could reach up and pluck one out of the sky. Still smelling the sweet aroma of camas, a fire flickered in the middle of their circle.

"Grandfather, tell us again how our people were gifted with horses," Istukus asked. The discovery of the horse had been a pivotal event in their tribal history that greatly enhanced their mobility. The storytelling of the event had been passed down from generation to generation since about 1730.

As the firelight danced across his lined face, his grandfather smiled, gave a big sigh, and began his favorite tale:

> We were on foot, and our hunting grounds were quite limited. Northern Shoshones from the Snake region were camped on the Malheur River, a tributary of the Snake River. They are our enemies, weak and unworthy people. A war party of our brave and noble Cayuse and our neighbors, the Umatilla, were preparing to attack the Shoshones. Chief Ococtuin sent scouts to spy on them. Our scouts peered over the bluffs with

much cleverness and cunning, like Coyote. "Oh, Great Spirit," one scout whispered in amazement to the others, "Our enemies are riding on elk!" The scouts inched closer, dumbfounded.

After the Shoshone braves had ridden away on top of these "elk," our scouts descended the bluffs to survey the prints. "The imprints are not split but solid and round. Look at the size of this beast! It is larger than an elk! We must find out about this strange animal that is able to carry a man on his back." When the scouts returned, they reported this story to Chief Ococtuin and mimicked the men who rode on the back of elks.

The children all rolled over with laughter at the thought of the "elk" being ridden. Then his grandfather continued:

Chief Ococtuin wisely decided, "We will not attack. We will make a truce with the Shoshones. We must find out about this new creature of the Creator." His curious mind was full of possibilities.

The war party advanced in peace the next day, and the Shoshone chief welcomed them into their camp.

"These animals are called horses. Men called Spaniards brought them from far across a great ocean in the east. We traded for them with tribes to the south, along the great ocean of the Pacific," the Shoshone chief explained.

The Shoshone men demonstrated how to ride, pack, and carry firewood and lodge poles.

They, of course, could never be an expert in the riding and breeding of horses as we Cayuse.

The grandfather paused to allow all the people around him to nod and say yes in agreement with their superiority. He continued:

"I wish to trade for two horses," said Chief Ococtuin. "What is your price?"
By the end of the day, our men laid down all their possessions in a pile until the Shoshone chief said, "I see that you have nothing else to give. We will have pity on you, even though you have been our enemy. You may have a mare and a stallion in goodwill and friendship."
Destitute but excited and pleased, Chief Ococtuin returned home with his prizes.
The following spring, the mare foaled. Cayuse are wise and strong. We knew the Shoshone were weak and beneath the Superior Ones, so we sent another party. This time we raided their camp and stole horses from them! It was easier and smarter for us to increase our herds by stealing than by years of breeding.

The boys laughed and danced around the fire in their people's joyful pride and cunning.
Cayuse became formidable horseback riders. The horse strengthened their warring and raiding skills and quickly adapted to maneuvering the elk and deer on hunts, a task they previously performed on foot. Horses were excellent pack animals, carrying up to three hundred pounds of gear and supplies, such as lodge

mats and robes. They stood twelve to fifteen hands high. Sure-footed and able to withstand hunger and rough treatment, their speed and endurance were exceptional. When they were adults, Istukus' cousin Five Crows at Umatilla owned two thousand horses for recreation, travel, and trading purposes. All Cayuse were superb horsemen and owned many horses.

They met the Shoshone on more even terms, resulting in intensified hostilities between the tribes. They could break out of their limited homeland to hunt buffalo on the plains and go to the great Rendezvous. They went northward to the Columbia River and drove away any tribes standing in their path. Cayuse dominated the bands, which occupied a twenty-mile belt along the Columbia. They continued to push east before 1800, squeezing other enemy tribes farther away.

In the early 1800s, they shared common ground with their friends, the Nez Perce. They crossed the Blue Mountains and descended into the valley of the Grande Ronde during the spring, leaving the lush Walla Walla Valley at the end of the winter. Since they were the first tribe north of the Shoshone peoples to have horses in large numbers, they supplied them to the Nez Perce and the Salishan people farther north. The Nez Perce often goaded them with good humor, saying they had become more proficient than the Cayuse in the selective breeding of horses, even castrating their stallions to make them calmer and quieter.

Cayuse preferred white horses, and mottled black and white were their second choice. They decorated the animals' necks with streams of red and yellow paint and feathers and painted their tails black and red, which they clubbed in a knot and tied short. They decorated the horses' heads and tails with ribbons as trade increased. They mimicked the earth's colors by painting and decorating their horses as they did themselves, creating an illusion of physical union between man and horse to match their harmony. This union was most apparent in battle. As expert riders, they were able to throw themselves to the right side of their horse and the next moment to the left side of the horse, twisting and bending their bodies in a thousand different ways. The horses appeared to be riderless as they dodged or evaded enemies.

      The Cayuse people reached a position of dominance among the various tribes. They were aware of the marvelous goods ranging from beads to blankets that the white men brought to trade. These goods were an excellent means of displaying wealth and superiority. Now they had something to offer in trade--horses.

The Season of the Valley of Peace

Moving their lodges from place to place with the seasons was part of their way of life. Lodges glowed with ten fires of their family and friends. They camped every year in the valley of the Grande Ronde. Many tribes came together to fish, hunt for elk and deer in the surrounding mountains, compete in games, and share stories. Never had a battle been fought between tribes in this valley. The tribes always called it the Valley of Peace. It was Istukus' favorite place as they moved with the seasons. His people had come there for eleven centuries. It was a huge valley entirely encircled by mountains full of pines, tamarack, fir, berries, and rich with game.

The floor of the Valley of the Grande Ronde was marshy in places, with cattails and tall reeds waving a welcome to their band. It was rich with high grasses, golden by the summer's heat. Tall shady cottonwood trees were swaying in the wind, and how the wind could blow at times in this valley! He recalled once when the mighty wind pinned his brother, who was the size of a full-grown beaver, against the lodge as he hollered for their mother.

The women gathered the reeds and willows for fishnets, baskets, bags, and mats. The river snaked and twisted through the valley ending up in Nez Perce camps over the mountain range to the east. The river gifted them with brook trout, steelhead, salmon, and fresh-water clams. The marshes offered ducks, geese, and camas, his favorite food besides salmon.

Istukus' mother gathered a plentiful supply of berries she had dried on mats in the sun for winter. When it was cooler, she dried them before slow-burning fires. Children collected huckleberries, gooseberries, wild currants, serviceberries (the fruit of the service tree), pine nuts, wild carrots, onions, and black mushrooms shaped like miniature pine trees called morels. His mother, aunts, and sister butchered and dried eight mule deer, an elk, dozens of ducks, grouse, seven geese, and two swans that the earth offered to them. His father said the snow season would be mild and that this should be enough for their family to winter on.

"Help me, my son. I need water from the river, holes dug for cooking, and firewood," Istukus' mother ordered him one day.

He stood up straight with his arms folded in front of him, his feet firmly planted on the ground, and he declared, "I am a Cayuse warrior. I do not carry water. I do not dig for camas. I do not carry firewood. I do not take down the lodge. That is woman's work."

His father did not share his vision of his manhood. At eleven years old, his father threatened him with the Whip Man for his disrespect to his mother. The Whip Man scared the children. He would come from another village and whip them on their backs when misbehaving.

"Istukus, go hide. The Whip Man is coming," his grandmother warned him a week later. He did, and the dreaded man did not find him--that time.

Successful hunting ensured the survival of each family. Each family needed the fresh meat of one buffalo from the plains, equal to seven or eight deer and four or five elk. They needed twenty to thirty hides from elk and deer for clothing, patching lodges, and buffalo hides for sleeping robes. They made food containers, war armor, and shields from animal hides. Hides were used to make lodges, and they were quiet in the wind, unlike the canvas that the traders offered them in later years, which rustled and flapped in the breeze and were thunderous in the strong winds. Women fashioned shirts from hides of elk, deer, mountain goats, and bighorn sheep. Usually, the women made their dresses from soft deer hides. His mother saved every scrap from the large animals, including the horns and antlers used for tools. They wasted nothing.

The Cayuse had great hunters in their band. Patience was the virtue a good hunter must learn. Making a bow the old way took up to five years. Finding the right limb and hanging it to dry was an art form. Expert hands slowly turned obsidian into arrowheads after hours of chipping and flaking. A hunter needed to get within a stone's throw to get to his animal for, hopefully, the animal's quick death with an arrow through the heart. After hours of waiting, crawling, and hiding, hunters were rewarded by offering their children and elders fresh meat. Impatience brought no rewards.

Istukus' father had taken him with the men to hunt when he was twelve years old. His first attempt throwing the spear at game brought a big laugh. His father said he was very brave and cunning, like the Coyote, to get close to the deer without her smelling him. When he threw the spear, he was shaking so much that it ricocheted off the trunk of a tamarack and bounced back at him, landing at his feet. The second attempt wounded a mule deer buck, and his uncle relieved the deer of his suffering. His father taught him to honor the animals who sacrificed themselves for their family. They gave thanks to the plentiful Earth Mother, who blessed them with abundance. The deer and elk that grazed on green grasses provided sweet and tender meat.

What a feast they had in celebration of Istukus's first hunt! His mother and sisters cooked his favorite treat, camas, which were plentiful in the valley of the Grande Ronde. His mother was the best camas digger. With her hardwood crutch-handled digging stick, she would gather two full sacks in a half day.

"These camas bags are your weight, son. However, camas taste sweeter than you. You taste like bitterroot because you think you are a man. Next season, you will grow into manhood," she teased.

He dug a hole in the ground for his mother. She threw in stones and heated them until they were red hot. She covered the rocks with green grass, placed the camas bulbs upon the grass, and covered the hole with earth. Camas are black when it is cooked and tastes like figs. Sometimes she would make bread with it or flavor it with huckleberries.

The band headed towards the setting sun over the majestic Blue Mountains to their salmon fishing grounds at summer's end. On the trip back to their winter village on the Eu-o-tal-la, now called the Umatilla River, his mother softened the deer hide over the saddle horn and used that piece for a shirt for her son in honor of his first hunting and fishing season. His aunt, whose Spirit Source guided her to be a medicine woman, took side trips in remote areas on their journey back to winter camp for herbs and medicinal plants.

Istukus had his spirit quest when he was fourteen years old in the Grande Ronde Valley, located near present day La Grande, Oregon. It was his third year hunting for elk and deer. His father and the elders taught him a great lesson about bragging about his hunting when Istukus told them that if he came across a bear, he would wrestle him and take him to the ground. While on that hunting trip, Istukus was separated from the men and came across a bear. The bear was right in front of him, stood on his hind legs, and wrestled, taking *him* to the ground. Then he released the boy and let him go. The elders said the bear let him live because he was his spirit guide, and the bear was there to teach him not to brag because the animals could hear him.

In the valley's river, the steelhead trout were sometimes the length of a man's arm, beaten and bruised from their trip from the great ocean of the Pacific. They also caught fresh-water clams and rainbow trout. His father and the elders showed Istukus how to fish the river of the Grande Ronde. The river in the valley was small, which made catching the steelhead manageable.

The men gathered and waded in a line upriver, funneling the fish through rock dams. Some used spears, and others used nets. They placed rocks close to the banks of the small streams to narrow the channel. They speared the steelhead and used a dip net that his mother made from wild hemp. The men set traps in calm water stretches, and dip nets were used at rapids and deeper pools.

Catching fish was a grander project on the Columbia River. They would dry salmon there for long-term storage. His father taught him how to fish on that life-sustaining river that spring, and his father said he could go to Celilo Falls with him.

But in this valley, they ate fish fresh, and every member shared in the bounty — the sick, the elderly, even some who were lazy. His grandfather told him, "You must eat the eyes so you can see better." The head and eyes were his favorite.

"Go take your bath, Istukus," his mother ordered each morning. It did not matter where they were or if there was ice on the river. "This will toughen you and prepare you for hard times. It will make you strong." The boy loved to protest, but he loved it more to dry himself in the summer sun lying on the grass or the rocks by the river.

Life was simple, abundant, and as predictable as the rising sun. Their day-to-day activities were dictated by the changing seasons. They greeted spring in a ceremony as the plants and migrating salmon appeared. In summer, they traveled and traded with their brothers: the Nez Perce, Palouse, Walla Walla, Yakima, and other regional tribes. Later in the year, they moved to the high mountains to pick berries and hunt deer and elk. As the days shortened, they returned to the lowlands in anticipation of the winter.

Umatilla was in the Columbia plateau. Their nation of people was diverse. Cayuse, for instance, boasted that they were brave and mighty warriors; their neighbors, the Nez Perce, were considered more peace-loving. Istukus's mother's heritage gave him a gentler side than some of his Cayuse brothers. Associations and intermarriages with the Nez Perce were a good match. The Walla Walla and Shoshone were considered inferior to the Cayuse, and they raided Shoshone camps and took them for their slaves. Interactions were governed by food gathering, kinship with inter-tribal marriages, ceremony, trade, and sometimes warfare.

The principle of *na'ymu* or kinship governed Cayuse society. It provided community structure. It defined the roles and responsibilities of gender and all age groups. Men, women, and children were valued equally as contributors to the success of their village. They lived their lives in their culture, religion, and society for the beauty and preservation of life and the "Earth Spirit."

His father said, "The sacred foods strengthen our bodies and renew our spiritual belief in our maker, the Great Spirit, and all he has created for us." He was a good and wise man.

Their winter village at the Umatilla was not far from Waiilatpu, the Place of the Rye Grass, a favorite camping ground of their great Chief Umtippe. That is where his white friends lived, Dr. Marcus Whitman and his wife. Whitman had saved his life, and they were friends for eleven years until one day, a series of unfortunate events led to a tragic climax, and his people, the mighty Cayuse, were reduced to a handful.

Sacred Waters & Fishing Grounds

People of the Pacific Northwest tribes have always treated water as medicine because it nourishes the earth's life, flushing poisons out of humans, other creatures, and the land. The people of the tribes knew that to be productive, water must be kept pure. When water is kept cold and clean, it takes care of the salmon. For hundreds of years, their people have known how to care for the water.

Istukus' band fished nearly year-round in rivers and streams, catching Chinook salmon, sockeye salmon, Coho salmon, steelhead, cutthroat trout, whitefish, sturgeon, lamprey, chisel mouth, squawfish, and suckers. They used hooks and lines, spears, harpoons, dip nets, traps, and weirs. His father and the men set up basket traps in stone weirs in streams for the smaller species. They ate these fish fresh since they were too small to dry and store. Salmon and steelhead were their greatest gifts from the waters. These would be dried to feed them through the winter. Sometimes they used the dried fish for trade as far away as the Rendezvous in Montana country.

Istukus' Nez Perce cousins told him of an explorer, David Thompson, and ten of his men who arrived at one of their sacred fishing places in 1811. Their people referred to it as *Tum-tum*, the name they gave great waterfalls. White men called it Kettle

Falls because the water dug out circles in the rocks as smooth as the inner surface of their cast-iron kettles. These were the highest falls on the Great River, now called the Columbia River, whose width is about a thousand yards. They fished there with baskets made of wicker supported by long poles. When the fish tried to jump the falling water, they would strike the broad frame and fall into the baskets. Thompson saw many local people fishing there because the salmon were concentrated in that section. He said, "A man might almost cross the river upon the backs of the salmon."

The chief in charge of fishing told him, "You must respect the salmon. Your men must keep the shores clean. Do not throw anything into the water. By doing this, the salmon would continue to offer themselves in great numbers."

Thompson did not heed the chief's warning. His men dumped some horse bones into the water. All the salmon fled, and no more were caught that day. Thompson had his men remove the bones, and the salmon returned.

Another great waterfall, Celilo Falls, had been the cultural hub of the Pacific Northwest for over a thousand years. Here they fished, traded, feasted, and renewed friendships. Istukus was stunned the first time he saw the falls. He could hear the continuous, thunderous roar of these sacred falls from miles away and had to yell to be heard when he stood near its beautiful mist. He could smell the fish before he could see the falls, and after they arrived, the odor of salmon lingered in their hair, hands, and clothes.

Lodges lined the banks of the Great River for four months during the salmon run. Bands from the Northwest came in peace. The first salmon caught was the harbinger of good news. The tribes knew the fish would come in about five days. The first fish was part of their First Fish Ceremony, a feast they called *ka-oo-yit*. They honored and gave thanks to earth's bounty. The first fish was divided into small pieces and given to each child in the village to hasten the arrival of the salmon and ensure that the salmon would return next season.

Some fishermen built scaffolding, while others fished from giant rocks. Nets, weighing over one hundred pounds, were laid out to catch the precious salmon. Fishing there could be dangerous. If a man fell into the river, they knew he would not return because the raging water would swallow him forever, so most men used safety lines. However, one old man called Water Ouzel, defied the odds. He was named after a small water bird that swims under the water to catch its food. This old fellow caught his salmon in a dip net where there was hardly room to pull it out. He would not tie himself with a safety rope. Young Istukus saw him catch a huge salmon, and it pulled him into the river and the boiling white water. He put his hands over his eyes, knowing the Water Ouzel would go to the spirit world.

"Keep watching, Istukus," the other men reassured him. "Soon, he will pop out of the water."

Indeed, his head popped up in a short time, and he was still holding the netted salmon. He looked unconscious but then jerked his head from side to side and swam to shore with his prize. Several men ran over as he spat out water. They asked, "How are you doing? Are you all alright? Can I get you anything?"

"Water, I need water!" he gulped, and everyone laughed at his sense of humor. The men told Istukus that he got pulled in all the time and still wouldn't tie himself to a safety line.

Bones and fish heads covered the ground around the falls, and he had to hold his nose the first day until he got accustomed to the smell. He recognized the stench as a blessing to his people, and somehow it smelled sweeter. The women pounded the fish and set them to dry on large platforms. He watched them hammer the dried fish between two stones, and they pressed them tightly into packages that weighed the same as he did that twelfth year of his life. They covered the bundles with matting and wrapped cording around them to haul them to the storehouses where customers came to buy or trade.

This magnificent, abundant river was their Life Force. It had nourished his people for thousands of years and provided life-giving water. The falls were sacred and treasured by many bands. The first night visiting the falls, the air had cooled the earth from the heat of the day, and his grandmother began her story around the open fire:

> Coyote was walking up the river on a hot day, and he decided to cool himself in the water. He floated downriver to where maidens had made a fish dam, which kept the fish from going up the river. Coyote saw a maiden and disguised himself as a baby, floating down the river on a raft in a cradleboard, all laced up. He cried like a baby, and maidens ran over to save the child from drowning. The eldest maiden gasped with delight, "Oh, what a cute baby."
>
> The youngest maiden retorted, "That's no baby. He is Coyote."
>
> The others scolded, "Stop saying that. You will hurt the baby's feelings."
>
> They took the baby home and cared for and fed him. He grew very fast. When he asked for some water, they said to him, "You go get it

yourself, you are big enough now." He then began to crawl, but when he was out of sight, he ran to the river.

One sister noticed, "He certainly can move fast. He is out of sight already."

"That is because he is Coyote," said the youngest.

When Coyote got to the fish dam, he tore it down, pulling out the stones so that all the water rushed free. Then he crawled up on the rocks and shouted gleefully, "Mothers, your fish dam has been broken!"

The sisters ran down and saw that it was true. The youngest maiden repeated, "I told you he was Coyote."

Coyote said, "You have kept all the people from having salmon for a long time by stopping the fish from going upstream. Now people will be happy because they will get salmon. The salmon will now be able to go upriver and spawn."

This is how Celilo Falls came to be. Because Coyote tore down the fish dam, salmon are now able to go upriver to spawn on the upper reaches of the Great River and its tributaries.

"That's a wonderful story, Grandmother. Will you tell us more?"

"Tomorrow night, my child. Tonight, you sleep and dream of our great teacher, Coyote."

Istukus was sad to leave this place of the great falls for their hunting grounds. People from many tribes along rivers shared delightful, informative stories with him about their legends, culture, and bravery. They were all in good humor because of the bounty of salmon. It was important to know how others lived. He also had seen beautiful girls there. As reliable as the sun rose in the morning, they came every year to this sacred place, and each year he was filled with wonder.

The Noble People

Typical dress of Umatilla tribes
These are wax figures at the Whitman State
Historical Site

Tribe members live and travel in bands. The village on the Umatilla mainly consisted of Istukus' family, which were his aunts, uncles, cousins, and grandparents. White men identified their bands by the geographical locations of the villages or by their fishing and hunting sites. Some of his people were Upriver People, and some they called Downriver People, which referred to the Columbia River. Leaders specialized in activities to develop skills as warriors, hunters, fish catchers, spirit leaders, conflict resolvers, and healers. Men of prominence in the villages were council members for their village. The councils were involved in all levels of activities. Each band had its own fishing and hunting places, and they respected the fishing and hunting places of other bands.

The Cayuse called themselves *Te-taw-ken*, which meant "Superior People." Their people were great warriors. French traders and trappers called them *Cailloux,* meaning "People of the Flint Rock." The Americans turned *Cailloux* into Cayuse. It was amusing when the Americans first translated the name for their enemy, the Shoshone. The Shoshone gave the sign language for a salmon as it swam upstream, as their name meant "Salmon Eaters." The white men misinterpreted the sign, as they did most of the tribes' customs, thought the waving of the hand and arm was the sign for a snake and named them "Snakes," a name that stuck with them today. The Cayuse thought this was a great language slip, for they also considered them venomous creatures.

Cayuse men felt it beneath their dignity to marry Walla Walla women, although Walla Walla men often married Cayuse women. Even though the Walla Walla were considered inferior, it did not prevent them from trading salmon in exchange for horses.

Raids were a part of Cayuse's heritage. Why raise these new animals called horses when they could steal them and have herds that would have taken years to develop? Each nation of Native Americans throughout the continent is called a tribe. Each tribe has several bands that are wintered in different areas, compared to Europe, with separate countries with their own language and often divided by geographical boundaries. They developed their own cultures, and each country has year-round settlements called towns, villages, or cities. The Europeans also fought with other nations for centuries and took slaves and property of their neighboring villages or countries. Indeed, white people fought against those who spoke their language, such as in their great Civil War, with brothers fighting against brothers.

Istukus friend, Dr. Whitman, told him that the countries of England and Ireland still were killing each other over their unique way of praying to and believing in a higher spirit, or God. The indigenous tribes had no understanding of this. What they referred to as The Great Spirit may have different faces to each of them, but they did not kill because of another tribe's way of honoring the Great Spirit. Honor, glory, slaves, and horses were proper reasons to wage war. They protected their people. They shared an abundance of food and water. They freely roamed the land. The women raised the children collectively and taught them gentleness, patience, and oral history. In the summer months, many nations came together to trade and show their skills as archers or horseback riders in games and merriment.

The Cayuse waged war with other nations, and their power grew. Fighting was less for territory than for glory. Young males learned that by bringing home captured women, children, and horses, they could raise their status in the eyes of their people.

Warriors practiced ceremonial preparations for combat. Young men fasted and purged themselves, swallowing fish oil and shoving willow sticks down their throats to induce vomiting. The purifying sweat bath and ceremonial smoking of the pipe followed. The chiefs and elders joined in the smoking ritual and recalled past deeds of glory, which encouraged and taught the young warriors to perform in battle. Then the warriors danced, and many would perform feats and maneuvers on their horses. They ended the festivities by decorating themselves and their horses with paint, feathers, and other regalia.

Dying gloriously in defense of their people was the ultimate sacrifice. Whenever possible on the battlefield, they gathered up their dead warriors and buried them in rock-covered holes to prevent detection and desecration by man or animal. It was not always practical to return later to the battlefield to exhume and re-clothe the bones of their warriors to comfort their spirits on the long journey to the spirit world. When the warriors returned to their villages and announced the names of the brave dead, the people wailed. The deceased's property was burned, and widows and their children were taken into another's lodge and always cared for, which their missionary friends called polygamy. To them, it was kindness and mercy to care for their own.

With the mobility horses gave them, they freely roamed the hills and valleys of the Blue Mountains. They found adventure by raiding nations west of the Cascade Mountains and ranged as far south as present-day northern California, where they took slaves from the Shastas. The Klamaths and other tribes of the Northwest region of the great ocean also fell victim to their raids for enslaved people. Enslaved people gave them high status and were used to gather fuel and perform women's chores.

They often raided other tribes for horses and slaves, and occasionally for a wife. They had their differences; however, they all had great respect for each other's burial and sacred grounds. They respected and appreciated buffalo, elk, deer, antelope, and salmon, giving thanks for their sacrifices to feed and sustain their people. All the Indian nations shared a root belief in the reverence for "Earth Mother."

The First Encounters with White Men

Istukus' grandfather had a vision in a dream when he was young. He sat at the council and told this story to the elders: "I had a dream about men with white faces who would bring new things and ideas to our people. They would trade with us and bring new ways to see the Great Spirit. Our people will be forever changed. I see parallel lines in our Earth Mother with a long chain of carts that go on forever, like a string of ants. We must welcome our strange visitors and trade our salmon and buffalo robes for their goods."

Perhaps his grandfather's vision was why he welcomed and befriended white men, especially Dr. Whitman.

His grandmother had a Lakota friend who had a dream when her grandson was very young. His grandmother often repeated her friend's story as people gathered around. She dreamed of a two-faced giant with an endless appetite. He ate everything and trampled the land, smashing all that lay in his path. The more the giant ate, the larger it grew until it could leap across lakes and shake the earth when it ran.

Many years later, the Lakota encountered such a two-faced giant: hunters and soldiers who bragged that they could kill one hundred buffalo a day with their rifles, which they called long knives. The tribes had no understanding of slaughter and waste. The white men used the tribe's life-sustaining buffalo as targets, merely stripping the hide and leaving the meat to rot. When Istukus was an older man, he saw them pile the bones into mountains, and they sent the bones away on iron boxes on rails to use as fertilizer. What kind of man would destroy their sacred *tatonka* in a wasteful way just for sport? They knew stories of huge herds dominating the country and that a single pack took six days on horseback to ride through it.

During the summer buffalo hunts, Lakota friends told stories of the Americans crossing in endless numbers from spring to late summer. They watched from afar, leaving the travelers unmolested due to fear of sickness. The tribes could never understand the Americans polluting their water holes with dead carcasses or leaving behind loved ones who died on the trail. They, like the soldiers, were like the two-faced giant, consuming everything in its path.

"We are like the Earth," friends told the Cayuse. "If they were like the wind, we wouldn't mind, for the wind passes, bends the grass, and breaks a branch here and there, but it passes and becomes a bad memory. These whites are like a prairie fire, desecrating everything in their path. We could never understand what brought them on this trail. Where was their heritage? Where were their families and friends? Where were they going? When would they find what they were looking for?"

Santana, a Kiowa chief, expressed their love for the prairie based on his speech at the Treaty of the Medicine Lodge when he said so eloquently, "I don't want to settle. I love to roam over the prairies. There I feel free and happy, but when we settle down, we grow pale and die.

"A long time ago, this land belonged to our fathers, but when I go to the river, I see camps of whites on its banks. They cut down the timber, they kill the buffalo, and when I see that, my heart feels like bursting. I feel sorry. Has the white man become a child that he should kill and not eat?"

In 1792 Captain Robert Gray named the Great River "Columbia" after his ship. He was looking for a place to acquire sea otter and beaver pelts from the neighboring tribes near the great ocean of the Pacific.

The white men came, as Istukus's grandfather's dream predicted. They were explorers, fur traders, and trappers. Thirteen years after his grandfather's vision, while fishing on the Great River, he met a party of men whose leaders were named Lewis and Clark. They followed the Great River to its mouth from an overland route, coming toward the setting sun from the American states. They told his grandfather of a great ocean on the other side of our world. His grandfather said they brought new goods to their people, but the price was misery from a disease they called smallpox. It killed about half of the indigenous of the Pacific Northwest before 1800.

A party of Cayuse, Walla Walla, Umatilla, and others visited Fort George in 1814, previously called Fort Astoria, established in 1811. A Cayuse chief spoke to the men, saying, "Come and visit our lands. We have many beavers. You may trap beaver only. You are not to hunt anything else. You and your guns are not allowed on our ancestral hunting grounds, for you would drive the deer away, making them so wild that they could not be killed by bow and arrow."

A white man from Astoria hanged one of their people for stealing his silver goblet the year prior, which angered the chiefs throughout the Snake-Columbia country. Six major tribes attended a large spring root gathering in the Yakima Valley. The leaders expressed their displeasure over the killing to Alexander

Ross, who had come to trade horses. Ross was known among the native people as a fair man and understood many of their customs. The chiefs addressed him, saying, "These traders at Fort George are the men who kill our relations, the people who have caused us to mourn."

Ross said, "I am aware that you desire trade goods. I know you must be compensated for the death." He understood their ways: if a man took the life of one of their people, the band members must be paid in gifts for that life. After some discussion, Ross gave them a knife, beads, buttons, and rings. The chiefs allowed him and his men to leave the camp without harm.

The tribes made peace with the men who sold furs but not with their enemies, the Shoshones, which seemed to be of great concern to the traders, who in 1817 assembled the chiefs to talk with them about it. Walla Walla Chief Tumatapum was very supportive of trading with the white men and had significant concerns when the traders insisted on peace among the Shoshones and Cayuse. "If we make peace, how shall I employ my young men? They delight in nothing but war, and besides, our enemies, the Snakes, never observe peace." He paused, then continued, "Look," pointing to his slaves, scalps, and firearms. "Am I to throw all these trophies away? Shall Tumatapum forget the glory of his forefathers and become a woman?"

Then Chief Quahat, powerful from the days before the white men came, rose to speak. He possessed more authority than many chiefs along the Columbia. He asked, "Will the whites in opening trade with our enemies, promise not to give the Shoshones guns or balls?" Other chiefs spoke in the same vein.

The trader said, "We want peace between your people and the traders. We need peace between your tribes, including the Snakes. We will provide you with blankets, beads, pots and pans, and many comforts. You will have much pleasure to gain from our peaceful trading."

The chiefs held several meetings to discuss this problem. Finally, one day a messenger notified the traders that the chiefs were of one mind and asked them to present themselves in council to announce their decision. An entourage of armed and painted chiefs, headmen, and warriors dressed in their full regalia, arrived to speak with the traders.

There was a profound silence until the pipe had circled the seated group six times, which was the custom to show friendship. As the sun dropped behind the hills bordering the west banks of the river, the chiefs promised to make peace with the Snakes and let them pass to the Snake country unmolested. The chiefs threw their garments on the ground as a peace gesture with the hope of obtaining new clothing from the whites. After another smoke, the final seal was stamped on the treaty, but the white men did not provide new clothing because they did not understand how to make proper peace offerings.

In the same year, a trader's boat en route to Fort George tried to slip by the Columbia-Snake forks in mid-steam to avoid detection by some indigenous men camped there. The men fired two warning shots for the traders to bring their boat to shore. Before the craft reached shore, the local men jumped into the water to beach her and explained, "You may not pass this place without bringing your canoes to shore and asking permission to travel in our territory. This is our way. Now we will sit and pass the pipe six times."

The white traders did not understand the tribes' ways and kept smoking the pipe until they became drunk.

Some traders tried to pole through a rapid the following June but stopped in still waters above. A party of local men met them on horseback and plunged into the river, grabbing the boats. In the scuffle, two tribesmen were killed, and a third was severely injured. Three were swept downstream, and traders crossed to the opposite shore and moved to an island for the night. The next day they met with Alexander Ross traveling with a Cayuse delegation. After a three-hour negotiation, the traders paid the people for the two deaths, according to custom, and took their leave in peace and safety, ending the disagreeable affair.

Fort Nez Perce, later called Fort Walla Walla, was built by Donald McKenzie, Alexander Ross, and ninety-five men in 1818. The Cayuse were stunned by the audacity of white men building such a structure on their land! It had massive walls twelve feet high, twin towers at each end a hundred feet apart, large swivel guns, and a mortar mounted over the main gate. The local bands, including Cayuse, Spokane, Palouse, and Coeur d'Alene, protested and demanded payment from these men for putting such a formidable structure in their hunting path between the Great River and the Walla Walla River. Ross was proud of the fort, called it the Gibraltar of Columbia, and said it would allow peaceful trading. To the Cayuse, this did not seem like a gesture of peace.

Traders permitted no more than two or three people, and occasionally a few chiefs, to enter the fort at one time. Trade was carried on through an eighteen-inch square opening in the wall, secured by an iron door. The chiefs viewed the restrictions as an insult. "Are the whites afraid of us?" they asked. "If so, we will leave our arms outside."

"No," replied Alexander Ross, "but your young men are foolish." The chiefs had to agree that they did like war. The local people gathered around the fort, demanding guns, ammunition, flints, and knives in payment for putting such a monster on their land, forbidding entry, and then arming it with canons. This territory belonged to the Cayuse for centuries. Now the traders were saying that they could not enter their reinforced lodge. They provided a peephole to do trading, which was an insult to the local bands. This monstrous structure was on their traveling path. They did not understand why they were not welcome on their land, so continued the disappointment and the decline of the relationship with the white men. Neither of their cultures understood the other's ways. The traders said they now claimed the land for their own. The tribes did not understand this concept of ownership of the land.

Years later, when the American government wished to buy the lands of his people, Chief Seattle, one of the bravest and most respected chiefs of the Northwest Nations, sat at a white man's table to sign a deed presented by the new commissioner of Indian Affairs for the territory. However, before he signed it, he rose to speak, and his voice was the voice of all our people:

> How can you buy the sky? How can you own the rain and the wind? My mother told me, "Every part of this earth is sacred to our people: every pine needle; every sandy shore; every mist in the dark woods; every meadow and humming insect. All are holy in the memory of our people."
> My father said to me, "I know the sap that courses through the trees as I know the blood that

flows in my veins. We are part of the earth, and it is part of us. The perfumed flowers are our sisters. The bear, the deer, the great eagle, these are our brothers. The rocky crests, the meadows, the ponies--all belong to the same family."

The voice of my ancestors said to me, "The shining water that moves in the streams and rivers is not simply water, but the blood of your grandfather's grandfather. Each ghostly reflection in the clear waters of the lakes tells of memories in the life of our people.

"The water's murmur is the voice of your great-great-grandmother. The rivers are our brothers. They quench our thirst. They carry our canoes and feed our children. You must give to the rivers the kindness you would give to any brother."

The voice of my grandfather said to me, "The air is precious. It shares its spirit with all the life it supports. The wind that gave me my first breath also received my last sigh. You must keep the land and air apart and sacred, as a place where one can go to taste the wind that is sweetened by the meadow flowers.

"When the last red man and woman have vanished with their wilderness, and their memory is only the shadow of a cloud moving across the prairie, will the shores and forest still be here? Will there be any of the spirit of my people left?"

My ancestors said to me, "This we know: The earth does not belong to us. We belong to the earth."

The voice of my grandmother said to me, "Teach your children what you have been taught. The earth is our mother. What befalls the earth befalls all the sons and daughters of the earth.

"Hear my voice and the voice of my ancestors. The destiny of your people is a mystery to us. What will happen when the buffalo are all slaughtered? The wild horses tamed? What will happen when the secret corners of the forest are heavy with the scent of many men? When the view of the ripe hills is blotted by talking wires, where will the thicket be? Gone. Where will the eagle be? Gone.

"And what will happen when we say goodbye to the swift pony and the hunt? It will be the end of living and the beginning of survival.

"This we know: All things are connected like the blood that unites us. We did not weave the web of life--we are merely a strand in it. Whatever we do to the web, we do to ourselves. We love the earth as a newborn loves its mother's heartbeat. If we sell you our land, care for it as we have cared for it. Hold in your mind the memory of the land as it is when you receive it.

"Preserve the land and the air and the rivers for your children's children and love it as we have loved it."

For eleven hundred years, indigenous life had been consistent and simple. The horse gave them the most change. It gave them mobility. Then, within Istukus's lifetime, he witnessed changes that shattered their world, way of life, freedom, and future. The Cayuse population was nearly annihilated. For eleven hundred years, they existed in harmony with the "Earth Mother," and, in an instant, their lives were altered forever.

Artist Drury Haight's conception of the Whitmans
based on sketches by artist Paul Kane.
Narcissa had no portrait painted of her while she was living.

WIND

"Wind passes, bends the grass, and breaks a branch here and there, but it passes and becomes a bad memory."

This section accounts for the impact the first two missionary families settling in Oregon country had on the Indigenous people, stirring up a wind that resulted in a firestorm of settlers.

Terrie Biggs

The Call for Missionaries

Judge Prentiss lifted the pitch pipe and set the tone. The choir, mainly consisting of his children dressed in white robes, blessed the air with *Amazing Grace*. The lovely soprano voice of his oldest daughter Narcissa filled the eager ears of the congregation. Her clear, strong voice was under perfect control and as sweet and musical as a chime of bells. Her brothers Stephen, Harvey, Edward, and Jonas stood behind her; her sister Jane to her left, and her sisters Mary Ann, Harriet, and Clarissa (named after her mother), to her right.

Her voice was filled with joy, for the night before, she had taken the first step on the path to change her life forever. Narcissa, a spinster at age twenty-six, taught a science course called Natural Philosophy at a school that was considered the best in the district. The previous evening, a cold November night in 1834, Samuel Parker arrived in Amity, New York, and had spoken at the log schoolhouse that was Narcissa's classroom during the week. He began: "Good people of Amity, opportunity, and adventure abounds. Who among you has the courage to go west and venture into the Oregon country? The American Board of Commissioners has appointed me for Foreign Missions to take your application to join me in establishing a mission in Oregon country. Heathens from the tribes in the territory traveled to St. Louis to get our Bibles and ask us to bring back missionaries to their abundant land--a land filled with elk, deer, and a huge river so crowded with salmon that they jump right into your boat. The mountains are blue and mysterious and reach halfway to heaven. The valleys are green and rich with rivers that snake over the land to provide water for farms and livestock. The Indian tribes are peaceful and hungry for the word of God. We will deliver them from their sins. Who is with me to bring the word of Jesus Christ to these heathens? We have already received some volunteers. The fine, Christian people of Amity are just the people we need to give the word of God to the savages."

When she was sixteen, Narcissa had read the life story of Harriet Boardman, a pioneer American Board missionary to India. Ever since then, she has had a desire to be a missionary. Now she was ready and willing to go. After the meeting, she asked Mr. Parker, "Is there a place for an unmarried female in my Lord's vineyard?"

"Well, Miss Prentiss, I say...your question caught me unprepared. Quite unusual. Yes, this is the first request by a woman I have encountered." He paused to gather his thoughts. Parker had been looking for men to volunteer. "Miss Prentiss, you must understand that if you offer your services, the American Board will review your application and might send you anywhere in the world. It is quite unusual for an unmarried woman to make such an inquiry. However, I will immediately write to the Board and ask about their policy on unmarried females on your behalf."

She was intelligent and strong-willed. Her conversation was animated and cheerful, unlike her solemn mother and father. She loved to entertain company and, above all, was deeply religious. Narcissa had taken the first step to fulfill her dream.

Next month, Samuel Parker wrote a letter to the American Board asking, "Are females wanted? A Miss Narcissa Prentiss of Amity is very eager to be of service to the Indians. Her education is good, she has conspicuous piety, and she has a degree of influence. She is willing to go as needed."

Parker was amazed to discover that Miss McCoy also wanted to join the cause in the next town. In January, he wrote again to the Board on behalf of the two young women. He stated, "I told the young ladies nothing about their going among the Indians, nor to any particular part of the world, but only that if they offered themselves, it must be to go anywhere the Board should choose."

Upon its approval, the American Board of Commissioners for Foreign Missions made assignments to missionaries. As secretary, David Greene was the liaison and correspondent between the missionaries and the Board. Any work with people who could not speak English was considered a foreign mission, which began in 1816 with Native Americans.

Parker examined the letter from the kindhearted and tactful David Greene, which read, "I don't think we have missions among the Indians where unmarried females are valuable just now. Neither of the young ladies had made an application for an appointment." Parker was disappointed because he had instead encouraged the two women. Since neither had sent an application yet, he thought that the issue of unmarried females might have resolved itself. Still, because he had been moved by Miss Prentiss's desire to help, Parker wondered if there might be a way for her to go. An idea struck him when he remembered young Dr. Marcus Whitman, who Parker had recruited before visiting Amity. The American Board had accepted Whitman as an assistant missionary to accompany Samuel Parker on his exploring tour of the Rockies. In January

1835, Dr. Whitman rode to Ithaca, New York, to consult with Parker about their trek west that would begin the next month. "Marcus," Parker began, "I know you have a great desire to go into the Oregon country. It can be a very lonely place. Have you ever thought of taking a wife?"

"I have considered it. However, I have not had the time for courtship, nor have I met a woman yet that I feel would be suitable for a missionary's wife. There will be hardships, sacrifices, and arduous work."

"I have met a young lady from Amity who requested to go as an unmarried female, but the Board disapproves of an unmarried female being assigned a mission. She is a schoolteacher, lovely to look at, of great intelligence, and of great enthusiasm to give the word of Christ to the heathens. She is Narcissa, one of the daughters of Judge Samuel Prentiss. They moved last year to Amity from Prattsburgh. Did you ever meet the Prentiss family?"

"Why, yes. I met the family when they lived in Prattsburgh a few years ago. Samuel had a lot of active, healthy children in a tiny house. I attended a prayer meeting in his home. They were very hospitable. His daughter Jane made an impression on me, and I have fond memories of her. I did not meet Narcissa. They said she was away at Butler on an annual visit to see her cousin. They are a very handsome family. I also met Rev. Powell of Amity while I was in Prattsburgh."

Parker replied, "Rev. Powell is bother-in-law to Samuel Prentiss. I know you've only a few weeks left before leaving for this year's Rendezvous. Would you like me to arrange for you to be a guest at Rev. Powell's with the intent of introducing you to Narcissa?"

Marcus was practical and adventurous, so, in an instant, he said, "Yes."

"I will make the arrangements for you to visit Powell to meet this young woman. If she suits you, offer a proposal of marriage which would surely please the Board."

Marcus bid his mother and relatives farewell in Rushville, New York, east of Amity. A graveyard on the edge of the village beckoned him. He walked to the gravestone, a bit overgrown, which read:

<u>Beza Whitman</u>
Stop here, my friend, and think on me
I once was in the world like thee.
This is a call aloud to thee.
Prepare for Death and follow me.
Laid to Rest April 7, 1810

His father had died in his thirty-seventh year, leaving a widow with five children under twelve. Marcus had been only seven years old. The financial burden was overwhelming, so she asked her relatives for help. Marcus's mother sent him to live with his father's half-brother, Freedom Whitman, at Cummington, Massachusetts, when he was eight. The famous romantic poet, journalist, and editor of the New York Evening Post, William Cullen Bryant, resided in this village. Marcus had suffered a double tragedy: First losing his father and then separating from his mother, brothers, and sisters. Some people crumble under such conditions, and some, such as Marcus, gain inner strength and determination. Like his mother, Marcus was full of vigor and energy. He was a survivor and had great fortitude, which led him to medical school and ultimately to take on the challenge of going to Oregon as a physician and missionary.

Two years of apprenticeship with Dr. Bryant, followed by sixteen weeks at Fairfield Medical College, qualified him to practice medicine. Several of the graduates were famous men. No other school than Fairfield would have trained him for the work he was to do as a frontier physician. Marcus set up practice as a country doctor in Wheeler, New York, a town of 1,600 people. A memorial plaque now stands along the roadside, which states that the medical offices of Dr. Marcus Whitman once stood there outside of Wheeler. About two miles south of Wheeler is another roadside marker that indicates that Henry H. Spalding was born near there on November 26, 1803. It would be a stroke of fate that Henry would play a significant role in Whitman's future.

Muscular and sinewy, Marcus weighed about 175 pounds. Raw-boned with broad shoulders, he had dark blue, kind eyes that were sometimes on the gray side. He had brown hair, a broad forehead, and a straight and prominent nose. High cheekbones were a family trait, resembling those of Abraham Lincoln, a distant cousin.

However, the demands of his profession and a bout of poor health gave the young doctor no time to find a wife. He was once engaged to Miss Persia Saunders, who died four months before her twenty-third birthday. Since then, he got a glimpse of someone who haunted his thoughts during his lonely nights. In early spring, he visited Butler, a small town near Prattsburgh, when he was twenty-seven, to meet his childhood friend, Jonathan Pratt, a physician with a practice in Pennsylvania. Marcus had taken over his medical business for a couple of months while Pratt took a much-needed vacation two years prior. Jonathan's sister lived in Butler, and he got word to Marcus to join him there for a weekend getaway to catch up on a few years.

Sunday morning, they attended church services in a small quaint chapel with a tall steeple and a manicured lawn with beds of yellow, red, and pink tulips lining the walk. He sat to the right of Jonathan next to the aisle. Jonathan was intent on the services when Marcus's breath was taken away by a lovely young woman in a pew opposite him on the other side of the aisle. Her strawberry blonde hair spilled from under her hat, and a curl dangled over her eyebrow. She captivated him. Marcus could not focus on the sermon, and he lost his place in the hymn book when he heard her voice rise above the others, angelic without being pretentious. He only listened to *her* voice and saw her blue eyes as she glanced in his direction. For a moment, his heart stopped. "Maybe I could consider taking a wife," he thought. This lovely woman invoked a stirring in him like none before. "But she is such a refined young lady, and I am an oaf of a country doctor," he said to himself.

He nudged Jonathan and asked, "Do you know the young woman in the rose-colored hat?"

"Never seen her before," Jonathan whispered, "but I know her companion, Elizabeth Standish. Why?"

"I just thought I knew her. She looks familiar." Jonathan did not detect the lump in Marcus's throat.

Marcus stood outside the chapel by himself when the service was over, waiting for Jonathan, chatting with his sister and the pastor. Elizabeth and the young woman began to smile, whispering to each other as they exited the door. Although she did not glance his way, he could not take his eyes off her. Elizabeth saw him staring and nudged her cousin, but Marcus had turned away to hide his scarlet face. "Yes," he thought, "this woman will visit my dreams for a while," and she did for years to come.

During the previous November, the same month that Narcissa had attended the meeting in Amity, New York, Marcus had gone to the Wheeler Presbyterian Church and heard the words of Samuel Parker. Marcus, just like Narcissa, had unfulfilled dreams and aspirations to go west. His cherished dream as a young man had been to enter the ministry, but seven years of college and seminary was out of his mother's financial boundaries. Marcus was as eager to go with Parker as Parker was anxious to find missionaries to go with him. Parker asked him to make an immediate application to the Board.

Ten years prior, Marcus had written a letter to the American Board declining an offer to be assigned to the Marquesas Islands in the Pacific due to poor health when he had spleen inflammation. The American Board replied, "Millions of heathens are perishing for lack of knowledge of the Gospel....but your health is such that you think you cannot go to a warm climate and in such climates are the *immense* majority of heathen. Among no others have we a mission except among the Indians, .and among these, we have no demand for a physician at this time. Indeed, it seems doubtful whether your health would justify your going on a mission at all."

This time, though, the Board's letter from Rev. David Greene to Marcus displayed a different tone with wisdom and fatherly advice from Greene: "On such a tour as this, as well as in your missionary labors among any of the wandering tribes of our continent, great patience, fortitude, and perseverance are necessary. You must be willing to encounter hardships, dangers, self-denials in almost every shape, and discouragements without being moved by them from your purpose. Nothing but an unquenchable desire to do good to the souls of the Indians, originating and cherished by a supreme love of Christ and firm faith in the promises, can sustain you and carry you through."

The Proposal

    The Prentiss family had recently moved from Prattsburgh to Amity, New York. Their family had outgrown the twenty-two by the thirty-two-foot house they had lived in since 1805, and their new two-story frame house located on the west side of the village square accommodated the family adequately. The Prentiss home became the center for many happy gatherings of young people who were friends of Narcissa's lively brothers and sisters. Narcissa herself was vibrant and popular.

    Judge Stephen Prentiss was quite tall, finely proportioned, a little inclined to stoutness, and remarkably *unfriendly* for a man of his intelligence and standing. It was rare for him to indulge in laughter. He was an architect and a master builder and had a distillery at one time. He served at least one term as a county probate supervisor and a probate judge.

    After Judge Prentiss had been informed of Dr. Marcus Whitman's intentions toward Narcissa, Mr. Parker had spoken to Rev. Oliver Powell. He asked him to arrange a private meeting with the judge. Prentiss replied to Powell, his brother-in-law, "Narcissa has longed to be of service in the name of God. We have discussed her appeal to Mr. Parker to be a missionary. The question of marriage to a man she has never met sounds unlikely. I will, however, welcome Dr. Whitman into our home again. Bring him over in the morning, Oliver. I will brief my daughter on his intentions, and we will leave it in the hands of

God. Narcissa is very independent and has adjusted herself to spinsterhood without the silly romantic yearnings of most unmarried women."

It was Saturday afternoon, and snow was packed along the roadsides. The northern February wind prevented a private walk through the garden, now asleep under a blanket of snow for the winter. Rev. Powell took Marcus to the Prentiss house and knocked on the door. To Marcus' relief, Jane answered the door. He remembered how fond he had been of her when they first met. She had thought of him as a kind and gentle man whom she liked very much. She also had a familiarity with her that took him back a few years. The family began gathering around to make introductions. He felt very welcome. Lively conversation always filled the parlor at the Prentiss house, and this certainly was one of those occasions. The kitchen door opened, and a vision filled his eyes. He was speechless. Could it be? Could this be the same young woman he had seen in the chapel at Butler seven years ago? She approached him, looking directly into his dark blue eyes. There was an instant connection, an instant of sizing each other up, and both were quite pleased. "Dr. Whitman, I would like to introduce my daughter Narcissa," Judge Prentiss said.

Marcus could not respond. His gaze never left her eyes. Finally, he cleared his throat, "Miss Prentiss, it is my pleasure to meet you," He finished his sentence to himself, "again."

The family managed to give Marcus time alone in the parlor with Narcissa on this occasion. Jane lingered as she left the room, catching Marcus's eye and nodding her head in approval. She had been very impressed with Marcus at their first meeting.

"I leave Monday on an exploratory expedition with Samuel Parker, whom you met in November," he began, and he saw a disappointed look from Narcissa. She had been very pleased and relieved to find Marcus tall, soft-spoken, with kind eyes. He was well-mannered and well-spoken at supper. Yes. She liked him immediately and felt a sense of emptiness that he would be leaving so soon.

He continued, "Mr. Parker told me that you had requested of him the possibility of an unmarried woman to accompany him in his missionary work. The American Board appeared to be unsupportive of this."

"Yes," she replied, with a graceful bearing, looking him in the eye, "When I was sixteen, I read about another woman, a missionary in India. I have dreamed of this for myself since then."

"So, it is not just a passing whim based on an eloquent sermon by Parker?"

"No, it is not."

"Miss Prentiss, the frontier of the Oregon country without a wife, would be a very lonely place." He turned to be received by her blue eyes. "Miss Prentiss...

"Please call me, Narcissa."

"Narcissa, please forgive me for being so bold. However, I do not have much time for formalities. Would you, could you, will you consider accompanying me to the Oregon country as my wife?"

Narcissa drew in a breath, corrected her posture, and said, "I would be honored to be your wife, Dr. Whitman."

He could not believe his good fortune. He certainly did not consider himself handsome, yet beside him was a tall, stately, fair-skinned, beautiful woman with blue eyes and strawberry-blonde hair. His knees were weak, and his heart was filled with wonder. "Miss...Narcissa," he continued, "my exploratory trip to the Rockies with Samuel Parker will take me away from you for six to eight months. We must make arrangements and be ready to marry when I return. Also, I suggest that you write the American Board for an appointment. The Powells are assigned to a Pawnee mission and expect to go next spring. Perhaps we can travel with them as far as the Missouri frontier."

They spent the rest of the evening exchanging information about themselves, which was their entire courtship. When Marcus left with Rev. Powell at the end of the evening, they both knew that they respected each other. They both recognized that they were very attracted to each other, and it would be easy to slide into love.

The following day Marcus came to bid farewell before heading for St. Louis. She walked beside him to his horse, pulling a wool wrap around her shoulders. He took the saddle horn in his left hand and put his foot in the stirrup to mount his horse. He slid his foot out of the stirrup and let go of the horn. Seconds passed until he faced her. "Why is he hesitating?" she asked herself. "Has he changed his mind?"

Slowly he turned towards her. His fingers barely brushed her ear as he put his right hand on her shoulder, looking deeply into her eyes. "I will come back for you. I will be back. Please wait for me."

Snow was falling, but the touch of his hand warmed her to the bone. She couldn't speak; she just nodded yes. She watched him ride away as he glanced back at her three times. He already had her heart.

"May God be with you until your return." Providence *had* brought them together, and her life would be forever changed.

David Greene of the American Board opened the envelope and pulled out the paper penned on February 23, 1835, the day Marcus left. Written in a clear, feminine hand, he read it to the members of the Board:

> Dear Brethren:
>
> Permit an unworthy sister to address you. Having found favor of the Lord and desiring to live for the conversion of the world, I now offer myself to the American Board to be employed in their service among the heathen, if counted worthy. It was requested of me to make some statements concerning myself, so I shall endeavor to be as brief as possible, knowing the value of your time.
>
> I was born on March 14, 1808, in Prattsburgh, Steuben County. In the beginning of the year 1819, a grand revival of religion was witnessed in Prattsburgh. I joined the Congregational church and remained a member for fifteen years. My advantages for acquiring an education have been good, having been situated near Franklin Academy--and most of the time, when not attending school, I have been engaged in teaching. My last effort in teaching was a children's school in which I took great delight. My brothers and sisters, nine with our parents, have all united with the same church. In June, we moved to Amity, Allegheny County, where we now reside.

> In regard to my feelings upon the subject of mission, I will say but little. From my conversion, I have felt a particular interest in the salvation of the heathen and an increasing desire for information on the subject and have not neglected to gratify that desire; but from time to time, with peculiar feelings, greeted the arrival the *Missionary Herald*. I frequently desired to go to the heathen but only half-heartedly. It was not until the first Monday of January 1824 that I felt the need to wholeheartedly pursue the missionary work, letting Providence lead me.
>
> Feeling it more my privilege than a duty to work for the conversion of the heathen, I respectfully submit myself to your direction and subscribe,
>
> Your unworthy sister in the Lord,
> Narcissa Prentiss

Greene turned the letter over to review three short testimonials. It was the footnote to Rev. Powell's testimonial that caught his attention, and he read it aloud to his associates:

> As it is probable that Miss Prentiss will hereafter become the companion of Dr. Marcus Whitman, should he be established missionary beyond the Rocky Mountains, it may be proper to add that he expressed a desire that she might accompany us on our mission as it will be a field of usefulness and an opportunity for her becoming acquainted with the work of a missionary.

"I believe, gentlemen," Greene said, addressing the Board members, "that Samuel Powell suggests that Miss Prentiss, the soon-to-be Mrs. Whitman, also be assigned to the Pawnee Mission until Dr. Whitman returns from his exploring tour of the Rockies."

A few weeks later, though, Narcissa learned of Mrs. Powell's pregnancy. The Powells felt that it would not be wise for them to undertake missionary work for the time being. This set into motion events that would affect the Whitmans in the years to come.

Terrie Biggs

Return from the Rendezvous

"This is to certify that Doctor Marcus Whitman is an assistant missionary to the Indian tribes west of the State of Missouri," Marcus read from the official commission that was mailed to him in St. Louis on his way to the Rockies. The *Missionary Herald* listed him as "physician" rather than "missionary" because Whitman was not ordained, whereas Rev. Samuel Parker was commissioned as a missionary.

In December of 1835, eight months after leaving Narcissa, Marcus returned to New York to find that the Prentiss family had moved six miles north to a small village called Angelica. Written communication was too slow to let her know of his estimated arrival. Narcissa had been sitting at her father's desk by the window when she saw him outside. Thin, worn, and dusty, Marcus lifted his foot out of the stirrup. As he dismounted, she ran to him outside, her heart racing. She reached out and took his hand, "You're back!" she said breathlessly.

"I'm back."

"Do come inside. Oh, Marcus. How thin you look. Your letters said you were ill at times on the trip. Are you now well, my dear?"

"I am...now that I am again with you."

The family heard her and gathered around them and led him inside. Marcus rested upon a down bed that night. The family gathered early the next day, refreshed in body and spirit as he recalled his extraordinary adventure to the Rockies with Parker. Word of his return went through the little village.

A wedding would be forthcoming when he returned and most likely occur in haste. Harvey and Stephen, Narcissa's oldest brothers, lived nearby and brought their wives to the Prentiss house. Jonas introduced his new bride to Marcus. The parlor of their home in Angelica was roomy and decorated with sage green velvet drapes over the two ample windows; two high-backed upholstered settees that provided good light for reading and comfortable conversation facing each other. Three comfortable chairs sat on a handmade print carpet. A blazing fire snapping with seasoned maple warmed the room with a portrait of Judge Prentiss over the mantle. The family brought in extra chairs from the dining room, and everyone began a barrage of questions at once. Marcus explained that his trip west had terminated at the annual Rendezvous among traders, trappers, and many indigenous tribes.

"When did you reach the Rendezvous? What did you do there?" asked Jonas.

"How did you sleep?" Jane inquired.

"Did you fight any Indians?" sixteen-year-old Edward asked.

Clarissa had to know, "Did you kill buffalo? Did you eat buffalo?"

The spirited family's bombardment amused Marcus. Judge Prentiss brought the house to order. The room grew quiet as Marcus leaned forward on the settee next to Narcissa and began, "Mr. Parker and I met up in St. Louis. I arrived there on April first, three days before Mr. Parker. We boarded the steamboat *Siam* with passage to Liberty, Missouri, to meet up with the American Fur Company. The eight-day trip took two weeks because of an accident; however, we had plenty of time to shop for provisions in Liberty since the Fur Company was to leave in mid-May. I made the acquaintance of Lucius Fontenelle, the caravan commander, and asked about supplies."

Marcus thought it improper to discuss his and Parker's disagreements throughout the journey. It began with the selection of provisions. The rough and ready practical Marcus, dressed in frontier garb, directly contrasted with the purse-lipped minister. Parker wore a plug hat and white stock around his throat. He was stoic and pompous; Marcus was robust and amiable. Parker refused to buy a second pack animal. They carried clothing, stationery, books, medicines, instruments, ammunition, goods for trading, bedding, a tent, an ax, and cooking equipment--all too great of a load for one weary pack mule.

"We each had a horse for riding and one mule for packing all of our gear. Fontenelle had about fifty or sixty men, two hundred horses and mules, and six wagons. When we started, I was an inexperienced packer, and the poor mule kept losing his burden. Very quickly, I learned to pack efficiently. Fontenelle did not want to help carry our provisions. However, a man named Merrill kindly let us stow some of our supplies in his wagon.

"Parker and I were steadfast about two issues that did not make us popular with our caravan. First, we stood fast to not traveling on the Sabbath, and second, we refused to partake in drinking alcoholic beverages."

The audience all nodded in agreement. Judge Prentiss, at one time, had owned a distillery but decided to let go of it to be a good example to his sons. He now whole-heartedly supported temperance.

"Due to the great animosity towards Mr. Parker and me, because we would not travel on the Sabbath, I tried to be of as much assistance as possible. I helped Fontenelle's men when we forged rivers by making rafts and bridges, which was exhausting work. The men in the caravan must have changed their feelings towards me because they stopped throwing rotten eggs at me."

"Oh, Dr. Whitman, how dreadful! They threw eggs at you?" asked Jane, aghast.

"It was only a couple of times. Another unpleasant incident happened one day as we were catching up with the caravan after the Sabbath when they had tried to destroy the raft they had used to cross a river to prevent us from following. We were very fortunate that the raft hung up in the trees along the bank, and we were able to repair it and cross the river.

"Parker, at 56 years old, either hadn't the stamina or didn't want to do the work needed to pack, unpack, build rafts, and generally be of service to the caravan and ourselves. I was raised to do my share of the work. The caravan was so distressed over our refusal to travel on the Sabbath that Parker was convinced that they had, at one point, plotted to kill us." There were gasps from the family.

"Cholera struck the caravan. Although it was deadly, the epidemic may have saved Mr. Parker's and my lives. In mid-June, Fontenelle's men drank from contaminated water in a river in a valley basin. Cholera raged through the camp for twelve days, infecting dozens, including Fontenelle. I attended the men night and day with medicine and was able to keep the number of deaths down to three by the grace of God. Having had experience with the dreaded disease, I moved the camp to higher ground and clean water. Fontenelle, along with dozens of his men, began to recover. From that time on, Fontenelle bestowed on us every favor in his power."

Narcissa had received letters from Marcus and knew of the many perils of his journey. However, it was still disturbing to hear how close her betrothed had come to death--first from the men in the caravan and then from the dreaded disease.

He kept glancing at Narcissa, yearning to have some time with her alone, knowing it would come in due time. They recognized each other's needs. Meanwhile, she thought, "How refreshed he looks from last evening even though he must have ridden all night."

"So, the rest of our journey improved significantly, except that my health had been feeble from the stress of packing and unpacking alone, working for the caravan, and then tending the sick. My strength did not recover entirely after three weeks layover for cholera as I was struck with dysentery later.

"Three weeks' march brought us to buffalo country. We were entering Indian territory also, so Mr. Parker and I knew we must travel on the Sabbath not to be separated from the caravan." Still, Parker felt that working to pack and unpack was beneath his stature and that it was Marcus' job as his assistant. Parker never gained the respect of the men in the caravan, and he lost the respect of Marcus.

Marcus wanted to gloss over their disagreements and admitted that he did appreciate Parker's contribution. He said, "Mr. Parker had an observant eye and an inquiring mind. He gathered facts regarding the physical features of the country--its geology, fauna, flora, climate, the customs of the Indians, and the activities of the fur company. I am sure it will be useful to other companies, as surely there will be more to explore that country." However, no one used Parker's information, perhaps because mountain men led the pioneers in years to follow. They were already knowledgeable about the geography, climate, and customs of most Indian nations who lived in their trapping and hunting territory.

Marcus looked at Clarissa, who had asked about eating buffalo, and said, "I took no pleasure in witnessing the killing of the buffalo. However, I do admit I took pleasure in having fresh meat. I knew the meat was necessary to provide food for the caravan, and many men were eager to kill those magnificent wild beasts, but not I."

"What did buffalo taste like?" asked Clarissa.

"It is very lean and tasty, very similar to beef, and can be prepared the same way you cook beef." He answered other questions about buffalo and then continued to another subject.

"On August 7, we passed Independence Rock, then South Pass, which I predict will be the gateway to Oregon country. South Pass is considered the Continental Divide."

Judge Prentiss asked, "I've heard this term before. What does it refer to?"

"East of the Divide, rivers flow east; west of the divide..."

"Oh, they flow west," interjected Harvey.

"Yes. The elevation is 7,550 feet, but it is so gradual it was difficult to locate the summit. To answer your question, Jonas, it took us eight weeks to reach our destination at the Rendezvous. Our average day covered thirteen miles. We were a month late and held up the start of the two-week event, so we were greeted with boisterous enthusiasm. It was immediately apparent that the hearty welcome was for the *whiskey* the caravan brought for trading."

Entrepreneur William Ashley arranged the first Rendezvous on the Green River in 1825. The Rendezvous made it possible for the trappers to supply themselves with a year's worth of provisions and the fur companies to purchase months' worth of pelts in the wilderness.

Three significant companies brought their massive supply wagons of goods. Originally the Rocky Mountain Fur Company had the monopoly on the prices trappers paid for supplies and the prices they paid the trappers for furs.

The competition was sometimes brutal among the fur companies when the American Fur Company (that Parker and Whitman were traveling with) and the Hudson Bay Company joined the Rendezvous. Even with competition, the prices paid for supplies were high, and the prices they paid the trappers were low. The only people who prospered were those selling supplies and those manufacturing furs, especially those who fashioned the popular east coast hats made of beaver felt. Felt is a cloth made by pressing, heating, and treating animal hair with chemicals. It was valuable because it was waterproof, moldable, and didn't wear out easily. The best felt came from beavers because it was soft and warm. Felt hats dated back to the Continental Cocked hat in 1776, and production continued with hats for the Army and Navy and top hats such as the Wellington. The discovery of the beaver in North America had been a godsend to European hat makers. Man's desire to be fashionable had driven this industrious little creature to near extinction in Europe.

Trade items included tea from China, various candle holders, beads from Eastern Europe primarily made in Italy or Czechoslovakia, silver from world-renowned silversmiths in Germany, blankets from England, and the essential items to the traders--coffee and sugar.

Before trading began, the fur companies opened their wagons and popped off the lids from huge whiskey barrels to loosen the men up for trading. The drinking might last two days before trading began. Fueled by whiskey, the men got wilder.

Marcus continued: "The Rendezvous was held on a well-watered meadow on the Green River, a tributary of the Colorado River. The meadow was about twelve miles long and ten miles wide, which provided excellent pasture for the large herds of horses the various tribes brought to trade. They came with as many as ten thousand horses, representing two for each man. The tribes attending were the Shoshones--which mountain men nick-named the Snakes--the Bannocks, the Nez Perce, the Cayuse, the Flatheads, and sometimes the Utes." The family laughed when Marcus showed them how the Shoshones got their nickname, the Snakes. "The trappers, who we know as mountain men, came to barter with the Indians, buy supplies for the year, and sell their pelts."

"Narcissa said you met up with Jim Bridger," Harvey interjected.

"Oh, yes. I'll tell you about Bridger shortly, but first, I want you to get the event's flavor. After hunting and trapping months in the mountains, the Rendezvous is the year's primary or only social event. They displayed all their mountain skills in competitive games such as shooting, tomahawk throwing, horse racing, and wrestling with each other. There was also drinking, carousing, gambling, philandering, and fighting. The trappers cut loose, and it was a rowdy, riotous two-week event.

"I witnessed more than one trader losing all his money in a poker game, going away with nothing to show for a year's work. Many others tried to drink their year's wages in whiskey. One trapper with over $2,000 in his pouch from the sale of furs ended up owing the company after two weeks of gambling and drinking away his fortune

"Native tribes also came to trade buffalo robes and beaver hides for manufactured goods. There was constant whooping, howling, and quarreling with mounted Indians dashing into and through our camp. So, you see, Edward, we did not fight Indians. They came to trade, but we witnessed liquor's toll on the traders and the Indians. Alcohol had a devastating effect on them. It was culturally and physiologically alien to them, with destructive and corrosive consequences. The Hudson Bay Company has tried to prevent the bartering of liquor to the Indians and the mountain men for furs, but the American companies had no such scruples.

"Oh, you asked about Jim Bridger. Yes, I did meet him. He was loud, bulky, fun-loving, and told wild tales of his adventures. Most of the trappers knew his stories were a bit exaggerated, but we loved to listen to him. On the first day we arrived, Bridger asked me, 'Doc, would you take a look at this here back of mine. It gets to hurtin' when I puts ma rifle over ma shoulder.'

"'Why, Mr. Bridger, how did you get this arrowhead in your back?' I asked him.

"'Oh, I got hit 'bout three years ago in a skirmish with the Blackfeet. Can you fix me up, Doc?"

"The next day, I operated on his back. The arrow was hooked at the point from striking a large bone, and cartilage had grown over it. He bit on a piece of leather while I carved. He was very patient and brave, and even sober. I was told that this operation was the first ever performed by an American-trained physician west of the Rockies."

Jim Bridger

Jim Bridger was seventeen when he left Missouri and began his life in the mountains. Born in Virginia in 1804, he was one of the first trappers to discover the Great Salt Lake. Because he spun so many tall tales, at first, no one believed him when he told of an inland lake of salt that held a man afloat.

"Oh, I thought that was just a tall tale when I read about the Salt Lake," commented Harvey.

"No. It is true. I also talked with other men who saw it," confirmed Marcus.

Supper was served when they all gathered around the table. To everyone's surprise, Mrs. Prentiss, who usually did not allow colorful stories at the table, urged, "Please, do continue with your story, Dr. Whitman."

"The next day, I extracted an arrow from the shoulder of one of the hunters. It had been there for two-and-a-half years. It came out much easier than Bridger's." Marcus reached into his pocket and pulled out a three-inch arrowhead. "This belonged to that fellow. It had lodged in his right thigh. He said he was so grateful, and he insisted that I have it for a keepsake."

"Wow," exclaimed Edward, "this is a humdinger." The girls squirmed and shuddered.

"Another day, a French bully named Shunar challenged a mountain man named Kit Carson to a duel. Mr. Parker and I were witnesses to this event. The two men, each on horseback, fought with pistols. Both fired almost simultaneously. Shunar's bullet passed over Carson's head. Carson's ball entered Shunar's hand, came out at the wrist, and passed through the arm above the elbow. As Carson was reloading, preparing to fire again, the Frenchman begged for his life, and the duel was over. I attended Shunar's wound with his foul breath nearly gagging me."[1]

---

[1] One of Parker's letters to the American Board was the very first time Christopher "Kit" Carson was mentioned in the east. Short, freckled with sandy hair, Carson never boasted even though he was among the most accomplished and genuine of the mountain men. His fame came by way of John C. Fremont who hired him as a guide when his party of scouts, engineers and soldiers explored the West. Carson revealed a route to Fremont that would become the Oregon Trail. Fremont's journals published in 1844, made a national hero of Carson.

Marcus continued, "Two days later, a Shoshone came to me calling me a powerful medicine man, and from then on, the Indians called me a medicine man. Evidently, this was of high status with the tribes, for on the fourth day, Parker and I received a visit from the chiefs of the Flatheads and the Nez Perce tribes. They expressed great pleasure in seeing us and had strong desires to learn about the Bible and God. Little Chief of the Flatheads said he had greatly rejoiced when he heard there was a teacher from the Almighty and a medicine man coming among them. He had been told some things about the worship of God, but he said he did not practice them. But now, Little Chief said, if a teacher would come among them, he and his children, meaning all over whom he had authority, would obey all that the teacher would say.

"One of the Nez Perce chiefs arose and said, 'I had heard a little about God from white men, which had only gone into my ears. I wish to know enough to have it go down into my heart, influence my life, and teach my people about your God.' His speech was most eloquent. His Nez Perce name was Tackensuatis, but the trappers called him Rotten Belly because he bore the scars of a severe stomach wound he received in a battle.

"After mutual conversation and prayer with these tribes, I was satisfied there were no missionaries of any denomination among them. I suggested to Mr. Parker that if we had another associate with us, I should like to return home and, if the Board should approve, come out next year with others to establish a mission among them.

"I was surprised at Mr. Parker's immediate approval, which meant that Mr. Parker would go on and that I would return for our wedding," he paused to glance at Narcissa, "and prepare to journey to the Nez Perce country. The chiefs expressed great satisfaction that I should return with others to come and live among them and teach them the word of God. They readily promised the necessary escort to Mr. Parker, together with assistance to pack and drive his animals as he continued west. I turned over my pack mule to Mr. Parker with most of the camping equipment. I kept only my mount and the barest of essentials. I was eager to come back to New York." Saying this, Marcus looked directly into those lovely blue eyes of his fiancé, who was listening patiently next to him on the settee when they had adjourned to the sitting room after dinner.

"Since I dare not ask the Board to fund $100 for a fit pack horse, I bought a decrepit animal for $5, but he could not carry cargo because of his extremely sore back. I suggested that I take a Nez Perce lad I named Richard back to the States with me. Richard could speak English a little, and I could teach him more of our language on the trip. He would be able to serve as an interpreter and assist me in learning his language. Three days later, another Nez Perce chief also begged me to take his son, Ais. The chief told me, 'I have but one more son, but I am willing to part with this one that he might learn the religion of the whites.' I gave Ais the Christian name of John."

"Where are the lads now, Doctor Whitman?" asked Mrs. Prentiss.

"I took them to Ithaca to stay with Mr. Parker's family until I return for them. They will be attending school for a while."

"Are they wearing buckskin?" asked Harvey.

"Yes, they are quite an attraction with their fringed buckskin shirt, leggings, belts, and such. Buckskin is the typical attire of the trappers and the Indians. Fringes facilitate water drainage and are located across the back, the bottom of the jacket, the end of the sleeves, and the trouser legs. I was very impressed with the garb and may consider it for myself, but as for the boys, no doubt Mrs. Parker will clothe them in proper American attire.

"Mr. Parker and I parted company, and I joined the returning caravan on August 27, led by Thomas Fitzpatrick. About eighty-five mountain men were also returning to civilization. At Fort Laramie, Fontenelle took over the command from Mr. Fitzpatrick. Richard, John, and I landed in St. Louis on November 4, given free passage by Pierre Cabanne, who conducted a trading post where we refreshed ourselves and our horses."

The Prentiss boys had read about the mountain men, and they were excited to learn more since Marcus had a personal link with these legendary characters. He told them that although Bridger was illiterate, the only one who had a better knowledge of the geography of the western country was Jedediah Smith, born in New York. Smith set the record for the most beaver pelts in the history of the Rendezvous, selling 668 in 1825. Jed Smith was never without two things: his rifle and his Bible. In 1821 he had a confrontation with a grizzly bear. The bear slashed him from head to foot.

Marcus captivated them with more about Smith. "After other trappers ran the bear off, Smith lay on the ground with broken ribs, and his scalp was pulled off from his left ear to his cheek, taking his ear with it." The women shivered to imagine the gruesome sight as Marcus continued, "Since no medical facilities were available in the wilderness, he asked one of his companions to get a needle and thread and start sewing his scalp back on. After some coaxing, his friend reattached his ear. There it remained until he was killed by a Comanche in 1831, at age 32.

"Another example of the grit of the trappers the men told me about was Kentuckian Tom Smith--no kin to Jedediah. In 1827 his brigade was ambushed. A shot by a ball in the leg above his ankle shattered his bone. Nobody knew what to do, so Smith called for a knife and amputated his wounded leg by himself. Someone came forward and finished the job. They were sure he would die of infection, but Smith put an Indian remedy of a paste of arnica, comfrey, and yarrow on his wound. The paste he concocted is a remedy that I'll add to my medicine chest," and he added, "Smith then proceeded to make his wooden leg himself. He was known as "Peg-leg Smith" and lived another three decades from that time forward.

Marcus remarked,

"These men were tough souls," and his audience agreed.

Most mountain men thrived in the solitude and freedom of the wilderness, yet matrimony was one tradition of the civilization many partook in. Marriage to a tribe member offered companionship and sometimes status with the tribes that other mountain men did not have. In this way, many Indian wives became accustomed to white culture. The trappers were very proud of their wives at the Rendezvous and often showered them with gifts. The mountain men became cultural intermediaries between the settlers and the Indians. Often the trapper wintered with his wife's people and lived their lifestyle, becoming part of the tribe's culture.

All marriages were secured by offering gifts to the woman's family. The women were not "sold." The bride was a valuable part of the community and, therefore, the family required a valuable commodity in exchange, such as horses, blankets, or other trade goods.

Marcus knew the reality of the need for companionship in the Nez Perce country, and he felt he was fortunate to return to a beautiful woman waiting to be his wife--if she were willing to endure the hardships. Finally, alone with Narcissa after supper, he confided, "One major goal for my trip was to determine how well a woman might fare. Narcissa, dear, there is great difficulty in crossing the Rockies. It is not hospitable to a refined woman. The Indian women ride astride a horse. You may be riding on a horse, sitting in a bumpy, dusty cart, or even walking to get across rivers or through tight mountain passes. We will sleep on the ground, be exposed to the weather, and eat beans and jerky." Marcus paused, "You must consider this very carefully."

She looked up at him and said, "I intend to join you. My family and friends consider me a hearty and healthy soul. My commitment to the conversion of the heathens has never wavered. My commitment to join you as your wife has never wavered." He took her hand, raised it to his cheek, and closed his eyes at her softness.

Terrie Biggs

The Spaldings Join the Mission Party

Based on his upcoming marriage, Greene had given Marcus the decision of the Prudential Committee of the Board granting permission for him and his bride to go to Oregon along with another married couple (a clergyman and his wife) and three single men. He preferred that the single men have skills as teachers, farmers, and craftsmen proficient in carpentry. Reverend and Mrs. Oliver Powell had initially planned to go to Oregon with Marcus. Marcus had been a guest at their home when he asked Narcissa to marry him. However, Mrs. Powell had given birth to a child, and Greene and the Board would not allow a married couple with a child to go. Greene made it Marcus's responsibility to find another couple. With very little time to spare and slow means of communication, matters were approaching a crisis. Marcus had promised to return the two Nez Perce boys, Richard and John, to their families at the Rendezvous of 1836, where he was to meet up with Parker. The deadline was approaching. Marcus discussed his dilemma with Narcissa.

"Perhaps I can be of service," Narcissa offered to Marcus. "Rev. Henry Spalding and I attended the academy together. He married about three years ago, and they applied for missionary service. They have been assigned to the Boudinot station among the Osage Indians on the Neosho River.

"Mrs. Spalding had been with child, and I have heard that the girl child was stillborn in October. Perhaps if you were to write to them, they might be persuaded to be reassigned to our territory and be our companions on our journey to Oregon country."

Marcus got word to Henry, asking if they would consider being a part of their mission. Henry wrote Greene on December 28, 1835, stating, "If the Board and Dr. Whitman wish me to go to the Rocky Mountains with him, I am ready." However, Greene was unaware that the Spalding's child had died and discouraged them from going across the Rocky Mountains with an infant.

Greene's letter of January 22 to Marcus indicated that other prospective candidates had withdrawn their applications. He mentioned Henry as a last resort and may have felt a bit desperate for Marcus at that point because Greene previously indicated that no one with a child would be granted an appointment. "I have some doubt whether Henry's temperament will fit him for interaction with the traders and travelers in that region. As to laboriousness, self-denial, energy, and perseverance, I presume few men are better qualified than he."

Despite Greene's doubts, Marcus wrote a reply to his letter on January 29, informing Greene that Spalding's child did not survive birth. He asked if the Spaldings could be reassigned to their party, which was expected to leave for St. Louis by February 25.

Marcus would later find that the warning about Henry's temperament would be a problem of a different sort. The following incident was an example of the difficulties to follow. As of the first week of February 1836, the Spaldings were still preparing to leave for their Osage Indian station. They were staying in Prattsburgh, visiting Eliza Spalding's family. Rumors had reached his friends that Marcus asked him to be reassigned to Oregon.

"Why is Whitman still looking for associates?" a church member asked Henry.

"Why are you and Mrs. Spalding not going with the Whitmans?" another asked.

Tall and bony, with sunken cheeks and eyes, Henry was a man of touchy pride and smoldering resentments. After many friendly inquiries, he made this bizarre remark, "I do not want to go into the same mission with Narcissa Prentiss as I question her judgment." Henry's comment about Narcissa never reached Marcus's ears, or undoubtedly their destinies would have been altered.

As it turned out, Narcissa had rejected him when he tried to court her, and he had never forgiven her. However, she had been the one to suggest his name, never aware that Henry still harbored resentment towards her after three years of marriage.

When Marcus received permission from the Board, he took immediate action since time was running out to find a couple to accompany them. He rode to Prattsburgh to appeal personally to Henry, unaware that the Spaldings had left for Howard, a village about twenty miles southwest of Prattsburgh. Henry had a speaking engagement there in the Presbyterian Church on Sunday. Marcus overtook them on the road shortly before they reached Howard.

Marcus greeted them with, "We want you for Oregon!" Marcus rode with them to the village of Howard, where they got a room at an inn. "Listen, Henry. We need you to accompany us to Oregon. We must leave immediately. The Board will only allow us to go if we have a married clergyman with us. Without you, there will be no Oregon mission founded this year." He turned to Eliza. "Mrs. Spalding, I know that you are still recovering from the difficult birth and the death of your child. You need to know that this will be a very tedious journey. No white women have ever crossed the Rockies. You will be required to ride horses. Despite how much I need you both, you must know about the hardships."

"I am very concerned about Mrs. Spalding's health for such a journey," Henry replied.

"Your wagon will be of great value to us, Brother Spalding," Marcus urged.

Eliza's strength of character was displayed when she determined, "I like the command just as it stands, 'Go ye into the world,' with no exceptions for poor health."

The Spaldings had prepared to leave, but now their destination was Oregon country. They were already heading for Cincinnati, where they would wait for the Whitmans with their light, two-horse Dearborn wagon. It had wooden springs from one axle to another made from hardwood. The bed was dark brown, and the wheels were yellow with blue stripes.

By February 15, 1836, Marcus knew that his Oregon mission was assured. He asked Henry, "Since you will be passing by Angelica, would you please deliver this letter to the Prentiss home? Miss Prentiss should be advised that we must hastily prepare for our wedding. I will arrive on February 17."

Judge Prentiss, Narcissa's father, had been informed of Henry's comment about his daughter. When Henry arrived in Angelica with Marcus's letter to Narcissa, Judge Prentiss was furious and took Henry aside.

"I demand an explanation about the remark you made in Prattsburgh about my daughter. What is this nonsense that you did not want to go on the same mission with Narcissa? In the name of God, Henry, you have known each other for years. You must know how dedicated and unwavering she has been in her desire to be of service."

Henry gave a weak excuse to Prentiss: "I certainly never intended to suggest that Narcissa was in question. I was very concerned about the dangers and hardships of traveling with women. I am sorry if my words were misconstrued. As you know, I am very fond of all of your family."

"Are you sure this apparent bitterness is not a result of her rejecting you when you were younger?"

"No, sir. My only concern is for the safety and comfort of the women."

Judge Prentiss seemed to be appeased by Henry's response. "Well, my son, then go with my blessings, and may God be with you."

The bitterness that Judge Prentiss suspected of Henry had a far-reaching impact later.

Henry Harmon Spalding
He paraphrased Whitman's philosophy: "While we point them with one hand to God, it is equally our duty to point with the other to the hoe as the means of saving their famished bodies."

Henry Harmon Spalding had a painful entry into the world. One child who would later come to the Whitman Mission also had traumatic childhood experiences parallel to Henry's. He was considered a man of contradictions by history as a troublemaker, but he was more open-hearted than Marcus in his baptism of the indigenous people into his congregation.

Despite his seething jealousy of Marcus and his apparent loathing of Narcissa, it was more likely that he was still in love with her. Gaunt with narrow shoulders, black hair, scruffy beard, and dour personality, Henry would lend no humor to the long journey.

Henry and Marcus had never met in earlier years, even though Henry was born in Wheeler, New York, where Marcus later practiced medicine. Henry was born fifteen months before Marcus. They both had difficult childhoods. Marcus lost his father at age six, and his mother sent him to live with an uncle. Henry's father never married his mother, and she abandoned Henry when he was fourteen months old. The pious and staunch New England Christians judged him and treated him as an outcast.

"Bastard!" his foster father shouted at Henry. At age seventeen, he left that "home" after the brute whipped Henry and his foster mother. He felt he was a cast-off bastard and wished himself dead. In Prattsburgh, he found refuge in the home of Ezra Rice, a schoolteacher, with whom he lived for four years, working for room and board. Barely able to read or write at age twenty-two--which shows the lack of attention Rice gave him while he lived with him--Henry enrolled in the newly opened Franklin Academy in Prattsburgh, which was equivalent to two years of college. He attended school intermittently until he was twenty-eight. Five to six years older than the other students dressed in threadbare clothing, Henry felt awkward, ashamed, and embarrassed to be called upon to speak.

Still working for room and board, he moved to a farm nearby. He interrupted his studies at the academy to teach in small country schools to earn money. The year Henry first attended the academy, there were fifty-four young men, and Narcissa was among the forty-six young ladies. She was twenty-two. He had fallen in love with Narcissa and wanted her to marry him. Again, another rejection from one he loved added to the pain in his heart when she refused to be courted by him. She was his first love--lively, well-spoken, tall, fair-haired, self-assured, and spirited--everything he was not. Tenaciously struggling to further his education, he ultimately received a scholarship from the American Education Society and attended Western Reserve College in Ohio, from which he attained an A.B. degree.

Eliza Spalding was of medium height and slender. She had dark brown hair, blue eyes, and a slightly dark complexion. Her voice was coarse. She was very somber and well educated, having studied Greek and Hebrew. Devout to her Presbyterian Church, she had attended lessons on theology. Her grasp of languages would be invaluable in learning the Nez Perce language very quickly.

Terrie Biggs

The Wedding

Marcus returned to Angelica on Feb. 17, 1836. He had been preparing for their journey.

"Oh, my. Oh, dear." Mrs. Prentiss exclaimed, exasperated. "We have such a short time to prepare for your wedding. You know that your father is being ordained as an elder tomorrow. Our friends and family will already have gathered. The church is decorated, so we shall perform your marriage ceremony after the ordination. Narcissa, this abrupt, informal ceremony is not what I had planned for you."

"It's all right, Mother. Angelica's Presbyterian Church is lovely. We are being practical. My dress was finished last week, and I want my family to be together for our wedding." Narcissa, at age twenty-seven, was practical and had a black dress of bombazine, which is twilled silk, made for the ordination.

"Mother, it's bad enough that we are wearing black to show respect for her father's ceremony, but it is just bad luck for Narcissa to wear black for a wedding dress," whispered her sister, Jane, during the ceremony.

"Hush, Child," said Mrs. Prentiss. We had only a short time to prepare, and the dress will serve her as traveling clothes."

Missionaries leaving for stations often sang a favorite hymn called the *Missionary's Farewell*, by Samuel F. Smith, who also wrote *America*. The members of the choir sang two stanzas until the members of the choir and the congregation were unable to sing because they were touched by emotion as their cheeks became wet:

> Yes, my native land! I love thee.
> All thy scenes I love them well.
> Friends, connections, happy country,
> Can I bid you all farewell?
> Can I leave thee, can I leave thee,
> Far in heathen lands to dwell?
>
> Home! Thy joys are passing lovely.
> Joys no stranger-heart can tell;
> Happy home! – 'tis sure I love thee!
> Can I – can I say – Farewell?
> Can I leave thee, can I leave thee,
> Far in heathen lands to dwell?

Only a few, including Narcissa, were able to continue.

> Yes! I hasten gladly,
> From the scenes I love so well;
> Far away, ye billows! Bear me;
> Lovely native land! Farewell!
> Pleased I leave thee, pleased I leave thee,
> Far in heathen lands to dwell.

Narcissa's beautiful soprano voice prevailed until the last stanza, when sobs echoed in the church. The sentiment of the hymn overpowered her family and friends, but Narcissa continued the last stanza as a solo:

> In the deserts let me labor,
> On the mountains let me tell,
> How he died, the blessed Savior,
> To redeem a world from hell!
> Let me hasten, let me hasten,
> Far in heathen lands to dwell.

There was no dry eye in the church. Her clear and sweet voice left its music in the hearts of all present.

The married couple spent the night of their wedding visiting with friends and family. Marcus was getting better acquainted with her family and meeting her friends for the first and possibly the last time. They were celebrating in joy yet preparing to part in sorrow. Marcus gave her practical advice on choosing and packing her personal belongings. They both knew this was not the night to consummate the marriage. Still, in awe that this tall, vibrant, beautiful woman had accepted his hand in marriage, he walked her to the base of the staircase leading to her bed-chamber. She was exhausted. The joy of her wedding and the realization of her life's dream to be a missionary were offset by the pain of leaving her home, classroom, and family, knowing it was likely that she would never lay eyes on them again. Agony and ecstasy.

"My dearest," Marcus said softly, as he faced her with both hands on her upper arms, "we will have a lifetime together to get more," he paused for the right words, "more intimately acquainted. You rest now, for we have a great deal of traveling ahead. Rise early, for I will be here before dawn." He leaned forward, wanting to kiss her forehead, but he felt it was not appropriate at this time. He left for Rev. Powell's house, where his gear was stored.

    Tearful goodbyes sent them on their way, with everyone promising to write. They rode away in the early dawn, silhouetted by the brilliant red and orange sunrise. The words of her song haunted her:

>Home! Thy joys are passing lovely.
>Joys no stranger-heart can tell;
>Happy home! 'Tis sure I love thee!
>Can I, can I say farewell?
>Can I leave thee, can I leave thee,
>Far in heathen lands to dwell?

    "Red sky in morning, sailor, take warning," Jane whispered, sobbing.

    "Royal Coach Inn" was the freshly painted sign that hung over the door, swinging from chains in the cold February wind. It was the end of Narcissa's first day of travel, riding side-saddle. Her bones were sore, but her groin muscles would have taken a toll had she ridden astride. Her right leg was cold and numb from being bent over the saddle for so long. Marcus dismounted first and helped her off her gelding. She used him for balance as she was a bit unsteady at first. "I know this inn. The proprietor is very kind. There's always a warm fire and good victuals." He was a bit shy and looked away as he added, "We'll get a room for the night."

    "I do admit that I need some refreshing," she confessed.

The supper was warm and hearty. The potato soup was seasoned with leeks and was quite delicious, followed by roasted pork baked with carrots and parsnips.

The stairs creaked as they ascended to their assigned room, the third door on the left. "Well, my dear, I believe we will just have to make this door our official threshold. May I?" He tenderly scooped her up and carried her through the doorway. The proprietor had lit a fire, and the reflection danced on the ceiling. The muslin curtains were closed, and the down comforter was already turned back.

"No need to light the lamp," she said softly, "Let's sit in front of the fire on the bearskin rug for a while."

He sat down on the rug and helped her lower herself in front of him. She leaned back into his chest. Instinctively his senses longed to be drowning in the smell and the softness of this woman's luxurious being. Softly, his cheek, nose, and mouth slid in, though, and over her hair. He loosened her combs, and her shiny, silky hair slipped down her back. She felt his heavy breathing and the rhythm of his heart beating against her back. His arms, so strong and masculine, wrapped around her. How tender, she thought. What a safe harbor he gave her.

Life had taken such a drastic turn in the past year. She was with a man she instantly knew was sent by God as her life partner when she walked out of her mother's kitchen into the parlor last February. He was still amazed that this was the same young woman who had taken his heart and drifted into his dreams seven years ago in a small chapel.

Tonight, she would give herself to her first lover, not just her body but also her whole being. She had never known the sheer ecstasy of making love and then sleeping next to a man all night. This first encounter in a lover's embrace was worth the wait, worth the unspoken words of those who were sorry for her spinsterhood. She had a feeling of rapture with his body curled against hers. "Thank you, my Lord, for the blessings you have bestowed upon me." The glow of the embers mirrored the glow in both of their hearts as they gave in to slumber, wrapped in each other's embrace.

Journey to the Rendezvous

"The Lord would provide," was the optimistic view of the missionary party. The Board gave Marcus $184 traveling expenses for himself, Narcissa, and the two Nez Perce boys to go the fifteen days from Rushville to Cincinnati. The missions were expected to be self-supporting. Since fundraising for the trip was one of Marcus's responsibilities, he appealed to many churches interested in his proposed mission. Marcus had received $26 from the Angelica church and $200 from the Rushville congregation.

On Sunday, February 21, they arrived in Ithaca, New York, at the home of Samuel Parker to pick up the two Nez Perce boys, John and Richard, who were staying with Parker and attending school. They returned to Rushville to bid their final farewells. On March 3, they started for Pittsburgh by horse-drawn sleigh. They met up with another party comprised of Dr. Satterlee, his bride, and a traveling companion on their way to a Pawnee mission. They rested for a day due to the ill health of Mrs. Satterlee until Marcus felt she could continue.

When they reached Pittsburgh, they stayed at the Exchange Hotel. Narcissa was suffering from a headache and stayed in her room. At the same time, Marcus and the two Nez Perce boys created quite a sensation at the East Liberty Presbyterian Church when their identities became known.

In the meantime, while traveling to Pittsburgh with his small wagon, Henry Spalding and Eliza met George Catlin, the famous painter of Indians. Catlin had firsthand knowledge of the far west, as he had been on an expedition in 1832. His advice was, "I would not attempt to take a white female into that country for two reasons. First, the enthusiastic desire to see a white woman, everywhere prevailing among the distant tribes, may terminate in unrestrained passion, consequently in her ruin. Second, the fatigue of the journey will destroy the women. It is 1400 miles from the mouth of the Platte. They will be on horseback, with rivers to swim. Every night they must sleep in the open air and endure the sun's heat, the blowing dust will tear their tender skin raw, and terrible storms will hammer them. They will have to live on buffalo meat and collect dung to be used to fuel the campfire. No female has yet made the trip." This description gave Eliza a realistic glimpse into the future, and she became even more determined to endure.

The next day Marcus and Narcissa secured passage on the 127-ton steamboat *Siam,* leaving Pittsburgh and sailing down the Ohio River for Cincinnati, the same vessel that Marcus and Parker had sailed on that spring up the Missouri River to Liberty, Missouri. They left at ten o'clock, cruising at a rate of thirteen miles per hour, and Narcissa was delighted at the rapid pace they made. The motion of the steamer was agreeable to her in their spacious stateroom, except when she was writing. Narcissa was a gifted writer, and her letters and diary provided vivid descriptions of her surroundings, the people she met, entertaining anecdotes, the journey, and missionary life. She was fully aware that this was a ground-breaking journey for American women.

Two days later, when the *Siam* docked at Cincinnati, Narcissa met Eliza Spalding for the first time. She was concerned about Eliza's health and her ability to endure the journey after her miscarriage. Still, she liked Eliza very much and thought she was steadfast and well-suited for Henry. Narcissa commented that there was "no shrinking with her" and felt that Eliza would fearlessly stand up to their future challenges.

They all stayed in Cincinnati a few days while Marcus and Henry secured some provisions. Steaming down the great Mississippi on the *Majestic*, one of the largest boats on the river, they arrived in St. Louis. Accommodations were better than the other ships they had boarded, and Narcissa enjoyed the excellent food and servants who stood at their elbows, ready to fulfill any wish.

Greeted by dense fog in St. Louis, Henry checked for mail at the post office and received a letter from Greene dated February 25 with the Board's official consent for the change of destination. It permitted them to establish a mission among the Flathead and Nez Perce Indians and to be teachers.

At the post office, Marcus found a letter from Greene and one from the War Department, Office of Indian Affairs, issuing letters of introduction and permits to enter and reside in the Indian country. Oregon was then a foreign land with both the United States and Great Britain exercising joint occupancy under the Treaty of 1818. The permits were called "passports" in the official records.

The letter from Greene gave him his final instructions and sound, wise advice: "Let your conduct be exemplary and free from the appearance of evil. Do not feel it necessary to be critical of everything wrong among this class of persons, remembering that your business is almost exclusively with the Indian tribes.

While you are strict and uncompromising about your principles and conduct, do not be harsh and dictatorial to others. Do them good and be kind to all at every opportunity. Let Christian love shine brightly in all that you do."

As was the strict custom of that period regarding the Sabbath, he continued, "Keep it strictly and let the Indians and all others see that you do so. Make the distinction between that and other days as broad and obvious as possible. You must introduce the Sabbath to explain its meaning, design, and use. You must fix the standard of its sacredness." The travelers needed no reminder of this. Their refusal to travel on Sunday delayed their trip and would create problems and conflicts while going with their escort, the American Fur Company.

Greene, continuing his wise advice, told Marcus that his most important duty was to concentrate on benefiting the Indians. He added, "Avoid all secular and political interference with any class of men. Engage in no trading that is not absolutely necessary to obtain the necessities of life for yourself and your families. Let all of your worldly and secular concerns be as limited and compact as your circumstances permit."

Upon returning from the post office, Marcus had to tell his bride that there were no letters from her loved ones.

"Why have they not written, Marcus? This is the last opportunity they will have to bring me news from home--my home sweet home--and the friends I love."

Marcus had no answer and held her in his arms.

"But I am not sad," she said, feeling the joy of her love for him. "My health is good, and I am enjoying the beautiful scenery while we are sailing. However, I wish, my dear Marcus, that my mother was here so that I could whisper in her ear many things that I dare not write. You are the kindest husband and the best in *every* way. I have such a good place to shelter--under your wing."

The *Chariton* sailed from St. Louis after dinner on Thursday, March 31, headed for Liberty, Missouri, with the mission party numbering nine. The newlyweds of six weeks were on deck to witness leaving the Mississippi River and going into the narrower channel of the Missouri River.

Narcissa observed, "Isn't it interesting that there are rugged, high bluffs on one side of the river and a different world of low plains on the other? That is, of course, when we can see through the fog."

As the newlyweds were enjoying the confluence of the two mighty rivers at twilight on that beautiful evening, Henry Spalding climbed up the stairs and saw the new lovers. Henry's stomach twisted in jealousy when he saw them. Marcus had his left arm around her waist and whispered into her right ear. Silhouetted by the moon, thoroughly enjoying the glorious view from the bow, love and intimacy glowed on her face. Henry reached the top of the stairs and called them to prayer. They gave each other a look of resignation and followed Henry below.

Mrs. Satterlee was still very sick with a bad cold and cough. All others were well except for side effects from drinking the river water. Narcissa's health was the exception. Weighing 136 pounds, she was complimented by everyone who saw her as the best able to endure the journey over the mountains.

Liberty hosted the Whitman group for twelve days. It was halfway between their homes in New York and their destination near Ft. Walla Walla. The Board had hurriedly appointed William Gray as a mechanic. He caught up with the Whitman party in Liberty on April 9. Gray was also a teacher, cabinet maker, and house joiner but was an incredibly dull scholar. His ambition exceeded his qualifications. Secretary Greene had some reservations about Gray's appointment but felt it was better to send one with mediocre skills than none.

The remaining supplies for their expedition were purchased, and Marcus's final financial report to the Board in September totaled $3,063.96. Henry brought his small wagon for the women's use and lighter supplies, and Marcus and Henry bought a large farm wagon to carry the heavier baggage. They spent more than one-third of their total cost on animals. They bought tools, furniture, guns, ammunition, clothing, books, stationery, seeds, medicines, instruments, and side-saddles for the women.

Marcus hired a young man named Dulin to assist with the packing and care of the animals. Samuel Temoni, a young Nez Perce whom Richard knew, was returning to his country and joined their party. Miles Goodyear, a nineteen-year-old from New Haven, Connecticut, attached himself to the party, making a total of ten. Five were missionaries--the Whitmans, the Spaldings, and Gray--three were Nez Perce, and two were hired men. Dulin left them at the Rendezvous, but Goodyear continued with them to Fort Hall. Narcissa grew quite fond of the Nez Perce boys, Richard and John.

The travelers split up at Liberty. Henry, Gray, the two hired men, and Richard and John went overland with the wagons, supplies, and animals to join the American Fur Company. Sadly, the new bride, Mrs. Satterlee, died. She was just twenty-three years old. Marcus performed an autopsy and determined that she undoubtedly had tuberculosis. This incident was the first of many deaths and illnesses the Whitmans would encounter. Marcus and the two women, Narcissa and Eliza, were scheduled to travel on the fur company's boat, the

Diana, to Bellevue. However, as the funeral service was about to begin the next morning, the fur company's ship suddenly hoisted its anchor. It cut through the water, the whistle blowing to announce its departure. The captain, unaware of Marcus's arrangements for the boat to pick them up, refused to stop when Marcus frantically yelled at the captain for him to stop his boat. The three were very distressed when the captain hollered back, "There's no more room. We can't haul you."

After the steamer disappeared around the bend, they finished the burial service on the grassy bank of the river. It was a blow to Marcus. His responsibility to protect his small party through hostile Indian country grew heavy upon him. Ironically, the *Diana* later snagged herself and sank, although no lives were lost as she went down in shallow water.

They had to travel about 300 miles overland to join Henry, or the whole venture would fail that year. Satterlee had stayed for his wife's burial service with his other traveling companion, Allis. They had one wagon drawn by three teams of oxen. Marcus had no choice but to join the Satterlee group hastily. The oxen traveled slowly, and Marcus was afraid they would miss their Rendezvous destination, so he sent Allis ahead to overtake Henry and to bring back the light wagon for the women. When Allis arrived, Marcus and the two women left the slow-going wagon and continued in Spalding's small wagon.

While laying over in Liberty, Narcissa and Eliza had made a tent of bed ticking, which was large enough for seven of them to sleep under, but it had gone with the supplies in the heavy wagon with Henry. The three had only their hand luggage and bedding they had taken with them on the steamer. They slept in the open air but could gaze at the brilliant stars. The adventures of pioneer travel and hardship had already begun.

Marcus and the women caught up with Henry within eighteen miles of the Oto Agency, their original meeting place. After many anxious and challenging days of traveling, their hearts were thankful when they met up with the Fur Company at one o'clock in the morning while the caravan was still sleeping. The Company, commanded by Captain Fitzpatrick, had failed to take axle grease, and the Company had to stop for several days to slay two oxen to render fat to make axle grease. Without the caravan's delay, the Whitman party would have missed their opportunity for the Oregon Mission one more time. The missionaries felt that this was God's protective care over them.

Narcissa was given her choice between a horse and a mule to ride. She chose the mule and rode side-saddle. The pair of "gentlemen's" boots she had made for herself in Rushville was perfect for riding and protected her ankles and calves.

Of her mule, Richard commented, "That's very bad mule--can't catch buffalos," but the animal seemed steady and reliable to Narcissa.

They raised a tent with a center pole at night and fastened it down with pegs. It was tee-pee shaped, covering a large circle. They spread India-rubber cloth on the ground and put Mackinaw blankets over the cloth for the beds. During the day's rides, the Mackinaws covered the saddles. Each member had a plate, knife, fork, and tin cup. When the timber was no longer available, buffalo dung fueled their fires. A hunter brought the women their first taste of buffalo meat. Marcus cooked the meat for them, and they found it very satisfying. Narcissa became healthier and more vibrant on the prairie diet, while Eliza became sickly. Henry was more and more disagreeable as Narcissa flourished, countering his prediction about her.

They often ate all three meals of buffalo meat, which was lean and hearty and tasted very similar to beef, as Marcus had described to her family what seemed like a lifetime ago. Often Richard and John hunted and killed the buffalo, which were sacred to them, and they gave thanks to the spirits and the buffalos for offering themselves for nourishment. Richard's common sense and knowledge proved very valuable to the Whitmans.

The Whitman party of ten began the journey with seventeen cows, including four milk cows, fourteen horses, and six mules. The American Fur Company, consisting of seventy men, had nearly four hundred animals, primarily mules loaded with packs strung in a line. They had seven wagons, and the Whitman party had two. At night the caravan camped in a circle of wagons, tents, and baggage. Horses and mules were inside the ring for protection, and cows were picketed outside the circle. The Company posted guards day and night, afraid that local bands would steal the livestock.

At daybreak, a member of the Company called, "Arise, arise," which startled the mules who bellowed and made such an uproar that they woke up the whole camp. Everyone quickly ate breakfast, and they were moving by six o'clock. Lunch was from eleven until two o'clock, and the caravan stopped about six in the evening unless they found an ideal campsite earlier.

After spreading the oilcloth, they ate their meals on the ground, serving as a rain cloak. The tin plates held up well. They had several pans for meat and milk. The women sat on the oilcloth on the ground, sometimes on a blanket or a box. Occasionally they had the luxury of a cup of tea. The ten of them went through three loaves of bread each day. The flour almost ran out, and they reserved it for thickening broth. The travelers ate breakfast and dinner in their tents and lunch in the open air. Marcus prepared most of the meat. The women had baked several loaves of bread before they left Missouri, and when it ran out, they learned how to bake over an open fire.

Terrie Biggs

The Rocky Mountains to the Blues

The women were about to discover how unique their presence was. They were near the foot of the Rocky Mountains in the latter part of June, at the Platte River, about six days from Fort Laramie, when they met a large party of Pawnee on the way to Fort Laramie. The Pawnee were very surprised to see the missionaries and especially taken aback by the white females. The next day the mission party passed the villages the men had come. When they camped, the Pawnee visited them. They stood around their tents, peeking in with curiosity and astonishment at Narcissa and Eliza, their first glimpse of white women and strawberry blonde hair.

A messenger was sent ahead from Independence Rock to inform the impatient trappers and Indians when the caravan was expected to arrive. The Fur Company carried trade goods for the Rendezvous. "White women! White women, two of 'em, with the missionaries," the messenger hollered to the trappers, bringing his horse to an abrupt stop, spraying them with dust. Yelps and whoops belted out from the trappers who had not seen a white woman in years. Two days before the caravan reached the Green River, the missionaries were alarmed by ten Indians and five white men dressed in buckskin yelling and waving a white flag from a raised rifle. The self-appointed welcoming party barreled down one side of the camp and then the other, shouting wildly and firing rifles in the air. At first, they frightened the weary travelers until they realized they were not in danger and that it was indeed a *welcoming* party. The camp invited two Nez Perce men for dinner: Chief Lawyer, whose tribal name was Ish-hol-hol-hoats-hoats, and Tackensuatis. Chief Lawyer had earlier heard Spokane Garry read from his Bible, and he carried Garry's teaching back to the Nez Perce. He had been the connecting link between Spokane Garry and the Nez Perce delegation that went to St. Louis in 1831 to get teachers and more information about Christianity. Parker had met Chief Lawyer at the previous year's Rendezvous. Another member of the welcoming party was Kentuc, who had accompanied Parker on his exploration tour of the Pacific Northwest in 1835.

Twenty-six-year-old Joe Meek, whom Marcus had met at the previous year's Rendezvous, also joined the welcoming party. Meek became enamored with vivacious Narcissa. He rode by her side the next two days while accompanying the caravan to the Green River location.

Joe Meek

Narcissa was amused by the language of the Company men from the West as to how they referred to a quantity: "A heap of man, a heap of water, she is heap sick." Meek entertained her with his colorful language and adventures. He was nineteen years old when he went to the Rockies. "The first fall on the Yellowstone, Hawkins--that's Jake Hawkins, my hunting partner--well, he and I were a'coming up the river in search of the camp when we discovered a large bar on the opposite bank." It took Narcissa a moment until she realized that the "bar" he referred to was a bear. "We shot across and thought we had kilt him, for he lay quite still. As we wanted to take some trophy of our victory to camp, we tied our mules and left our guns, clothes, and everything 'cept our knives and belts, and swum over to where the bar was. But instead of being dead as we expected, he sprung up as we come near him, and he lit out after us. Then you ought to have seen two naked men run!"

Narcissa jerked her head and was stunned at first to hear such frank language. Soon, though, the corners of her mouth curved into a lovely grin as she adjusted to his raw but colorful descriptions. He continued, "T'was a race for life, and a close one, at that, but we made the river first. The bank was 'bout fifteen feet above the water, and the river ten or twelve feet deep, but we didn't stop. Into the river we went, the bar after us, and he was 'bout as quick as we were. The current was very strong, and the bar was about halfway 'tween Hawkins and me. Hawkins was a-tryin' to swim downstream faster than the current was carryin' the bar, and I was not holdin' back. You can reckon that I swam fast as a jackrabbit on hot rocks!"

Narcissa imagined the scene of a bear and the two men frantically swimming to save their "hides."

"Every moment, I felt myself bein' washed into the yawnin' jaws of the mighty beast, whose head was lookin' up the stream with his eyes on me. But the current was too strong for him and swept him along as fast as it did me. All this time, not a long one, we were lookin' for someplace to land where the bar could not overtake us. Hawkins was the first to make the shore, unbeknownst to the bar, whose head was still facin' upstream. Hawkins set up such a whoopin' and yellin' that the bar made shore, too, but on the opposite side. I made haste to follow Hawkins, who had landed on the side of the river we started from, either by design or good luck, and then we traveled back a mile or more to where our mules were left--a bar on one side of the river, and two bare-naked men on the other!"

"My word, Mr. Meek!" exclaimed Narcissa. "God certainly had his hand on you that day."

On the second day of travel, after becoming accustomed to his company and his tales of adventure, Narcissa noticed his coarse narrative improving with each story he told. She inquired, "Are you not lonely for female companionship?"

"Well, ma'am, there ain't no white women in these mountains, but I'll tell you the story of a Shoshone beauty and how she became my wife last year. My friend Captain 'Billy' [Milton] Sublette had secured this lady for his wife through his wealth, power, and kindness. I admired her from the first moment I saw her, but I respected their union. Billy received a very troublesome wound in the leg and had to go back to the states. We got word that his leg was only cured by amputation, and he weren't a-comin' back 'cause you need two good legs to maneuver these mountains.

"Isabel is what Sublette called the lovely Umentucken. The ways of the Shoshone are different when it comes to what we might call divorce in the states. She was of free will when he left, and she joined me without the ceremony of serving a notice or payin' a plug nickel to her former lord.

"She was the most beautiful woman I ever seen, and when she was mounted on her dapple-gray horse, which cost me three hundred dollars, she made a fine show. Her hair was braided and fell over her shoulders, a scarlet silk handkerchief tied on hood-fashion covered her head, and she wore the finest embroidered moccasins. She rode like all the Indian women, astride, not side-saddle like you, and carrying on one side of the saddle the tomahawk for war, and on the other, the pipe of peace.

"The name of her horse was All Fours. His ornaments were as fine as his rider's. The saddle, crupper, and bust girths cost $150, and the bridle $50. All these articles were decorated with fine-cut glass beads, porcupine quills, and hawk bells that tinkled at every step. Her blankets were of scarlet and blue and the finest quality. Such was the outfit of my wife, Umentucken, Tukutey Undenwatsy, the Lamb of the Mountains."

"Why, do you refer to her in the past tense, Joe? Where is she now?"

"A trapper's life is very dangerous, and she was put in great peril because she followed me on long marches through hostile territory. What tales I could tell you of her bravery and pluck. One time while a-huntin' berries with other women, her party was attacked by a band 'a Blackfeet. Some of the women were taken prisoners. But Umentucken saved herself. She ran and jumped into the Yellowstone and swam while a hundred guns were leveled on her, the bullets whistling about her ears. Oh, I have lots of stories of her courage."

He paused and looked towards the mountains, and she noticed that the sparkle in his eyes turned to pain as he continued. "This summer, she met her death by a Bannock arrow. She died like a warrior, my Mountain Lamb, one year after she became my wife."

Joe moved Narcissa with such openness. Her hand reached out to him and touched him softly and kindly on his buckskin-covered arm, then he lifted the reins, and his horse, knowing his master's body language, trotted forward. He took some time alone.

She thoroughly enjoyed this handsome, adventuresome young man. Five years later, Joe would bring her a most unusual gift.

On the evening of July 6, 1836, they arrived at the Green River, the destination of the American Fur Company and the location of the Rendezvous. They were greeted with great anticipation and excitement by the one hundred trappers and about two hundred members of the Nez Perce and Flathead tribes and various other tribes, including Cayuse. The Cayuse was the band that lived at "the place of rye grass," which they called Waiilatpu near Fort Walla Walla. Chief Umtippe of the Cayuse camped there every year, with the rye grasses as tall as his head.

Narcissa and Eliza dismounted to meet the tribal women who surrounded them. One after another, the women shook their hands and kissed the two ladies. Narcissa and Eliza had never been exposed to such a warmhearted, uninhibited display of affection. They were seated when a Nez Perce chief brought his wife over and politely introduced her to Narcissa and Eliza. The chief said, "We like you very much. I thank God that we have seen you and that you will come to live with us."

After two days of observing the native women, Narcissa said to Eliza, "I feel such pity for the poor Indian women. They are continually traveling during their lives and know nothing of comfort. Have you seen how they do all the work and are complete slaves of their husbands?"

Eliza replied, "How fortunate that we have such thoughtful and kind husbands."

In later years, settlers at her mission would observe Narcissa's workload and feel pity for her similarly.

Richard and John were brought to tears of joy to see their friends and brethren again. They formally greeted each friend by taking off their hats and shaking hands, as they had been taught in Rushville.

The mountain men were in awe of the two lovely women. Scrubby and hardened, the men tipped their hats to the ladies like Eastern gentlemen and vied for their attention, jumping at any chance to talk with the genteel women in dresses and bonnets. Some attended morning or evening prayer meetings with Narcissa's lovely singing voice beckoning them.

Narcissa naively thought the men were drawn to them simply to bolster their turn to Christianity. She declared, "This is a cause worth living. Wherever we go, we find opportunities for doing good. If we had packed one or two animals with Bibles and testaments, we should have had abundant opportunity of delivering them to the traders and trappers of the mountains who would have received them gratefully. Sadly, we have given away all we have to spare."

Trapper Osborne Russell recalled his impressions of the two women in his book *Journal of a Trapper.* He wrote, "The two ladies were gazed upon with wonder and astonishment by the rude savages, they being the first white women ever gazed upon by these Indians, the first that had ever penetrated these wild and rocky regions." However naïve the women were about the trappers' motives for attending services, Russell received a Bible from Narcissa. He converted to Christianity while reading his Bible in his lonely hunter's cabin in the Rocky Mountains.

Another mountain man who met the women, Isaac P. Rose, who published his book, *Four Years in the Rockies*, described the women: "Mrs. Whitman was a large, stately, fair-skinned woman, with blue eyes and light, auburn, almost golden hair. Her manners were dignified and gracious. She was, both by nature and education, a lady and had a lady's appreciation of all that was courageous and refined, yet not without an element of romance and heroism in her disposition strong enough to have impelled her to undertake a missionary's life in the wilderness. Mrs. Spalding, the other lady, was more delicate than her companion yet equally earnest and zealous in the cause they had undertaken. The Indians would turn their gaze from the dark-haired, dark-eyed Mrs. Spalding to what was, to them, the more interesting golden hair and blue eyes of Mrs. Whitman, and they seemed to regard them both as being of a superior nature."

While Narcissa was intent on improving the faith of the white men, Eliza was more interested in the Indian people. Even though Eliza was not feeling well, she began learning the Nez Perce language. She was the first among the missionaries to become proficient in their tongue.

The Cayuse and Nez Perce felt there were significant benefits in store for them if the missionaries were to settle on their lands, so a rivalry developed over the missionaries. The Cayuse were under the impression that they would be compensated for the land, and that misunderstanding may have come from Parker, even though no record of it exists. The Nez Perce simply had a sincere desire to learn about Christianity. Narcissa wrote her family about a quarrel between the two tribes, "The Nez Perce women said we were going to *live* with them, and the Cayuses said, no, we were going to *lie* to them. The contradiction was so sharp they nearly came to blows."

After refreshing themselves at the Rendezvous for two days, the missionary party was about to get underway again. In parting, Marcus went to Captain Fitzpatrick, the leader of the American Fur Company, saying, "Captain, we thank you for your kindness and our safe passage thus far. I wish to get our bill for all the favors you have bestowed upon our party. You have fed us and shoed our horses and mules. How much do we owe you?"

Fitzpatrick asked him in return, "How much is our Company's bill for your medical services rendered to my men?"

"I have no bill," he replied.

"Then," Fitzpatrick countered, "Neither have I."

With that leg of the journey settled, Marcus needed an escort from the Rendezvous to Fort Walla Walla. Parker's expedition in 1835 had taken thirty-five days. Marcus estimated it would take their party six weeks when an unexpected event occurred, which he felt was divine intervention. John McLeod and Thomas McKay of the Hudson Bay Company arrived at the Rendezvous with a letter for Marcus, advising them to travel under the protection of McLeod and McKay and their small party. McLeod and McKay had purchased Fort Hall, built in 1834, and were on their way to finalize the deal; thus, the Whitman party, traveling with about two hundred Nez Perce going for their homeland after the Rendezvous, headed for Fort Hall. The caravan usually made two camps a day; however, the Nez Perce stopped only once a day, so to keep up with the Nez Perce, the travelers doubled their pace. They now covered as much as twenty-one miles a day than their previous ten. The Nez Perce moved fast because they were afraid of the Blackfeet. Narcissa and Eliza became exhausted.

The route was rugged through narrow, steep mountain passes in which the wagon got stuck and overturned twice. The axle of their wagon broke, and the men converted it to a cart using the back wheels. Narcissa had pressed Marcus not to leave the trunk with shirts and clothes her family had provided him as a gift earlier in their journey. He had kept the articles, but now she decided to abandon the trunk because they had only the cart to haul their belongings.

McKay saw her distress and approached Narcissa: "Please, ma'am, I would ask you for the privilege of taking your little trunk along on my wagon."

"Mr. McKay, it would have been better had we not brought any baggage. It has cost us so much work and required animals to pack it. If I were to make this journey again, I would make quite different preparations. Packing and unpacking so many times and crossing so many streams, where the packs frequently get wet, is such tedious work, besides the damage to the articles. I understand now that the custom of this country is to possess nothing, and then you will lose nothing while traveling."

That night Narcissa stood by the trunk her sister Harriet had given her and lamented, "Poor little trunk. You have come with me so far, and now I must leave you here alone. Poor little trunk, I am sorry to leave you. You must stay here alone, and no more will you remind me of my dear Harriet. Twenty miles below the falls on the Snake will be your resting place. Farewell, little trunk. I thank you for your faithful service, and I am grateful to have been cheered by your presence for so long."

The mountainous trail turned into a flat, sweltering August desert. "Oh, Marcus, this heat is so excessive. Truly I feel that the heavens over us were brass, and the earth is hot iron under our feet," the exhausted Narcissa paraphrased from a Bible passage.

Fort Hall was a welcome sight on August 3, 1836, located on the south bank of the Snake River and about twelve miles from present-day Pocatello, Idaho. Since leaving the Missouri frontier, both couples were treated to a room with a bed for the first night. Their host invited them to dine at a real table with stools and served turnips and fried bread as an accompaniment to dried buffalo meat and stewed wild serviceberries for dessert. Their two-day visit ended, and they headed for Fort Boise.

John and Richard continued to travel with the Whitmans. Since the band of two hundred Nez Perce stayed at Fort Hall, they could slow down their pace, which was more suited to the women struggling with the long days and scorching heat, but their progress was still arduous. They traveled through swamps where the mosquitoes were so thick that they could hardly see the Portneuf River, the wildest river they had crossed on horseback. The livestock nearly went crazy because of the mosquitoes.

Riding side-saddle could be very dangerous for women. Eliza's horse stepped on a hornet's nest and threw her, and her foot caught in the stirrup, and the horse dragged her for some distance. She miraculously had no serious injury. One day they rode fifteen miles over the parched, barren earth where only sagebrush could survive. Finally, after six days, they enjoyed their first taste of fresh elk meat. A few days later, at Salmon Falls, the Indians gave them fresh salmon.

River crossings could be challenging and dangerous, and traversing the Snake River was very difficult. They picked a place where several islands broke the river flow, making it possible for the two women to cross safely on the tallest horses. They went a half-mile across the current riding side-saddle, with the water up to the horses' flanks. Both mules and the cart capsized in the water, and the mules got entangled in the harness. Both went upside down in the river. Marcus desperately struggled and succeeded in getting them to the north side of the river. Narcissa had anticipated that crossing rivers would be the most challenging part of the journey, but she was now proud to say, "I can now cross the most difficult stream without the least fear." Unfortunately, many of the emigrants to follow her lost their lives at the river crossings.

They reached Fort Boise on August 19. That evening Narcissa put her clothes in water to soak and finished doing laundry early the following day to avoid the day's heat. It was only the third time she had been able to wash clothes since she had left home.

Marcus's determination to keep his wagon-turned-cart ended at Fort Boise. The horses were physically exhausted from pulling the cart. The Blue Mountains lay between them and Fort Walla Walla, and they would be more challenging to travel than any other terrain they had encountered. Thus far, mountain passes parted the mountains, but not so in the Blues, which rose at a steep rate to reach the highest altitude on the journey. So dear to Marcus and Narcissa, the little cart had to be left behind. Bringing the cart that far had been a grand accomplishment. It proved that it was possible to bring a wheeled vehicle for the first time. When a group of one thousand Oregon-bound pioneers was told at Fort Hall that it was impossible to cross with wagons, Marcus gave them the benefit of his experience and told them about his little cart.

After leaving Fort Boise, they crossed the Snake River at the fishing post of the local tribes. Branches of rushes were tied together and attached to a frame made of willow sticks to make a canoe for the women, and they boarded with their saddles. Two Indians on horseback towed the canoe by a rope across the river. The baggage was loaded on the tallest horses to avoid getting them wet. This experience was their first in a canoe and perhaps the first time white women rode in one. The women were quite captivated by their new adventure.

McLeod had been very kind and helpful to the missionaries. When they reached the Powder River Valley, he knew that Fort Walla Walla was only four days away on horseback. He suggested that the Whitmans proceed with him while the Spaldings travel slower with the cattle, guided by Chief Tackensuatis (Rotten Belly). McLeod's group descended a steep hill from the Powder River Valley high desert into the Grande Ronde Valley. They saw a cluster of trees ahead, a beautiful sight to Narcissa. A river snaked through the valley surrounded on four sides by lofty mountains--a refreshing change from prairies and barren deserts. The valley had marshes lush with grasses and cottonwood trees lining the river.

McLeod came to their camp loaded down with twenty-two ducks and gave the Whitmans nine. The river was full of fresh-water clams and trout. Ocean-going trout called steelhead, prevalent in the valley's stream, weighed up to five pounds, and Richard caught a large one. There were berries and fresh, cold water. The mountains looked blue and mysterious, covered with evergreens and tamarack. McLeod explained to them that Tamarack trees resemble evergreens but drop their needles in the winter, and the wood of tamarack is denser than pine, providing hearty, long-lasting fires.

Camas, the prized root of the Cayuse and Nez Perce, grew in abundance. Narcissa enjoyed watching John and Richard delight in gathering and cooking their favorite sweet treat. The missionaries found it very delicious, tasting like fig, and understood why the tribes who gathered the camas in the Grande Ronde Valley treasured it as their primary food source in the winter. They ate their meal in the valley, but McLeod wanted to push on despite the vibrant green trees and grasses delighting their weary eyes, even though there was no more danger of hostile tribes. They were now in the Valley of Peace.

Century-old trails lead out of the valley, gaining altitude quickly and leading into timber as the air-cooled from the hot August day on the valley floor below. It was reasonably comfortable traveling the trails the first day, still climbing and reaching the summit of the Blues by late evening. They camped in a high meadow, and the evening fire felt comforting against the nippy night air. Marcus whispered that the stars were so close and bright that he could catch one for his bride's finger.

Before noon the next day, though, the Whitmans were on their horses looking down at an unbelievable scene. The ground broke away suddenly into a deep ravine of several hundred feet. It was the most terrible descent for steepness and length they could have imagined and, in some places, almost perpendicular. The horses appeared to dread the plunge as much as their riders. They would turn and wind in a zigzag manner as they ascended down. The loose, black broken basalt in the path made footing difficult for the horses, and the unshod hoofs were very sore, and they would stumble and lose their footing. The men usually walked, but Narcissa had no desire to walk. Holding her breath and clinging tightly to the saddle horn, she rode astride for the first time, rocking back-and-forth and side-to-side, nearly lying on her horse's rump from the steep decline.

No sooner had they gotten to the foot of that descent than another confronted them steeper and more dreadful than the last. They rested and ate dinner before attempting the next dangerously steep incline.

They could not locate water that night and stayed on the crest looking for a place to camp. They looked into the valley floor ahead at that elevation, and they could see the Columbia River and two distinct mountains--Mount Hood and Mount St. Helens--far off on the horizon. The sun hid its rays behind Mt. Hood's cone capped with snow, glowing violet in the distance.

The rolling foothills in front of them broke into an extensive valley as far as the eye could see with dry grasses blowing on soft knolls, turning greener to mark the riverbanks. From the top of the world at forty-two hundred feet above sea level, the view was magnificent as they witnessed the brilliant sunset of vermilion, purple, and blazing orange. It faded away into the darkness of night, and despite the frightening ride, the day ended in glory.

The Arrival

The scenery changed as they descended the mountains into rolling foothills, and the valley opened into a vast expanse of golden grasses waving in the breeze like a friendly welcome. Here Marcus and Narcissa would begin a new phase of their lives, a rebirth in a new, unfamiliar land. Hope and wonder filled their hearts

On August 31, they made camp about eight miles from Fort Walla Walla on the river banks of the same name. McLeod had left the day before to notify the fort that the missionaries were on their way. Early in the morning, two miles from the site initially called Fort Nez Perce, the Whitman's saw their first sign of civilization: the greenery of a garden against the dry summer grass. Excitement welled, and they galloped the rest of the way. They entered the fort after the usual introductions and salutations, forgetting the long journey's fatigue. They were seated in cushioned armed chairs and served breakfast. Fresh grilled salmon, potatoes, and bread and butter filled their white China plates. Tea was served. It was a taste of heaven.

"Marcus, listen. How long has it been since we've heard a rooster greet the day?" asked Narcissa.

"My dear, he is celebrating his first sight of a beautiful woman," Marcus returned.

Their host, Pierre Pambrun, said, "He certainly has something to crow about--your incredible journey. We honor your bravery, Mrs. Whitman."

"Or out of compliment to the company, perhaps. Either way, his morning greeting pleases me greatly," Narcissa exclaimed.

Pierre Pambrun, a French Canadian, was the Hudson Bay Company man in charge of the fort. He was an active, dapper little man, full of backbone and eager to be helpful. His wife, an Indian, spoke French but very little English. He was leaving in a few days for Fort Vancouver, following McLeod. Dr. McLoughlin governed Vancouver. Marcus had expected to get all his supplies at Fort Walla Walla, but instead, he discovered, he would have to get them at Fort Vancouver because the storeroom did not have adequate supplies. In the meantime, they ate melons for the first time at their noon meal, and they dined on pork, cabbage, turnips, tea, and bread and butter. Their taste buds were delighted by the fresh food.

The Spaldings and Gray arrived two days after the Whitmans with only eight head of cattle left of the original seventeen, and only eight of fourteen horses survived the trip. Two calves were born en route, two calves were lost, two cows were butchered, and five cows were left at Fort Boise because of their poor condition. The Hudson Bay Company gave them five cows to replace the five left at Fort Boise. All in all, they fared well in stock, considering the treacherous journey.

After they had rested, Gray, the Spaldings, and the Whitmans boarded a thirty-foot long boat with Pambrun on September 6, rowing with the current of the mighty Columbia River headed for Fort Vancouver. This journey would take six days and require several portages. Portage often consisted of the people hiking around the rapids and the men towing the boats (fully loaded with supplies) up the falls. Sometimes they lifted the boats over rocks; sometimes, they went around the falls. The men from the local bands were willing to help carry the freight and the boats on a full portage if given a little tobacco. It took from thirty to forty men for the task.

    On one of the portages, when all passengers got out of the boat and walked past the falls, Narcissa found some hazelnuts and sat in the shade of a rock, awaiting Marcus's return. She felt something unusual on her neck. She put her hand under her cape and retrieved two fleas. She looked down at her dress and was horrified that every fold of her dress was black with fleas. The creatures were on her neck and in her ears, and she screamed. Immediately she climbed up on the rock, waving and calling frantically to Marcus. He rushed to her and helped her brush the fleas from her. Narcissa shook her dress for an hour, knocking the creatures off, for there were too many to kill. A young chief following the party kindly gave her his horse to get through the sand back to the boat. They were still on her in private places, but she finally got relief when she changed clothes. It was a harrowing experience, and she felt the creatures crawling over her long after they were gone.

    They were amazed at the grandeur of the thunderous Celilo Falls, one of the Northwest tribes' prized salmon fishing grounds. On the fourth day, the scenery changed from basalt cliffs, dry grass, and sagebrush of the high desert to a moist, lush landscape. The beautiful land was the most breathtakingly they had ever seen. The riverbanks transformed as if by a miracle into lush forest-lined cliffs, and the forest floor was thick with ferns.

Then they saw the magnificent cascading waterfalls: Wah Gwin Gwin Falls plummeted into the Columbia River 208 feet high; Multnomah Falls and Bridal Veil Falls cascaded inland into streams racing toward the great river.

"The Indians have legends for most of their landmarks. The legend of Multnomah Falls began with two lovers," Pambrun began, "and, of course, we French are very romantic, *oui*? I will tell you the sad Indian legend:

> Many years ago, the head chief of the Multnomah people had a beautiful young daughter. She was especially dear to her father because he had lost all his sons in fighting, and he was now an old man. He chose her husband with great care, a young chief from his neighbors, the Clatsop people. Many people from the tribes along the lower Columbia and south of it came to the wedding feast.
>
> The wedding feast was to last for several days. There were swimming races and canoe races on the river. There were bow-and-arrow contests, horse racing, dancing, and feasting. The crowd was merry, for both the maiden and the young warrior were loved by their people.
>
> But without warning, the happiness changed to sorrow when sickness came over the village. Children and young people were the first victims, then strong men became ill and died in only one day. The wailing of the women was heard throughout the Multnomah village and the camps of the guests.

"The Great Spirit is angry with us," the people said to each other. The head chief called together his old men and his warriors for counsel and asked gravely, "What can we do to soften the Great Spirit's wrath?"

Only silence followed his question. At last, one of the medicine men arose and said, "There is nothing we can do. If it is the will of the Great Spirit that we die, then we must meet our death like brave men. The Multnomah has always been a brave people."

The other council members nodded in agreement, except one, the oldest medicine man. He had not attended the wedding feast and games, but he had come in from the mountains when the chief called him. He rose and, leaning on his stick, spoke to the council. His voice was low and feeble. "I am a very old man, my friends. I have lived a long, long time. Now you will know why. I will tell you a secret my father told me. He was a great medicine man of the Multnomah, many summers and many snows in the past.

"When he was an old man, he told me that the Great Spirit would send sickness upon our people when I became old. He said that all would die unless a sacrifice was made to the Great Spirit. Some pure and innocent maiden of the tribe, the daughter of a chief, must willingly give her life for her people. Alone, she must go to a high cliff above Big River and throw herself upon the rocks below. If she does this, the sickness will leave us at once."

Then the old man said, "I have finished. My father's secret is told. Now I can die in peace."

Soon a dozen girls stood before him, among them the chief's daughter. The chief told them what the old medicine man had said, and the chief commented with sadness, "I think his words are words of truth."

The sickness stayed in the village, and many more people died. The daughter of the head chief sometimes wondered if she should be the one to give her life to the Great Spirit, but she loved the young warrior, and she wanted to live.

A few days later, she saw the sickness on her lover's face. Now she knew what she must do. She cooled his hot face, cared for him tenderly, and left a bowl of water by his bedside. Then she slipped away alone, without a word to anyone.

All night and the next day, she followed the trail to the great river. At sunset, she reached the edge of a cliff overlooking the water. She stood there in silence for a few moments, looking at the jagged rocks far below. Then she turned her face toward the sky and lifted her arms.

She spoke aloud to the Great Spirit, "You are angry with my people. Will you make the sickness pass away if I give you my life? Only love and peace and purity are in my heart. Let some token hang in the sky if you accept me as a sacrifice for my people. Let me know that my death will not be in vain and that the sickness will quickly pass."

Just then, she saw the moon coming up over the trees across the river, the moonbeams kissing her face. It was the token. She closed her eyes and jumped from the cliff.

The next morning, all the people who had expected to die that day arose from their beds, well and strong. They were full of joy. Once more, there was laughter in the village and the camps of the guest.

Then someone asked, "What caused the sickness to pass away? Did one of the maidens...?"

Once more, the chief called the daughters and granddaughters of the headmen to come before him. This time one girl was missing--his daughter. The young Clatsop warrior hurried along the trail, which leads to Big River. Other people followed. They found the girl they all loved on the rocks below the high cliff. There they buried her.

Then her father prayed to the Great Spirit, "Show us some token that my daughter's spirit has been welcomed into the land of the spirits."

Almost at once, they heard the sound of water above. All the people looked up to the cliff. A stream of water, silvery-white, was coming over the edge of the rock. It broke into a floating mist and then fell at their feet. The stream continued to float down in a high and beautiful waterfall that thundered into two pools.

Even today, the white water has dropped from the cliff into the pool below, like the flowing of her hair. Sometimes in winter, the spirit of the brave and beautiful maiden comes back to see the waterfall. Dressed in white, she stands among the trees on one side of Multnomah Falls. There she looks upon the place where she made her great sacrifice and thus saved her lover and her people from death.

Vertical basalt pillars lined the banks, standing guard over this sacred land. Moss clung to any flat spot and climbed down the sentinels of rocks facing north. The river can be as calm as a lake; however, that day, the headwinds were ferocious, causing two days layover. While they camped for the evening, a party of Indians passed close to them. The men had oddly shaped heads. The following day at the Cascades, Narcissa saw an infant whose head was in a "pressing machine," and she thought it was a pitiful sight. The mother took great pride when she unwrapped the child's head and showed the flattened head to them. The child was lying upon a board with a squirrel pelt between his head and the board. A bandage was drawn tight over his forehead, protected by a square cushion, and it would press his head against the board for at least four months, ultimately permanently flattening the back of the head.

Cayuse mother with child

Narcissa was concerned about the tribe's tradition of flattening heads. She understood it was fashionable in their culture, but she considered it mistreatment when she saw a child's recently exposed head that was purple with bruising. Much to her relief, only a few tribes of the Columbia River still practiced the custom.

Fort Vancouver, called the New York of the Pacific, had a large harbor with many ships moored, one having just returned from the Sandwich Islands, a popular destination.

Many men, including Dr. McLoughlin, greeted the Whitmans and introduced them to Mrs. McLoughlin and Mrs. Douglas, both women from local tribes.

Mural in the Oregon State Capitol
depicting the Whitman-Spalding party's arrival
at Ft. Vancouver in 1836.

The party was delighted by the abundance of fruit and vegetables in the neatly tended garden. McLoughlin often liked to tell the story of how new emigrants introduced apples and grapes to the Pacific Northwest. A twelve-year-old boy had eaten the fruit in London, had put the seeds into his vest pocket, and had taken a voyage around the Horn and landed in Fort Vancouver. He gave the seeds to Mrs. McLoughlin, and miraculously a garden of grapes and apple trees grew! [Could his name have been Johnny?]

Their school was in session, and the fifty-one children attending sang for the visitors. Narcissa sang with the children during her stay and enjoyed teaching them songs. McLoughlin came to listen to her sweet voice every evening. He asked Narcissa to become a tutor for his daughter. Rev. Beaver, who had arrived one month before the Whitmans, was teaching the children of the fort. Beaver was intimidated by the women at "his" school. Though he protested, McLoughlin reminded him that the supervision of the school was under his direction and not Beaver's. Despite that, Beaver wrote a letter to "Mesdames Whitman and Spalding," informing them they had interfered with the English system without his permission and asked them to refrain from teaching, in any respect, the children of the school at Vancouver. McLoughlin was furious when he learned of this letter, and he let Beaver know it was a direct insult to the honorable ladies. Beaver replied in writing with a form of apology, which somewhat satisfied McLoughlin. The women continued their work in the school.

They toured farms that grew wheat, peas, oats, barley, potatoes, and turnips. Cattle, hogs, sheep, and goats were abundant, along with chickens, pigeons, and turkeys. Butter and cheese were plentiful in the dairy, and they observed advanced methods of raising cream from the milk. In contrast, the mill was horse-drawn and produced low yields of flour.

The stores had every article they could need or want for their new mission. They purchased gifts for John and Richard, who stayed at Fort Walla Walla. Narcissa and Marcus loved them deeply and had sworn to treat them as their own. Dr. McLoughlin gave Marcus a pair of leather trousers since riding a horse and carrying a gun is destructive to cloth britches. McLoughlin was incredibly generous with the missionary party in selling them necessary supplies at a great bargain.

Bunks had rough boards for support. A dozen Indian-made blankets laid on top with a pair of pillows covered in calico. The early emigrants filled their beds with wild duck, geese, and crane feathers and covered them with sheets made of brown linen. The local women made their sheeting from deerskin. Narcissa made her own feather bed.

Meals were feasts compared to the food on their journey. First came a bowl of soup with various vegetables chopped finely and boiled in water. Rice, tomatoes, duck, or fowl meat were added along with spices. After the soup came platters of meats, including roast duck, boiled pork, tripe, fresh salmon, or sturgeon. The last course of dessert was pudding or apple pie. Wine was served, and, of course, it was rejected by the missionaries as it passed around the table. There was plenty of milk and sugar for their tea and lots of fresh butter for the baked bread, still warm from the oven.

French was the dominant language spoken there. The laborers were French Canadians, and those married had wives from local tribes. Narcissa observed that some men had adopted native ways, one of which was not allowing their wives to eat with them.

Guided by Pierre Pambrun to find the location of their missions and new home sites, Marcus, Henry Spalding, and William Gray said goodbye to Narcissa and Eliza twelve days after arriving at Fort Vancouver. They initially expected to settle in the Grande Ronde Valley, but the harsh winters would have left them isolated, and game was not predictable. On October 18, Henry returned to Fort Vancouver with a letter from Marcus informing Narcissa that Marcus had selected a location called Waiilatpu, which was among the Cayuse on the Walla Walla River. Marcus stayed at Waiilatpu to begin building a shelter. On their way to Fort Vancouver, the missionaries had passed Waiilatpu, which was twenty-five miles east of Fort Walla Walla. Narcissa recalled meeting Chief Umtippe in July on the trail, who said his band traveled every year to "The Place of the Rye Grass."

The Cayuse and the Nez Perce wanted missionaries, so they decided to open two stations. Both of the tribes were wealthy and influential. Henry chose to settle in Lapwai with the gentler Nez Perce on the Clearwater River to the northeast. McLoughlin was consulted and agreed with the locations, but neither Marcus nor Henry knew the contrasting dispositions of the members of the two tribes.

Although Narcissa and Eliza were very fond of each other, Henry's humiliation and bitterness continually interfered with any harmony they might have had. Marcus and Henry quarreled three times on their journey across the country, which disturbed Marcus, who was a peaceful and gentle soul. The Whitmans were not aware that the reasons for Henry's hostility most likely stemmed from Narcissa's rejection a few years earlier.

When William Gray asked Henry why he had located so far from Marcus, he answered, "Do you suppose I would have come to Lapwai alone with my wife, a hundred and twenty miles away from them, if I could have tolerated living with him and Mrs. Whitman?"

Neither family realized the strategic importance of the proposed site for the Whitmans. Waiilatpu would become a vital station on the highway between the States and the Columbia River. All who entered Oregon country by the overland route would be passing their home, including mountain men, Hudson Bay Company officials, explorers, adventurers, and emigrants. The number arriving annually over the Oregon Trail would be thousands within the next seven years.

On November 3, 1836, after six happy weeks at Fort Vancouver, the ladies left with Henry and McLeod in two boats loaded with provisions for their new stations. The school children bid the missionaries Godspeed by singing some of the songs Narcissa had taught them. Dr. McLoughlin tried to get the ladies to stay through the winter, as Narcissa was in her fifth month of pregnancy, and he was disappointed when the women wanted to return to Fort Walla Walla.

Eight of the crewmen were Iroquois from Montreal, men accustomed to the water since childhood and well acquainted with the dangers of the river. The largest river in volume of water carried in North America, the Columbia was the main artery of travel connecting Fort Vancouver with the Hudson Bay Company's forts in the Pacific Northwest and its activities east of the Canadian Rockies. The fall season brought rain and more rain, typical of the Pacific Northwest.

The boats were water-proofed by gumming, and each full portage would remove the protective coating so they would spend the evening re-gumming them for the next day. The

Dalles area of the Columbia River had exceedingly rapid and robust water, full of whirlpools. Narcissa remained in the boat while the men climbed, at times on their hands and knees, with ropes to pull the vessel through a narrow channel between high, craggy, perpendicular bluffs. The line would catch on rocks, requiring someone to crawl over the precipice to loosen it, putting his life in danger. They had one daring and challenging rescue. While the men climbed the steep and difficult ascent, the rope lodged upon a rock and remained there until all hands had reached their point and commenced hauling. The endeavor was going well until one man prematurely shoved the boat off. The current took the boat downstream rapidly, some of the men nearly being dragged down the precipice by the rope. The crew scrambled to pull them to safety, and no one was severely injured.

Traveling upriver with rain falling nearly every day took them ten days after leaving Fort Vancouver to reach Fort Walla Walla, twenty-five miles from Waiilatpu, where the Whitmans would settle. Marcus and Gray were still building a shelter at Waiilatpu when Narcissa and the Spaldings arrived at the fort. Marcus joined them on Friday, November 18, 1836, and all five were together for a church service on Sunday, the last time they would be together until the fall of the following year. Narcissa remained at Fort Walla Walls while her husband returned to Waiilatpu to work on their house.

Chief Tackensuatis (Rotten Belly) was very unhappy that Marcus had selected a site with the Cayuse and warned, "The Nez Perce do not have as much difficulty with the white man as the Cayuse. No chief is more eager to have you join our village as I." The chief then said to Henry, "This is all my country. Where you settle, I will settle. Just let me know what you want done, and it will be done." Tackensuatis's words would haunt Whitman's memory in times to come. Marcus never enjoyed such wholehearted cooperation and welcoming from the Cayuse at Waiilatpu.

Rotten Belly arrived at Fort Walla Walla with thirty Nez Perce to escort the Spalding party to their new home site at Lapwai. The Nez Perce took charge of everything: pitched their tents, saddled their horses, and packed and unpacked their cases and bags weighing about 125 pounds each on twenty horses. Clothing, farm utensils, furniture, books, building materials, and food supplies comprised their cargo. They divided the cattle between the two families at Waiilatpu. Henry took five cows, the bull and two calves. Henry, Eliza, and William Gray reached Lapwai in a week, thus beginning the isolation of the women from each other for a year, as there were no other American women in the Northwest.

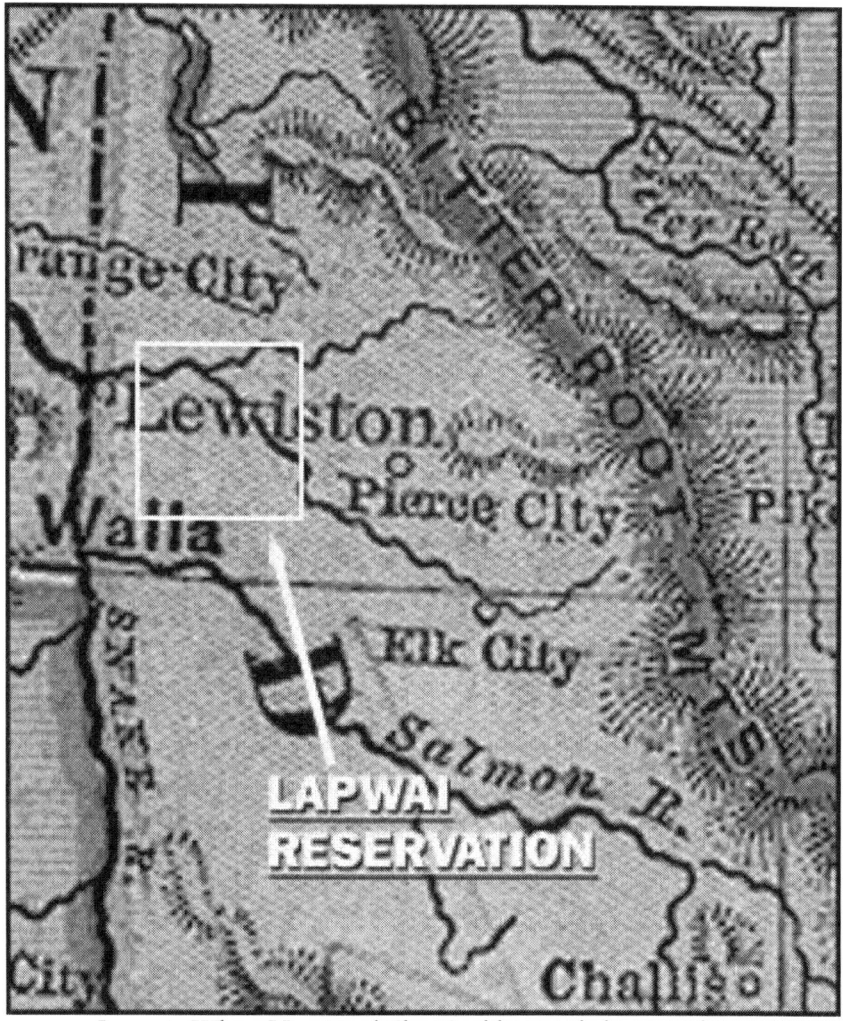
Lapwai. Where Henry and Eliza Spalding settled among the Nez Perce.

Marcus returned to Fort Walla Walla for his wife on December 9. The next day, they made the trip to Waiilatpu, their new home, thus ending an incredible journey taking nine months and covering twenty-five hundred miles.

A New Life at Waiilatpu

With blankets serving as windows and a door, Marcus and William Gray had built a small lean-to made of split logs on the west side of the unfinished house, which measured thirty-six feet long. Marcus had planned to build a two-story house measuring thirty by thirty-six feet, using a combination of small logs and adobe bricks. The project did not go as timely as he and Gray had anticipated. Thus, the lean-to added temporary shelter. All houses in New York had basements, so Marcus wanted one, too. He used the mud from the basement excavation mixed with dried grass to make adobe bricks. The green cottonwoods they had cut into framing material warped and twisted.

True to her nature, Narcissa did not complain and said she was grateful that they had a comfortable shelter. "Oh, Marcus, my dear parents made a similar beginning and perhaps a more difficult one than ours," she said to her husband, expressing only joy upon her arrival as she went into her new home where he had lit the fireplace.

About 300 yards from the lean-to was a cone-shaped hill. How significant this little hill would be in their lives! At 100 feet above the valley floor, it would give her a lovely view of the country, including the confluence of the Walla Walla River and Mill Creek. She could see about fifteen miles to the slopes of the Blue Mountains, which would provide more suitable timber for lumber. Indeed, it was an excellent location at a horseshoe bend of the river lined with cottonwoods and grass promising to return to green in the spring.

A week later, eighteen inches of snow fell. By Christmas eve, they were able to install some of the twelve-pane windows in the house. They made partitions in the lean-to, giving them a pantry and a bedroom for privacy.

Two months after her arrival at Waiilatpu, Narcissa said to her husband, "Today is the first anniversary of our marriage. I feel so fortunate to have had such a grand adventure and a fine location to live. However, it marks one year without a word from my family and friends in Angelica. Who can tell how many are sleeping in their graves by this time?" Marcus understood her loneliness. Her yearning to hear from her friends and family would not be satisfied for two years and three months after leaving New York. Despite receiving no communication, she wrote continuously, usually writing each letter over some time.

They passed a comfortable winter relying on the Cayuse village and the Hudson Bay Company food. Ten wild horses supplied most of their winter meat, and the cows provided milk. Marcus made two chairs with deerskin bottoms. Narcissa had a special barrel to clean clothes, and Mrs. Pambrun had the only other barrel for washing that side of the Rocky Mountains. Mr. McLeod, so fond of Narcissa, gave her a cat and a dog they named Boxer.

Narcissa had saved all the seeds from the fruit she ate in Vancouver. Along with vegetable seeds purchased, these seeds began their first spring garden. Neither of them was able to tend to the first garden with the arrival of their child, Alice Clarissa, in early spring. The Cayuse were not interested in farming, nor did they understand the perennial benefits. Also, since the bands traveled most of the year, only a few Cayuse spent the winter at Waiilatpu, and they roamed to different locations, which yielded year-round food sources. However, Hawaiians were outstanding workers, in addition to transients and passing mountain men. Two single Hawaiian men joined them that spring. One Hawaiian, Jack, stayed at the Mission for years. The residents harvested 250 bushels of potatoes and 200 bushels of corn that first summer, and the gardens continued to provide a plentiful supply of vegetables throughout the season. The mission inhabitants planted apple and peach trees, grapevines, and strawberries. Narcissa wrote home asking for seeds for growing walnut, chestnut, and locust trees. She also requested broom corn seeds because she was using hemlock boughs for a broom, and they didn't work as well as the brooms at home.

  Marcus added hogs, sheep, cattle, chickens, and turkeys to the mission. He had a passion for raising sheep, which thrived in that country and were prolific breeders. Marcus remarked, "This is a country where a man can winter a thousand sheep easier than he could feed half the number from a well-stored barn in the states. They exchanged the wool grown here and manufactured in this country for domestic articles. No foreign fabrics," he prophesized, "can compete with this fine wool." Indeed, the Pendleton Woolen Mills in the region of Whitman's home are world-renowned today. Likewise, Henry's abundant crop was the potato, for which the future state of Idaho would become famous.

Terrie Biggs

The First White Child in Oregon

Alice Clarissa, named after her grandmother and her aunt, arrived on the eve of Narcissa's twenty-ninth birthday, on March 14, 1837. She was the first child born to white American parents in the Pacific Northwest. Mrs. Pambrun and her two children arrived two weeks before Alice's birth, but she wasn't much help. Marcus delivered their baby after two hours of labor and tended to his wife and child himself. He also did the washing and cooking during her one-week convalescence before she resumed her duties.

Tiloukaikt (who would succeed Umtippe as Chief) came to see the child the day after she was born. The entire village anticipated her birth. "Your child is a Cayuse *te-mi,* which meant Cayuse girl. She was born on Cayuse *wai-tis*" interpreted as Cayuse land. Throngs of chiefs and principal men and women from the camp came to see the Cayuse *te-mi.* This ten-pound bundle (Narcissa's description at two weeks old) with light brown hair and a beautiful round head enamored the local people. They gazed at her complexion, size, and dress with a sense of wonder. The Cayuse were continually surprised at her strength and development. Flattened heads of their children were their custom, so when the local women saw Alice Clarissa's round head, it ended the tradition, which had already been abandoned by most of the other regional tribes. This little child would be the darling of the village and an unexpected emissary between the two cultures.

Alice Clarissa gave such comfort and joy to them both, but especially to Narcissa during her husband's long absences. At eighteen months, she was remarkably healthy and was a great talker, and was beginning to sing with them in the family worship. Little Alice ran to her mother's arms when the singing commenced and especially loved the Nez Perce hymns. Many Cayuse children played with her, running in and out of the house, and she was learning their language. Chief Umtippe, whom Narcissa referred to as "old chief Cut Lip," loved the little girl. He was ailing, and he did not expect to live long, so he gave all of his lands to Alice Clarissa. This act of kindness was quite a transformation from his hostility towards the Whitmans when they arrived.

Alice Clarissa was so much quicker to develop than the children of his band. Her blond curls bobbed as she scampered about on her sturdy little legs. She could speak his language, sang with them, and played with their children. Through the innocence of this child, there were no boundaries, no racial distinction, no judgment. She saw everyone as a friend, and she loved Chief Umtippe. This child touched his heart!

After she had visited a lodge nearby where twins were born, Narcissa shared her concerns for the Cayuse babies, who were stark contrasts to her lively little darling, in a letter to her parents dated March 14, 1838:

> The babies were both boys and appeared very well. We found the mother with them in a small lodge made of a single mat, about half as high as a man, scarcely room enough for three persons to sit in it comfortably and without a fire.

She had plenty of dried grass for her bed with a few old skins. Her babies were laced to a board, as small as they were. Their mother's comforts at such a time would be death to us. The pregnant women usually go from the main lodge and build a temporary hut for their lying-in hospitals. Many infants die because their mothers do not have enough milk for them, and they do not know how to prepare food to feed them and have no means to do it. They usually nurse them until they are three or more years old.

In January, a child about a year-and-a-half old died a few moments after its mother had given birth to another baby. Afterward, we found that the older child died of starvation because the mother had only enough milk for her infant, and the older child was too young to eat their roots.

Marcus & Stickus Meet

It was May of 1837, and Istukus was thirty years old when he became very ill, so he traveled twenty-five miles from his village on the Umatilla River to Waiilatpu to ask Dr. Whitman for help. Whitman invited him into his home, and the doctor gave him medicine and personal attention. His eagerness to heal overrode his fear of what his fate would be if Istukus were to die.

Mrs. Whitman held their girl-child, Alice, in her lap the entire day, as she had no cradle yet. She stayed by Istukus' side until after midnight and finally joined her exhausted husband and five-week-old daughter in bed. He recovered with the doctor's medicine, and he considered Whitman a friend and gave him his loyalty as long as the doctor lived.

The Whitmans and the traders translated Istukus as "Stickus," and this name will follow references to him from this point on.

Terrie Biggs

Civilizing, Evangelizing, & Doctoring

William Gray, who had been commissioned for his carpentry skills and presumed to be able to help with the construction of the homes for the missionaries, was lazy and incompetent. He helped Marcus for about six weeks and then helped Henry for four weeks before leaving for Fort Vancouver and then returning to the States. Marcus and Henry, however, were very energetic and versatile. They supervised and engaged in all the activities to keep themselves and their families comfortable and self-sufficient. They farmed, built fences to protect the crops, tended animals, milked cows, butchered a horse as needed, sawed logs to make boards, made adobe bricks, and performed various other duties to begin a home in the wilderness.

Henry and Marcus were committed to "civilizing" their tribal neighbors. They both had witnessed the buffalo slaughter by the white men, which gave them an awareness that the semi-nomadic way of life of *following* the food would quickly need to change to *growing* the food. They knew that the tribes must learn to adapt to white man's ways of farming or perish. Marcus and Henry taught them to grow vegetables, including corn, peas, potatoes, grains, wheat, and oats.

Henry and Marcus helped the tribes to obtain and raise cattle by teaching them to trade their healthy stock with the pioneers' worn-out ones and then how to nurture the animals back to health. This method helped the pioneers get refreshed livestock and saved their lives. The Cayuse prospered through this type of trading and increased their herds of horses.

The Whitmans realized that the Cayuse men rejected manual labor. Females of the tribes traditionally did most of the hard work, such as dismantling the lodges when they moved and reassembling them at their new camp. Marcus and Narcissa felt their neighbors were ungrateful, lazy, childlike, sometimes threatening, and occasionally obedient.

Marcus knew he must teach the Cayuse to farm to keep them in the village year-round for them to learn about the Bible. As author Drury described it, his philosophy began with the plow and ended with the sermon. He appealed to the Board for two hundred hoes and fifty plows. It took two years before he heard their decision and four years before enough plows were delivered to them to allow the Indians to begin cultivation.

Narcissa had come to this country to teach the Indians about Christianity. At first, the Cayuse were eager to learn about their God. The Whitmans began holding Sunday services on the Sabbath, which mainly consisted of singing, which the Cayuse loved. There was only room for men and boys from camp, who gathered in Narcissa's kitchen all day.

The language barrier presented a problem and much frustration, as it limited the missionaries' ability to teach Bible stories. They knew that the villagers would have to be able to read before they could appreciate the Bible. The language barrier began to dissolve as Marcus and Henry grew in their knowledge of the Nez Perce tongue. The two missionaries ultimately put the Nez Perce language into a written form for the first time by printing a primer and books in the Nez Perce language. They began a school for the children and replaced the tribal names with Christian names, as they had done with Richard and John.

However, the Cayuse and Nez Perce were becoming dissatisfied and disillusioned. One of the Cayuse on the Sabbath said to Marcus, "It was good when we knew nothing but to hunt and fish, eat, drink, and sleep. Now it is bad. Now you tell us we are sinners because we have more than one wife. You say we must have salvation through Jesus Christ. We do not understand these doctrines you set forth."

Meanwhile, the Roman Catholics at Umatilla were baptizing hundreds, while the Protestants were still trying to find any tribal men they felt met their standards. Pambrun, a Roman Catholic, had already introduced the Cayuse to singing and prayer. Before the Christian missionaries arrived, every morning at daybreak, every evening at twilight, and once on Sunday, the entire band of men, women, and children gathered at their chief's lodge to say prayers Pambrun had taught them and to give thanks to their Earth Mother. The service ended with Chief Umtippe giving them an inspirational talk.

According to author Clifford Drury, no group of individuals did more to help the natives bridge the gap from primitive, semi-nomadic life to "civilized" existence and to improve the material welfare of the Cayuse and Nez Perce, as Marcus and Henry. Looking at this from the indigenous people's perspective, though, the settlers also devastated a culture centuries old. Their ancient ways altered forever, along with the landscape. Years later, Stickus explained some of the cultural differences by saying, "Many tribes felt that plowing the earth was like taking a knife to the bosom of our Earth Mother and that cutting wheat or grasses was like cutting our mother's hair. The Whitmans had no understanding of our established way of life. Caring for the crops began a new idea of private ownership of land, but never had we known of the concept of ownership of Earth Mother. How can one sell the land or the air? Every part of the earth is sacred."

Primarily a physician, Marcus also wanted to minister to what he perceived were the "heathens." The Board wanted sermons first and foremost. Unfortunately, the daily struggle of building a home, gardening, tending to the livestock, butchering, preserving meat, and tending to his physician duties left very little time teaching the gospel. It took days or weeks for the doctor to make a professional call. As attending physician to many births and illnesses, he left for long periods due to the distances between settlements, forts, villages, and missions. These included one hundred twenty-five miles to Lapwai, sixty miles to Kamiah, Fort Walla Walla, Fort Vancouver, Umatilla, and villages.

Marcus found himself under an ever-present threat of death in an unforeseen manner. The Cayuse and Nez Perce had medicine men called *te-wats.* Unfortunately, relatives of deceased patients had the right to kill the *te-wat* if he were unable to cure the patient; thus, Marcus, as well, was under constant threat. Chief Umtippe, who was disagreeable to them from the beginning for settling near his favorite camp, called for Marcus to attend to his wife, who had inflammation of the lungs. He had heard of the doctor's healing skills at the Rendezvous. Umtippe told Marcus that he would kill him if his wife died that night while under Marcus's care. Marcus was relieved of his responsibility when Umtippe sent for "the Great Walla Walla *te-wat."* The Great Walla Walla *te-wat* performed several chants and pronounced her well after receiving a horse and a blanket or two. The next day his wife's condition had not improved. Umtippe directed his rage against the Walla Walla *te-wat,* and he said that he was "bad" and that they should kill him. Chief Umtippe's wife finally recovered, and the Great Walla Walla *te-wat* was allowed to live.

About three weeks later, Umtippe became ill, and everyone thought he would die. Umtippe came to Marcus for help, and the medicine Marcus gave him soon took effect, and his health returned.

A few days later, a vital war chief of the Cayuse died at Walla Walla, attended by the Great Walla Walla *te-wat.* That same day a younger brother of Umtippe went to Walla Walla and fatally shot the Great Walla Walla *te-wat.*

A Visit to Lapwai

On November 18, 1837, Marcus, Narcissa, eight-month-old Alice Clarissa, and Jack (one of the Hawaiian men living at Waiilatpu) began their 125-mile journey to Lapwai to assist with the delivery of Eliza Spalding's baby. The other Hawaiians, Joseph Maki and his wife, stayed at the mission to take care of the animals. Henry asked three Nez Perce to go to Waiilatpu and accompany the Whitmans, bringing with them a "leather lodge," which was a tepee wrapped in buffalo skin. Narcissa rode side-saddle with Alice Clarissa through rain and snow during the five-day trip. She had to nurse the baby and change diapers while riding to get ahead of the weather.

The Whitmans arrived on Sunday morning, riding ahead of Jack and the Nez Perce helpers who brought the supplies. It was a warm and welcome visit to both families. Eliza and Narcissa were delighted to be with each other again after one full year apart. Their separation and isolation even made Henry and Marcus glad to be reunited. They referred to themselves as "civilized" friends, meaning they were the only two American families in the Pacific Northwest.

On Wednesday morning, Eliza gave birth to a baby girl named Eliza. Baby Eliza was the first white child born in the future state of Idaho. Henry baptized both babies during the Whitmans' visit.

They returned by canoe down the Clearwater to the Snake River, the Columbia, and then down the Walla Walla River, preferring this to horseback. Jack and the three Nez Perce went overland with the gear. The river trip took four-and-a-half days; they had to clear away snow at evening camp. They returned to Waiilatpu a month after they had left.

The Whitmans observed that the Nez Perce were much friendlier and better-natured than their Cayuse neighbors during their visit. The Nez Perce had always been a more peaceful, gentle, and accepting tribe who looked forward to having a man of God among them. The Cayuse expected compensation from the missionaries, and some were disgruntled that the Whitmans settled and took ownership near one of their favorite camping grounds. Cayuse people were, by nature, a more war-like tribe and were people filled with pride.

Madame Dorion

Whitman's house was always full of company. The mission had many memorable visitors. One very colorful visitor was Madame Marie Dorion. She was Sioux and was the first woman after Sacajawea to have crossed the continent on foot. In 1811 she left Missouri with her husband, Pierre Dorion, and their two sons, joining the Astor Expedition, named for its financier, John Jacob Astor. It was the overland expedition of the Pacific Fur Company. The party was divided into three main groups and separated on the Snake River, all bound for Ft. Astoria on the Pacific Coast. Wilson Price Hunt was the leader of one of the groups, so his expedition was commonly referred to as the Hunt Party or Wilson Price Hunt Party. His party consisted of thirty-two white men, three Indians, and Pierre's family. The men were primarily hired as hunters, interpreters, guides, and Canadian adventurers. Pierre Dorion was their interpreter. They crossed the Snake River and moved up the Burnt River, heading towards the Blue Mountains on their journey west. Dorion's wife Marie was pregnant, and without murmuring or flinching, she went into labor and gave birth on December 30. Pierre told the rest of his party to go ahead, and they would catch up with them.

At this point, the exhausted explorers were close to starvation and not sure they would survive. One Canadian was so sick and his horse too weak to bear the weight that Hunt took the man upon his shoulders, making every step difficult due to Hunt's poor condition. The sight of the Grande Ronde Valley was a welcome sight. Hunt's diary described it as a "beautiful valley where a pretty stream meanders and the beaver seem plentiful." Snow was upon the bowl of mountains bordering the valley, but none was on the serene, sunny valley floor.

To their delight, they found six lodges belonging to a small group of Shoshones. The hospitable band accepted a rifle, an old musket, a tomahawk, a tin kettle, and a small quantity of ammunition in trade for four horses, three dogs, and some roots. The Shoshones butchered and cooked the meat they had given the explorers---a feast of roasted puppies and horsemeat. They dried the remaining meat for the expedition's winter journey over the Blue Mountains. This incident was one of the numerous times Indians saved starving travelers in this valley of peace.

The Dorions caught up with their party with Marie calmly riding astride her horse with her day-old baby in her arms and her two-year-old tied to her side in a blanket as though giving birth was just an interruption of her day. Hunt was anxious to move on; however, the Canadian trappers in the group, who never willingly gave up a holiday, for it was New Year's Day of 1812, talked him into spending the next day in the Grande Ronde Valley. Afterward, the Hunt party trudged through snow across the Blue Mountains. Unfortunately, on January 6, Marie's newborn died and was tenderly buried in an unmarked grave. They followed the Columbia River to their destination, Fort Astoria. The trail marked by Wilson Price Hunt would eventually become the famous emigrant road known as the Oregon Trail, stretching from Independence, Missouri, to the Willamette Valley in Oregon.

The Dorions returned to the Snake River Basin in 1814, along with other trappers and traders looking for a place to establish a hunting and trading post. Marie was tested once again for her extraordinary courage and tenacity. Marie told her remarkable story to the Whitmans:

> About the middle of August in 1813, we reached the Great Snake River, and soon afterward, following up a branch to the right hand, where there were plenty of beavers, we encamped; Mr. Reed, our leader, built a house to winter in. After the house was built, the people spent their time trapping beaver. About the latter end of September, three men called Hoback, Robinson, and Rezner came to us; they were very poor, the Indians having robbed them of everything they had about fifteen days before. Mr. Reed gave them some clothing and traps, and they went hunting with my husband. A man called Landrie fell from his horse, lingered a while, and died of it. Another one of our group, Delauney, was killed when trapping. My husband told me that he saw Delauney's scalp with the Indians and knew it from the color of the hair. The Indians about the place were very friendly to us, but when strange tribes visited us, they were troublesome and always asked Mr. Reed for guns and ammunition. On one occasion, they drove an arrow into one of our horses and took a *capote*, which was a cape from La Chapelle. Mr. Reed, not liking the place where we first built, left it and built farther up the river, on the other side. After the second house was built, the men went to trap, as usual, sometimes coming home at night, sometimes sleeping out for

several nights together. Mr. Reed and one man generally stayed at the house.

Late one evening on January 10, 1814, a friendly Indian came running to our house in a great fright. He told Mr. Reed that a band of bad Snakes, called the Dogrib tribe, had burnt the first house that we had built and that they were coming on whooping and singing the war song. After hearing this, the Indian went off immediately, and I took up my two children, got upon a horse, and set off to where my husband was trapping; the night was dark, the road bad, and I lost my way. The next day being cold and stormy, I did not stir.

On the second day, however, I set out again; seeing a large smoke in the direction I had to go and thinking it might be from a hostile group of Indians, I got into the bushes again and hid. On the third day, late in the evening, I got in sight of the hut where my husband and the other men were hunting. But just as I was approaching the place, I observed a man coming from the opposite side and staggering as if unwell. I stopped where I was till he came to me. It was LeClerc, wounded and faint from loss of blood. He told me that LaChapelle, Rezner, and my husband had been robbed and murdered that morning.

I did not go into the hut but putting LeClerc and one of my children on the horse I had with me, I turned around immediately, took to the woods, and retraced my steps back to Mr. Reed. Le Clerc, however, could not bear the jolting of the horse, and he fell once or twice so that we had to remain for nearly a day in one place. In the night, he died, and I covered him over with brushwood and snow and put my children on the horse as I walked, leading the animal by the halter.

On the second day, I returned to the house again, but the sight was sad. Mr. Reed and the men were murdered, scalped, and cut to pieces. Desolation and horror stared me in the face. I turned from the shocking sight in agony and despair, took to the woods with my children and horse, and passed the cold and lonely night without food or fire.

I was now at a loss what to do: the snow was deep, the weather cold, and we had nothing to eat. To undertake a long journey under such circumstances was inevitable death. Had I been alone, I would have run all risks and proceeded, but the thought of my children perishing with hunger distracted me. At this moment, a sad alternative crossed my mind. Should I venture to the house among the dead to seek food for the living? I knew there was a good stock of fish there, but it might have been destroyed or carried off by the murderers, and besides, they might still be lurking about and see me. Yet I thought of my children.

After a sleepless night, the following day, I wrapped my children in my robe, tied my horse in a thicket, and then went to a rising ground that overlooked the house to see if I could observe anything stirring about the place. I saw nothing, and, as hard as the task was, I resolved to venture after dark, so I returned to my children and found them nearly frozen. I was afraid to make a fire in the daytime lest the smoke be seen, yet I had no other alternative. I must make a fire or let my children perish. I made a fire and warmed them. I rolled them up again in the buffalo robe, extinguished the fire, and set off after dark to the house. I went into the store and ransacked every hole and corner and found plenty of fish scattered about. I gathered, hid, slung upon my back as much as I could carry, and returned before dawn to my children. They were nearly frozen and weak with hunger. I made a fire and warmed them, and then we shared the first food we had tasted in the last three days.

  The next night I went back again and carried off another load, but when these efforts were over, I sank under the sense of my afflictions and was for three days unable to move and without hope. On recovering a little, I packed up and loaded my horse, and after putting my children on the top of the load, I set out again on foot, leading the horse by the halter as before. In this sad and hopeless condition, I traveled through deep snow among the woods, rocks, and rugged paths for nine days, till the horse and I could travel no more. Here I selected a lonely spot at the foot of a rocky precipice in the Blue Mountains, intending to pass the remainder of the winter.

  I killed my horse and hung up the flesh on a tree for my winter food. I built a small hut with pine branches, long grass, and moss and packed it all around with snow to keep us warm, and this was a difficult task, for I had no ax but only a knife to cut wood. In this solitary dwelling, I passed fifty-three lonely days!

I then left my hut and set out to cross the mountains with my children. I became snow blind the second day and had to remain for three days without advancing a step, which was unfortunate, as our provisions were almost exhausted. Having recovered my sight a little, I set out again. After leaving my winter encampment, I got off the mountains and down to the plains on the fifteenth day.

We had scarcely anything to eat for six days and not a mouthful for the last two days. Soon after we had reached the plains, I perceived smoke at a distance, but being unable to carry my children farther, I wrapped them up in my robe, left them concealed, and set out alone in hopes of reaching the Indian camp, where I had seen the smoke. I was so weak that I could hardly crawl and had to sleep on the way. The next day, at noon, I got to the camp. It proved to belong to the Walla Wallas, and they kindly treated me.

Immediately on my arrival, the Indians set off searching for my children and brought them to the camp the same night. Here we stayed for two days and then moved on to the river, expecting to hear something of the white people on their way either up or down.

Walla Walla Indians who found them adopted them into their tribe. In his book Astoria, Washington Irving would tell her story [from which I extracted her account]. She later married a French Canadian, John Toupin, who became the interpreter at Fort Walla Walla. In a twist of fate, her son, Baptiste, would play a crucial role in the Whitmans' destiny.

Don't Bet on a Full House

The location of the first house at Waiilatpu proved to be in the flood plain of the Walla Walla River. In December 1837, one year after they arrived, a Chinook melted the snow on the Blue Mountains, causing the river to overflow. The basement flooded, and the mud in the walls began to melt away. A few months later, water again damaged the house in early spring. The Hawaiians then went to the Blue Mountains to cut some pine boards to build a new home on higher ground. The mission began to expand with children of friends either sent to help or to attend school and would continue throughout their residency and would climax in a grand gesture of helping children.

The Whitmans had outgrown their second house, so it was a blow to Narcissa when Henry convinced Marcus that he needed a home more than the Whitmans. Marcus left for two weeks to help Henry build a log house at Lapwai. By this time, Narcissa's house was overflowing. Four mixed-blood children lived there to attend school: Mungo Mevway, a twelve-year-old Hawaiian/Indian mix, Maria Pambrun, Margaret McKay, and sixteen-year-old Sarah Hull, Thomas McKay's daughter. In her tradition of changing the children's tribal names, Narcissa named Sarah Hull after the pastor's wife who had married them.

By June of 1838, the Whitman household numbered twelve or thirteen. Joseph Maki, his wife Maria, and their baby came from Honolulu, which made the number of Hawaiians four or five. They were the only other married couple living there.

The mission became a convalescent home to many. John Hinds, a black man who had accompanied them from the Rendezvous for medical care, had been living there; however, a year after their arrival, he died.

French Canadian Charles Compo and his Nez Perce wife moved to the mission from Fort Walla Walla. The Whitmans employed Campo, but he and his wife had their lodge. He was a valuable assistant to Marcus and was left in charge when Marcus traveled. Both tribes spoke Nez Perce, and many of the Columbia basin tribes also spoke Nez Perce because of intermarriage and trade relations. Having both tribes speaking the same language became very important for the missionaries, so Nez Perce became the primary language of conciliation. The Whitmans were very frustrated with the language barrier, and Richard, the Nez Perce boy who came with them from New York, proved not to be of much value as an interpreter. John, who had also been their reliable translator, returned to his home at Lapwai; therefore, Campo's command of the Nez Perce language was a great benefit.

On July 11, 1838, twenty-seven months after their marriage, Narcissa visited Mrs. Pambrun at Fort Walla Walla when a Hudson Bay express rider arrived with mail from her family. The letters were dated January and August of 1837. Narcissa had agonized over having no word from her family in New York for such a long time, and she was genuinely ill at times yearning for a letter because it took almost three years to receive an answer to hers.

A month later, nine reinforcements for the Oregon Mission arrived at their house quite unexpectedly. It was a day of triumph and rejoicing. Except for Eliza Spalding, Narcissa had not spoken to another American woman since she left home. Included in the arriving party were William Henry Gray and his new wife. Gray had accompanied the first mission party to Oregon and had returned to the "states." Mary Augusta Dix of Ithaca, New York, where Marcus had practiced medicine, attended the Whitman wedding and married Gray two years later. The Whitmans were delighted to welcome English-speaking Christian missionaries.

Within a few days, though, disillusionment and reality hit the Whitmans. During their difficult and long journey, personality clashes developed between the reinforcements, so they were not on the best terms with each other when they arrived. Narcissa found the men very disagreeable, demanding, and ill-mannered.

"Marcus, you must make him stop. Brother Elkanah Walker is using my kitchen fireplace as a spittoon! It just disgusts me. Also, they drink wine," she uncharacteristically complained to Marcus.

"I know, my dear. What am I to do? I don't agree with a strong drink either, but they have had a long, perilous journey, and now they are our guests."

"My kitchen is thick with people. Our house provides just barely enough room for our family, and now there are twenty to tend to. Mr. Smith," referring to Asa Smith, "is always complaining. He went into our pantry and complained that there were only milk and melons. I have cleaned, cooked, washed, and made soap with very little help. Mr. Smith refused to let Jack [their Hawaiian assistant] help me! They seem to have no appreciation of the months it took us to grow our crops and raise and feed the animals they have eaten without even a thank you."

"I am out of patience with Mr. Smith, too," Marcus sympathized.

"The men keep gathering in our kitchen while we women are trying to prepare meals," she told him in total frustration, with tears welling in her eyes.

"It is apparent that this house is not suited for these many guests. The cramped space has made for short tempers," and he put his arms around his wife to comfort her.

Elkanah Walker's wife, also named Mary, was over six months into her pregnancy when they arrived. In December, Mary went into labor, and her husband complained that she did not have her bedroom because he didn't want her seen by others as her belly swelled with child. The Whitmans never knew why Elkanah left for Fort Walla Walla the day before his wife had their child. "I wish I had never been married," Mary admitted in her journal. "But just as I supposed the worst was at hand, my ears were greeted with the cry of my new tiny son." Narcissa, who was still nursing Alice, now had a newborn to add to her duties and caring for her maternity patient.

Narcissa often went to bed weeping. With no privacy in her own home, she went down by the river to cry where she was out of earshot of the house. She had cooked for twenty people over an open fire, and she washed clothes with little help from the other women. However, one day the women finally helped Narcissa when they made twenty-four dozen candles. This hard work and misery would go on for eight months until the last of them had left for their mission locations.

Another issue disturbed Narcissa greatly. The three men from New England--Eells, Walker, and Smith--had very reserved ideas about women praying aloud in front of men and would not allow their wives to pray in the services.

"In all the prayer meetings of this mission, only the men pray," she wrote. "I believe all the women would be willing to pray if their husbands let them. My husband has no objection to my praying, but if my sisters do not, he thinks it quite as well for me not to." It disturbed her greatly that Marcus caved into the piousness of the group. Narcissa tried to persuade her husband by saying, "After all, it is a new country, and one must adjust and be willing to adapt to modern times and the local environment." Still, Marcus held firm to the eastern tradition.

Finally, a get-away at the end of January relieved Narcissa's exhaustion and frustration. Since they had been married, this was their first vacation from the mission and their struggles to survive. They traveled fifty miles to the Tucannon River among the Nez Perce with Timothy, a prominent chief. Two-and-a-half weeks of camping and sleeping in a tent was glorious to Narcissa. The purpose of the trip was to live among the Nez Perce to get more proficient in speaking their language. It also provided a refreshing break from the tension at the mission.

Both experienced a deep feeling of joy and satisfaction when they witnessed the Nez Perce accepting Christianity. Marcus told them Bible stories. Because of their entirely different values and cultures, the Nez Perce sang, prayed, and could confess their "sins," whatever those might be. Chief Timothy sobbed, rose, and spoke of his wickedness and black heart. He wanted Christ to make him clean and save his soul from sin and hell. Timothy's brother then spoke, and so did their wives. Several others followed.

On January 27, 1839, Narcissa sat at the door of her tent that night, writing to her sister Jane: "While confessing their sins, their tears fell to the ground so copiously that I was reminded of the weeping Mary who washed her Savior's feet with her tears. You can better imagine my feelings than I can describe them on witnessing such a scene in a land unaccustomed to the teachings of the Bible. Most of the Nez Perce were not so hardened in sin, and they were not so proud of a people as our Waiilatpus.

"Oh, my dear Jane," whom, of all her siblings, she was closest to, "imagine us here on this beautiful eve, the full moon shining in all her splendor, clear, yet freezing cold, my little Alice sleeping by my side, my husband at worship with the people within hearing distance, and I sitting in the door of the tent writing, wearing my usual clothing except a shawl, with a handkerchief on my head, and before me a large comfortable fire in the open air. Do you think we suffer? No, dear Jane, I have not realized so much enjoyment for a long time as I have since I have been here."

In a letter to her father dated September 28, 1838, she wrote, "Home [in New York] has no attraction for me, compared with the satisfaction and enjoyment every day affords in living here and extending a silent and gentle influence upon these benighted minds. The Lord only knows what he has in store for us to pass through in this world. Frequently I feel as if our stay will not last long here." This letter was quite prophetic, considering later events.

Reinforcements Cause More Problems

As the winter grew colder, the friction at the mission grew primarily due to Gray's disillusionment and Asa Smith's sour disposition. Seven men, who included Marcus, Henry, Gray, Rogers, Smith, Eells, and Walker, held their first official Annual Meeting of the Oregon Mission. The women were not permitted to enter the discussions or to vote. One agenda item was to determine where each reinforcement member would be assigned. The Walkers and Eells would go to Spokane or Flathead country at Tshimakain. The Grays would go to Lapwai with Henry despite his wish to go among the Spokanes. The Smiths, at that time, were going to stay at Waiilatpu. Rogers could live where he wanted.

Five actions were voted and approved a month after the new missionaries arrived as follows:

I. All members of the mission were to apply themselves to the study of the language of the place where they lived and reduce it to writing.

II. That the natives be taught primarily in their own language, but they could also be taught some English.

III. Lapwai would get the printing press offered by a Hawaiian mission;[2]
IV. A corn and gristmill and a blacksmith shop would be established at Lapwai; and
V. Dr. Whitman would go to Fort Vancouver for supplies.

Unofficially the group of men collectively recognized that a new and larger house must be built at Waiilatpu. Smith was ranting again, and the personality clashes brought about a special mission meeting at Lapwai. Narcissa traveled there with Marcus, but the other wives, Mary, Myra, and Sarah, did not go. One resolution brought to the table was to replace the Whitmans at Waiilatpu and that they should relocate. Henry, supported by Walker and Eells, suggested that the Whitmans should open a new station on the Snake River near the mouth of the Palouse River to put the doctor in a more central location, making him more available in case of emergencies.

Smith had told the other men, "I will leave the mission rather than be connected with Mr. Whitman," thus creating the need for the special meeting. Then, driving a nail in the Whitmans' hearts, the other men, influenced by Henry's private complaints against Marcus, proposed that Smith replace Marcus. To the astonishment and shock of the Whitmans, the motion passed. The visitors completely disregarded their hospitality, hard work, and devotion to Waiilatpu.

---

[2] On April 29, 1839, a couple from Hawaii, the Halls, arrived in Fort Walla Walla with generous donations from Hall's church in Hawaii which included a printing press, type, paper, binding materials, sugar, molasses and salt. This was the first American printing press on the Pacific coast.

When they returned to Waiilatpu, Smith and Marcus came to a compromise. Smith agreed to move to Kamiah, which was in the heart of the Nez Perce country, temporarily to study the Nez Perce language. The Whitmans would remain at Waiilatpu at that time, and they would vote on the final decision in the September meeting. By April, Marcus and Narcissa were greatly relieved when most of the men decided that the Whitmans should stay at Waiilatpu since they had spent all of their efforts on establishing the mission.

On the last day of April, the Smiths left for Kamiah. The Walker and Eells had departed in March for their station.

By August of 1839, Marcus had made five round trips to Lapwai and many other visits to the other missionaries, totaling eighteen hundred miles on horseback, the equivalent of being in the saddle for two months.

The reinforcement party had jolted Marcus and Narcissa's lives. From the moment they arrived in August 1838, everyone bickered and did not get along. After eight months, their departure from Waiilatpu nearly cost the Whitmans their initial assignment. That was the most challenging time to date for the Whitmans--until June arrived.

A Tiny Angel

Great joy to poignant sorrow marked their third year.

Sabbath morning, Narcissa kissed Alice as she lay sleeping. She immediately awakened, stretched up her arms, put them about her mother's neck, and hugged and kissed her for a long time. Narcissa told her she would get some water in a tub to wash her and left the bedroom. Alice called her mother back, pleading, "No, Mamma. No wash Alice," trying to persuade her mother not to bathe her in the tub. This behavior was so unusual. However, Narcissa put her in there anyway. Alice mildly submitted, but there was something so earnest in her pleas that Narcissa was sorry that she did not listen to her. Narcissa realized later that Sunday, the Sabbath, made her daughter feel so reluctant about bathing, for it had been her usual practice to bathe Alice on Saturday.

Alice's appearance at family worship was profoundly moving. She had been in the habit of selecting the hymn she wished them to sing, and that morning her choice was "Rock of Ages, Cleft for Me," a hymn which she had been delighted in singing for some time at her precocious age, just three months past her second birthday. Narcissa had wished that her dear mother and father could have seen Alice's animation as she sang and heard how her sweet voice soared above theirs.

When they had completed the first verse, Alice rose out of her chair and said, "Mamma, should my tears forever flow?"

as if to remind her mother which verse came next, and when they commenced, Alice sat down and sang on as usual.

They held the worship with the villagers at noon. Most of the Cayuse left the previous week for another camp, so there were only about four or five at the station. The Whitmans let them come into the house for worship. Alice's appearance was solemn and attentive, and, to close, Marcus requested the same hymn as at the family worship earlier. Alice joined them again, with clearness and distinctiveness they never forgot, with such ecstasy that almost raised her out of her chair. And no wonder, for what words could have been more foreboding than these:

> While I draw this fleeting breath,
> When my eyelids close in death.
> When I rise to worlds unknown,
> And behold Thee on Thy throne,
>   Rock of Ages, cleft for me.
>   Let me hide myself in Thee.

After the service, her father took her out into the garden and picked a rhubarb stalk, which they called pie plant. She was very fond of the tart plant, and she ate part of it and then threw the rest down, "Too sour, Daddy," as Marcus laughed at her squinched face.

Marcus and Narcissa were sitting inside the house by the door. Alice ran in and out of the house. Margaret McKay, who lived there to attend school and assist Narcissa with chores, had been asked to set the table and get fresh vegetables for supper. Narcissa never felt comfortable when Alice was out of her sight, so the moment Narcissa ceased to hear Alice's voice or see her, she sent Margaret to find her. Margaret looked for Alice only a little while and then went into the garden to pick radishes and lettuce for supper. Margaret, distracted with her garden chores, did not come back into the house to let Narcissa know that she could not find Alice.

Alice had never gone near the river or appeared venturesome until the past week when she saw visiting children playing about the water. She observed their siblings and parents going to the river for water. She seemed to know what it meant when her mother told her, "Alice, you must not go near the river. If you fall in the water, you could die like Boxer, and Mamma and Daddy would have no little Alice." Boxer was their dog that Marcus had drowned because the animal was sick.

Later, while sitting on her mother's lap, Alice appeared in deep thought and said to her mother, with an inquiring look, "Alice fall in water. Alice die like Boxer. Mamma have no Alice." Her mother gently soothed Alice, reassuring her while reinforcing the dangers of the river.

Mongo, their devoted Hawaiian helper, followed Margaret outside to look for Alice, and he went to the riverbank. Immediately he came back to the house and said, "There are two cups in the river."

Marcus asked, "How did those cups get in the river? Which cups were they?" No one answered. "I suppose Alice put them there, so I had better fish the cups out of the water before they float away."

Narcissa was not alarmed because Margaret had not come back to let her know she could not find Alice and assumed that Margaret had found Alice and taken her to the garden to get vegetables. Suddenly, it flashed across Narcissa's mind like a dream. She recalled that while sitting and reading a little earlier that evening, she had caught a glimpse of Alice entering the house. On seeing the table ready for supper, Alice exclaimed with her usual animation, "Mamma, supper almost ready. Alice get some water." She went up to the table and took two cups that sat by her and Margaret's plates, for they drank water rather than tea. Alice disappeared outside.

Depiction of Alice in the Whitman Mission Video

The reality of the situation slammed her into a state of alarm, and she screamed, "Oh my God, Marcus. The cups! Alice must have taken them to the river to fill." She and Marcus frantically rushed to the riverbank, realizing that Alice must have fallen into the river.

"If she has just fallen in," Marcus panted to her as they ran, "if we can find her immediately, she may not be dead, and we could revive her."

Frantically they crossed a bend in the river downstream from the house and rushed back again and wildly searched upstream. Farther below them, Mongo and a few Cayuse who heard the parents' desperate cries waded into the river to look for Alice.

They gave up all hope of saving her, for they knew she had been in the water too long to revive her. As Narcissa and Marcus came upriver towards the house, they saw an elder entering the river and swimming underwater. He came up for air once, and then he found the child. He took Alice from the water, tenderly cradling her in his arms. He exclaimed, "She is found." It was Chief Umtippe who so dearly loved this child. Despite being wet from the river, the old man had tears streaming down his face.

Narcissa ran to grasp her to her breast, but Marcus outran her and took Alice from the arms of Umtippe. Marcus gently pulled her dress from her face. When her body shuddered, they hoped she had tried to struggle for breath, but they realized that her movement was only the effect of being pulled out of the water.

During the revival attempts, Narcissa dropped to her knees, looking up into the heavens, her left hand on her cold, wet child, and her right arm extended with her palm open as if making a conduit for her baby's spirit to travel to God. They tried every means to bring her to life for a long agonizing time, but to no effect. The tiny angel was already in heaven.

Narcissa wailed as she lifted the limp body of her little girl from the ground and held her to her breast, "Oh, my darling baby. My little Alice, you are the light of my life. How can I face another day without you?" She sobbed and rocked her in her arms.

After carrying Alice to the house, Narcissa washed her muddy body and prepared her for the grave. Marcus wrote a note asking immediately for Henry and Mr. Hall to come and assist in burying her. Night came, and they went to bed, but it was impossible to sleep while their dear child lay in another room. Dawn slid in, and they arose, but their child could not wake up. Narcissa prepared a shroud for her. They kept Alice for four days, and she did not change in her appearance for the first three days, which provided great comfort to her mother because as long as she looked natural and was so sweet, she could caress her. Narcissa could not bear to have her child out of her sight, but when she began to melt away like wax, Narcissa said that the grave would be a quiet, safe place for Alice to rest.

Alice had always slept with her mother. Never could Narcissa persuade her to sleep away from her, not even in her father's arms. The week before her death, Alice suggested that she sleep on the floor rather than in her parents' bed. Narcissa made a bed for Alice beside her, where she could reach down and touch her throughout the night. Alice would lie with her mother for a while and then go to her bed. Alice had recited this bedtime prayer with her mother each night, "O Lord, bless little Alice. May she be Your child, may she love You, and when she dies, may she go to heaven and live with Jesus and sing His praises forever and ever. Amen." Alice gradually went out of her mother's arms to the grave.

Although Alice was buried at the base of the hill in sight of the house, surrounded by a white fence, Narcissa's thoughts rarely wandered to the gravesite when she stepped outside. She felt that her child was not in the ground but that her spirit had gone to God. Narcissa looked towards heaven and contemplated, "My little angel is enjoying the full delights of that bright world where her joys are perfect, and she no longer needs the presence of her much-loved parents to make her happy."

Months later, in her October 9, 1839, letter to her mother, Narcissa penned, "My dearest Mother, after the shock of losing our precious Alice and after we laid her to rest, here is the prayer I said to our Heavenly Father: Lord, it is right. It is right. She is not mine, but Yours. She has only been given to me for a little while, and now, dearest Savior, you have the right to her. Thy will be done, not mine. I cannot wish her back in this world of sin and pain. Her tender spirit was too delicate to remain here longer and be subject to the ills of this cruel and unfriendly world. Jesus' love for her was greater than mine."

Alice was two years, three months, and nine days old when she died on June 23, 1839.

More Friends Lost

Alice's death was just one of many the Whitmans would endure. Joseph Maki, their trusted friend and loyal Hawaiian became ill and died in August of 1840. Narcissa's letter to her mother, dated October 9, that same year, described her sorrow:

> Our loss is very great. He was so faithful and kind--always ready and eager to help us in every way until his last breath so that we might give ourselves to our appropriate missionary work. He died as a faithful Christian missionary dies, happy to die in the field that he was permitted to come and work for the good of the Indians. In his dying moments, we witnessed him to be calm and serene because he felt it a privilege to be a missionary, to be the means of saving one such soul from the midst of heathen darkness. His wife is just so faithful. I don't know how I could do without her.
>
> Dear Mother, we feel that the Lord must be giving us a message by the events we have suffered through. Every year we have had a death in our family since we have been here. I feel it would be our turn soon, and we know not how soon.

> I have thought more about meeting my friends in heaven than in this world. We would prefer to live and die here--to spend our lives for the salvation of these people. Yes, dear parents, we have been contented and happy, notwithstanding all our trials, yet we would rather die in the battle than retreat. Our ardent prayer is, Lord, let not this mission fail, for our Board says it is the last effort they shall make for the poor Indians, and may the dear Christians at home pray more urgently to God on our behalf.

Cornelius Rogers, who was the one bright spot in the reinforcements when Smith arrived, asked Pierre Pambrun at Fort Walla Walla for Marie's hand in marriage. Marie was Pambrun's sixteen-year-old daughter, and he encouraged the relationship and promised much of his personal property to Marie with the pending marriage. The Whitmans, however, felt she was not suited for their young friend because she was uneducated, her mother was Indian, and her father was a French-Canadian. They also objected because Marie could not speak the English language well and because she was Catholic.

In May 1841, Pambrun and Rogers rode together when Pambrun's horse buckled and ran. He was repeatedly thrown against the saddle horn and then to the ground. Rogers got help to carry him back to the fort. Marcus attended Pambrun, who begged the doctor to give him something to put him out of his misery, but the doctor refused. Pambrun suffered for four days until he died, leaving behind a wife and nine children, the youngest being three weeks old. Marie then refused to marry Cornelius Rogers. Rogers went to the Willamette Valley and, in four months, married the daughter of a Methodist missionary.

Two years later, Rogers, his wife, and several others died when their boat tumbled over Willamette Falls. Two months before the Rogers drowned, a Methodist missionary also drowned.

In 1843, a couple with the last name Littlejohn and their twenty-two-month-old son were wintering at Lapwai with the Spaldings. The little boy crawled under the fence surrounding their house, scampered to the millrace pond, and drowned. It was dreadful for Narcissa and the Spaldings because his death had similarities to Alice's.

This tragedy made a total of two children and four adults drown within four years, in addition to the deaths of Joseph Maki and Pierre Pambrun. Premature death came in many forms and was not specific to race, sex, or age.

Terrie Biggs

A Safe Haven

Waiilatpu is referred to as the Whitman Station, and in later history, the Whitman Mission was in a strategic location for emigrants for several years. They hosted many weary travelers, and their house groaned from overload. Asahel Munger and his wife were one of two independent missionary families to arrive who were not sponsored by a mission board. Munger worked as a carpenter in exchange for room and board and eight dollars a month in wages. He drew the plans for a T-shaped new house on higher ground. It was built in sections, habitable in late 1840, and completed three years later.

The nearest timber was fifteen miles away. All the boards were cut by hand with a pit saw, using adobe bricks for the house, fireplace, chimney, hearth, and ovens. Even when finished, there were plans to make it larger.

Some Trails Never End

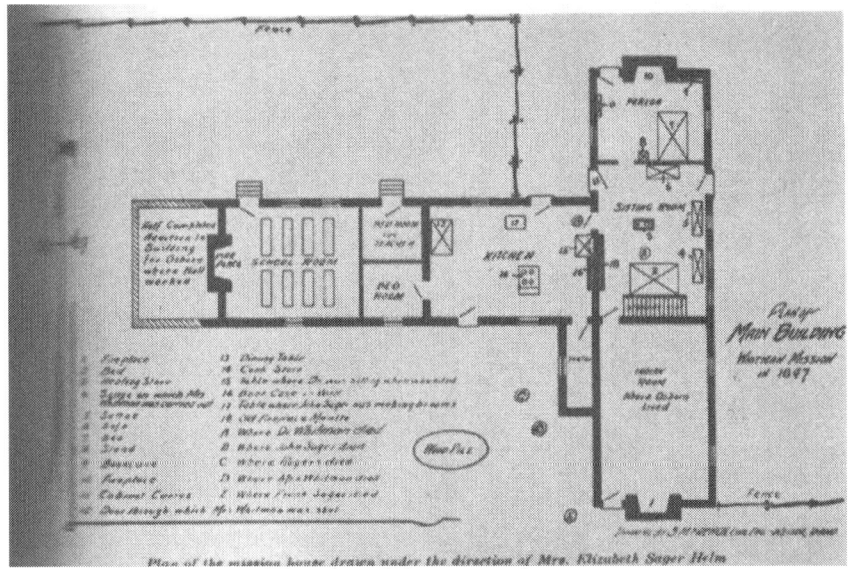

The plan of the mission house
by an artist following Elizabeth Sager Helm's memories

Narcissa no longer wanted the Cayuse to worship in her new house. She felt they were dirty and flea-infested, so when the Cayuse returned from their winter camp, the Whitmans asked them to put their lodges together to make a gathering place for worship within their camp. The Whitmans explained to the Cayuse that people in other areas who attended services helped build the house of worship, and they would use a section of their home for church services. The Cayuse refused to help and demanded that the missionaries pay them to use their land. They asked for more food and full access to the new house. Since they could not persuade the local band to help build their home, the Whitmans hired workers or exchanged labor for room and board, drawing the workforce from the emigrants and travelers.

The house consisted of the Whitmans' bedroom, sleeping quarters for visitors and residents, a parlor they referred to as a sitting room, a dining hall, a kitchen, a pantry, a cellar, storerooms, and hen houses. They included what they referred to as the "Indian Hall" for worship and allowed the Cayuse access only to this room and, reluctantly, to her kitchen. Never with any privacy when she cooked, Narcissa always had Indian and American visitors.

Munger had been quite helpful in the construction of the new house. However, he became increasingly irrational and unbalanced, which Marcus described as a "monomaniac" and felt Munger was unsafe. Marcus said he should return to his parents in the States. They attempted to send Munger, his wife, and their year-old daughter east with an escort, Mr. Ermatinger. However, it appeared the Oregon Trail was only westbound.

The young mountain man fascinated with Narcissa on the trail, Joe Meek informed Marcus that the fur trade had died off, and there were no more Rendezvous. Ermatinger could not find anyone at Fort Hall going east, so he returned to Waiilatpu in August with the Mungers. In September, the Mungers traveled to the Willamette Valley with two missionaries. Just before Christmas, Munger drove nails in his left hand, drew out hot coals from a fire, and burnt his hand to a crisp. He died four days later.

With Gray's help, they finished another house for company and passers-by in 1841. It was about four hundred feet from the main house, was one-and-a-half stories high, and could hold two families comfortably. It became known as the Emigrant House

Three children born to Indian mothers and trapper-trader fathers found their way to the mission by 1843. Helen Mar Meek, Joe Meek's daughter, was the first to arrive. Joe's Nez Perce wife deserted him when the child was born. Joe named the child Helen Mar after Lady Helen Mar, the heroine of Jane Porter's *The Scottish Chiefs*. Joe and four other mountain men traveled with the first group of emigrants to take wagons over the Blue Mountains. The mountain men knew their trapping days were over, so when they arrived at Waiilatpu in November 1840, Joe persuaded Narcissa to take his two-year-old child, who was dirty, covered in lice, and in pitiful shape. Narcissa bathed and dressed Helen in Alice's clothes. Helen was stubborn, fretful, and cried a lot when she did not get her way when she first arrived. Narcissa wrote to her sister Jane that she had quieted her so that she was a comfort to them, but she did keep tight reins on her. A small part of a large void was filled.

The second child to arrive was Jim Bridger's daughter. At the newly established Fort Bridger, when Ermatinger had tried to find someone to take the Mungers east, he met up with Jim Bridger. The fort was named after him. When the Mungers returned to the station, Bridger persuaded them to take his five-year-old daughter, Mary Ann, with them to Narcissa to raise and educate. Narcissa welcomed yet another daughter into their home and described her as being of a mild disposition, easily governed, and of little trouble.

The third child arrived the following year when two Indian women came by the Whitman house with a miserable-looking little boy. His Walla Walla grandmother said she was going to Walla Walla to dispose of the boy, who appeared to be between three and four years old. He was nearly naked on that chilly March day. His grandmother said that his mother had thrown him away and had gone off with a Flathead. The mother had several children with white men, and this child's father was a Spaniard named Cortez, who the Hudson Bay Company employed.

Narcissa asked his grandmother if she could keep the boy when the old lady said she intended to "dispose" of him, which may have meant that she would dump him in another village. The old woman was relieved to get rid of this burden and readily consented to give him to Narcissa with no hint of compassion for the child. His hair had a shaved cross in the center of it from ear-to-ear and forehead to neck, which some Indian boys had done to make him look ridiculous. They injured his foot by maliciously pushing him into a fire. Some boys also had burned his naked body with sticks on fire. Narcissa washed him, oiled his body, and bound up his wounds. She dressed him and cleaned the lice from his hair. She took the child into her home and her heart, deciding after cleaning him up that he was probably only two years old. She renamed him David Malin after a schoolmate in Prattsburgh who had married her friend, Mary Porter. Her letter to her sister Jane shows Narcissa's open heart for her new child:

> I am more and more pleased with my little boy every day. He is so mild and quiet and so happy in his new home that I have not had the slightest regret that I took him in. He is learning to talk English extremely well--much faster than my two girls, Mary Ann and Helen. The second Sabbath, he went about the room, saying, "I must not work. I must not work," and a part of a line of a hymn he had heard us sing, "Lord teach a little child to pray." All that he could say was, "A child to pray. A child to pray."
>
> He is learning to sing, also. He seems to have a natural voice, and he learns quickly. I think Marcus will have no objections to keeping him when he sees what a promising boy he is.

Marcus had been gone for three weeks when she took David into her protection. This sweet child would be broken-hearted and forsaken again before he reached ten years old in a dramatic turn of events.

Signs of Trouble

Chief Umtippe, who had been so enamored with Alice, died, and the new chief of the people who lived at Waiilatpu was Tiloukaikt. The village consisted of about fifty men, women, and children and was located one mile from the mission houses. Tiloukaikt had five or six children, among them Edward and Clark. It disturbed him that Marcus took Narcissa with him when he traveled. One morning he asked Marcus, "Why do you take your wife with you to Mr. Walker's? Why do you not go alone? You see, I am without my wife. Why do you always want to take your wife with you when you go from home? What do you make so much of her for?"

"It is good for her to go with me. We are as one, and wives are given to us as companions." The two men had the opportunity to learn each other's cultures, but neither had tolerance for the other's customs concerning a wife's role.

Narcissa described her band of Cayuse as exceedingly proud, arrogant, and insolent people who stretched her patience and forbearance. The people of the village often described her as proud and arrogant. The women and men of the village were also upset by her laundry hanging to dry outside. They were so poor that they viewed having more than one dress as a sign of too much wealth.

The Whitmans were very proud that the Cayuse people at Waiilatpu were becoming more independent through farming.

The missionaries saw this as a benefit because they could now grow their food and store it for winter rather than move from place to place seasonally to follow the food supply, as had been their custom for centuries. Narcissa was pleased with her neighbors' progress in farming, and their gardens were plentiful. The Cayuse and mission residents combined were harvesting two hundred and fifty bushels of wheat at that point. They all enjoyed the benefits of the grist mill, which could grind one-and-a-half bushels of grain in an hour.

Marcus vowed to help the Cayuse become true Christians as well as farmers. He spoke to Chief Tiloukaikt, who replaced Umtippe, "None of your people are Christians now. They are all on the road to destruction. They cannot be true Christians when they are sinners with more than one wife. Worshipping will not save your people unless they have a change of heart."

Tiloukaikt was confused by Marcus's condemnation and pleaded, "Please do not talk bad talk to my people. You must talk good talk. We just want you to tell us Bible stories. We want to learn about the great Jesus. When we traveled to the Rendezvous, we asked the men who spoke of Jesus to come among us. On our land offered to you in friendship, you tell us that our way of life makes my people unfit for your church. That is bad talk."

As friction escalated, the local band became angry with the Whitmans. Two men at the village had run cattle through their potato field. They also threatened to whip Marcus. Narcissa was very concerned about this incident, but Marcus assured her that he would not be intimidated by their actions. She approved of his firmness. Firmness in her was natural, and this quality, admired by the eastern white population, was detested by her Cayuse neighbors. She told Marcus, "This only makes us more resolved to plead for blessings to descend upon them."

More trouble was developing between the Whitmans and Spaldings, as well. Marcus and Narcissa were upset about Henry's mistreatment of his Nez Perce neighbors. There were two incidents in which Henry used or allowed the use of a whip for discipline. Marcus was a pacifist, and he neither believed in bodily punishment nor did he inflict physical harm.

In the first incident, Henry had performed a marriage ceremony between a mountain man named Williams and a Nez Perce woman. This gesture caused an uproar in the Christian group. At their first annual meeting, a resolution indicated that unless they were candidates for church membership, no one would perform a marriage ceremony again for a "heathen." They felt that Williams had no intention of applying for membership in their church, nor was he a suitable candidate. Williams mistreated his Nez Perce bride, and she ran off, so Henry permitted Williams to whip her. The Whitmans felt it was reprehensible for Henry to give the man permission to beat his wife, but that instead, Henry should punish Williams for his savagery against his wife.

Marcus was informed of another occasion when Henry allowed two boys to be beaten with the whip after stealing some corn. When Marcus told Narcissa about it, she exclaimed, "Two little hungry boys! Where is his heart?"

"In answer to that question, his heart may still be with you. I think that's why he's been so vile to both of us. He is still jealous," Marcus replied.

"He certainly doesn't seem so to me," Narcissa said. "He acts as if he hates us. I still have a hard time forgiving him for trying to get us to leave our station and let Mr. Smith take over. Our blood and sweat and our child's bones are in this land."

Demand for Payment

In 1842 the Whitmans were still having trouble with their neighbors whose fields were contiguous to theirs. As soon as the mission residents harvested their wheat, a few Cayuse men put their horses on the field to pasture. The horses ate and trampled a large amount of corn and potatoes.

A Cayuse named Tilkanaik from the nearby village put his horses in the mission's cornfield to feed, and Marcus sent some tribe members to catch and remove Tilkanaik's horses. When Tilkanaik heard this, he returned to the mission grounds to confront Marcus and said, "You are trying to get these men whipped. If you send *my* men to catch *my* horses, I will beat them. I put my horses there so that they would not stray. I have no servant to attend to them, and they will stay here and eat. If you put my horses out, I will take one of your horses and ride it to hunt for my lost horses until I tire him out. Then I will leave him."

Marcus replied, "Our field is a plantation and not a horse pen, but if you feel it is good for your horses to eat up our crops, I have no more to say about it."

"This was my land. I grew up here, and the horses were only getting nourishment from what grows from the soil of our Earth Mother. You do not own the land. What have you ever given me for my land?"

"Nothing," Marcus replied. "And I never intend to pay you anything."

"You should be full of shame," Tilkanaik scolded. "You have not paid us as is our way. If I take something of yours, I give you something in return. We trade with other white men at the forts. We do not take without giving except our enemies. You should feel shame for your insolence." And he turned to walk away.

"Please wait and let me speak," pleaded Marcus. Tilkanaik turned to face him again. "We came here by your people's invitation. We did not come by ourselves. This land was fully granted to us."

Tilkanaik grunted in disapproval and began to walk away again.

During this time, Chief Stickus, visiting from his band on the Umatilla, came over to his friend, Marcus. Stickus was also upset to see the horses eating up the corn. Marcus began explaining to Stickus what had just transpired when Tilkanaik, overhearing them, came back and demanded of Marcus, "How many times are you going to talk?". He struck Marcus twice severely on his chest, commanding him to stop talking.

Marcus replied, "I have been in the habit of talking from my childhood, and I intend to keep on talking."

Shortly after this incident, Peu-peu-mox-mox--whom the white men called Yellow Serpent--went into the house on the mission grounds where William Gray was living and sat by the fire in the kitchen. The woman preparing breakfast for Gray and his Hawaiian helper complained to Gray about Peu-peu-mox-mox. Gray then asked him to leave the house and told Peu-peu-mox-mox that he was not allowed there because many items were stolen from the home. Peu-peu-mox-mox was insulted by being asked to leave because Gray intimated that he might also be a thief. The visitor went outside to the horse corral and threw his rope on Gray's horse to ride off on it. Gray cut the line and forced Peu-peu-mox-mox out of the pen. That same afternoon Peu-peu-mox-mox rode back with his brother Tamsucky, who lived at Chief Tiloukaikt's camp near Waiilatpu, and started to take Gray's horse. At the time, Marcus and Gray were working together building the new house. Other band members, who were helping Marcus and Gray, gathered around.

"If you become a thief by stealing this horse, how can you cleanse yourself?" Marcus challenged Peu-peu-mox-mox.

Tamsucky egged his brother by saying, "It would be good also to kill their cattle."

Marcus countered, "You have now shown your true heart. Kill them if you think you must," but the two men rode off without stealing the horse or killing cattle.

Later that day, Chief Tiloukaikt and several of his men, having heard of the encounter, walked over to the house, demanding of Gray, "You must stop building this house. You must leave Waiilatpu."

Marcus told Gray to let him do the talking and answered, "Mr. Gray is not leaving. He is essential to me. Your men do not want to work, and I must have help building our new house, and Mr. Gray is a skilled carpenter."

"If I were to go to your country, I should be very careful how I conducted myself lest I be sent away," the chief warned.

Marcus replied, "If Indians come into Mr. Gray's or my house and refuse to do as we desire, it is right for us to put them out."

Chief Tiloukaikt took hold of Marcus's ear, pulled it, and struck Marcus on the chest, warning, "You will listen to me! We will do as we please in your house. This is *our* land!"

When the chief let go of his ear, Marcus turned the other ear to him--Biblically turning the other cheek--and he pulled the other ear also. The chief then took Marcus's hat and threw it in the mud. Marcus called the Cayuse helping Gray, "Please give me my hat."

One man cautiously ventured forth and handed Marcus his hat, obviously fearing a reprisal. The chief grabbed the hat again and threw it back in the mud. Once more, the Indians gave it to Marcus, and he put it on, looking Tiloukaikt defiantly in the eyes. Tiloukaikt was furious and yanked the hat off again and threw it in the mud and water. Once more, the Indians gave it back to Marcus, and he put it on, mud dripping off his head.

"Perhaps you are playing," Marcus suggested and turned and walked away, which was dangerous. He had made Tiloukaikt, Tamsucky, and some other men in the band angry.

McKinley, Pambrun's replacement at Fort Walla Walla, inquired about the incident after a few excited Cayuse told him about it. Marcus assured McKinley that things had settled down, but they hadn't. A day or two later, McKay, a man of mixed blood who was a Hudson Bay Official, made a forceful speech forbidding all the Indians to work for the settlers.

Tempers were flaring over the Cayuses' right to access dwellings on their land, as was their custom with their people. One day an old Indian threatened Narcissa at the window with a hammer while Tamsucky, inside the house, tried to unlock the door to let the others inside. Marcus ordered him to stop, but Tamsucky went into the kitchen and removed the door latch. Marcus followed Tamsucky as he opened the door to let others inside, and Marcus grabbed him and threw him out. Tamsucky took a hammer from an old man standing nearby, and the older man produced a large ax. Using these weapons, they broke down the kitchen door and entered to attack the Whitmans. Gray stepped forward and intercepted Tamsucky, snatching the hammer from him. Marcus went to the older man and disarmed him. There were chiefs present, and Marcus waited to see if they would speak to restore order, but they said nothing.

After Marcus grabbed the ax, the old man held Marcus's collar, struck Marcus with his fist, and tore his clothes. Narcissa got the ax from her husband, and Gray took the hammer and the ax upstairs. Tamsucky soon returned with a club and advanced toward Marcus. Marcus dodged the blow leveled at him as he rose to take the club from Tamsucky. The Cayuse men ridiculed him for evading death. After Marcus told them he was not afraid to die, Tamsucky came in again with a gun and held it across his chest defiantly, asking Marcus, "Do you not fear to die?"

Marcus answered. "I am not challenging you to kill me, nor do I want to suffer pain, but still, I do not fear death. If you kill us, you will suffer the consequences when the Americans hear of it. Also, you will be sending us to God ahead of you, and He will punish you."

"We do not want to kill you," Tamsucky said in a softer tone, "We are only asking that you do not shut us out of any of your doors again. If you do this, we will live in peace."

Marcus responded, "As long as we are allowed to live here and occupy our houses, we will lock some of our doors. If you wish to live in peace, you must not oppose such regulations."

Chief Tiloukaikt finally said, "It seems impossible to bully these Americans into a fight," but the Cayuse still demanded that they had the right to any belongings in the houses.

"You will not get anything from us for your bad conduct," Marcus warned them. "If you want property that way, you'll have to steal it."

"That is very harsh language," Tamsucky replied.

There was a long pause after the standoff. Marcus wondered what might have instigated this outburst and said, "It seems that this issue over our possessions is coming from another source and not from today's encounter. I feel it results from what Joe Gray told you on the Grande Ronde." Joe Gray, who was half-Iroquois, was stirring up discontentment in the band by telling Chief Tiloukaikt that the missionaries were bringing misery to the Indians and that they should pay to use the land.

Tamsucky, no longer being confrontational, admitted, "Yes. That is true. The Iroquois had told that to us. He had forbidden us to tell of it so he would not be blamed for any trouble it might cause." Then he told Marcus what Joe Gray had said about demanding payment. Gray said they could then live as brothers if they made proper payments.

The next day was the Sabbath. Not many attended the services because most of the Cayuse went to Fort Walla Walla carrying their firearms as a show of force. Those who stayed at the mission were disrespectful and reckless and acted violently by breaking windows and scaring the animals. Following their pacifist principles, the Whitmans responded with non-violence; however, they prepared to go to the fort for protection if the situation got worse. The following week the men at the mission met with the band leaders with an interpreter, and Marcus told the Cayuse, "Unless you are ready to protect us and enforce good order, we will leave you. We did not come to fight but to teach you. We came as your guest at your request."

The local band made more demands for payment for distributing the mission's cattle among them. Chief Tiloukaikt, who had been the leading voice for his people, spoke to his men: "I ask my brothers not to take this course. We must not take their cattle by force. I have been a bad example, and I ask you now, my brothers, to not act as I have done. McKinley at Fort Walla Walla called me a dog. We are not dogs. We will not act like dogs."

Stickus, a high-ranking Cayuse chief, was also attending the council meeting. He addressed the men, saying, "I advise you to be still and say no more about being paid for the land. You invited these people as your guests on your vacant land. Never had any mention been made of compensation. They did not understand our customs of trade. This conflict will now end."

Although the meeting was filled with tension and misunderstanding, they resolved the matter for the time being.

Narcissa's Frightening Night

As if the Whitmans had not enough problems with the Cayuse, Asa Smith continued to be disgruntled and wrote an endless string of letters to the American Board of Foreign Missions complaining about Henry and Marcus and demanding a station of his own. Gray and Rogers also wrote letters to the Board voicing their grievances. It took about a year for the letters to arrive in Boston, so the Board was unaware most problems were resolved. On February 25, 1842, Secretary Greene laid many complaint letters before the Prudential Committee. The Committee adopted five resolutions that essentially discontinued the Whitman and Spalding missions: the Spaldings, the Smiths, and the Grays were recalled and asked to return to the United States at their earliest opportunity. The resolution called to relocate the Whitmans and Cornelius Rogers and place the Eells and Walkers at their station.

Marcus had written a letter received four days after the Board mailed their letter, indicating that conciliations were resolved at the previous May's Annual Meeting. By that time, Rogers had moved to the Willamette Valley after Pambrun's death when Marie refused to marry him. The Grays were preparing to leave Waiilatpu also. Immediately, Secretary Greene wrote another letter to Marcus, telling him to disregard the resolutions. Unfortunately, the second letter had not arrived before Marcus had already left for Boston to plead his case in person before the Board after he received the resolutions. It was an unexpected and hastily prepared journey.

Narcissa watched him ride away that crisp autumn morning after kissing him goodbye. He had assurances from Chief Tiloukaikt and Tamsucky that they would look after his family and the mission property.

On October 3, 1842, he left, and Narcissa began writing her husband a long letter immediately upon his departure, mailing it two weeks later. She knew that it could be a year before she saw him again, and as an example of her love and concern for him, she wrote:

> In arranging the cupboard today, I found that you had not taken the compass as you had intended. I am afraid that you will suffer for want of it and I wish I could send it to you with the other things you have forgotten.
>
> Where are you tonight, precious husband? I hope you have been flourishing today and are sleeping sweetly. Good night, my loved one.

That night, he slumbered in the Blue Mountains, looking at the moon, missing her already.

The Grays left for the Willamette Valley the next day, leaving Narcissa alone for the first time with only her three children--Helen, Mary Ann, and David--along with their faithful Hawaiian, Jack. Marcus was counting on William Gray and McKinley to find someone to live at Waiilatpu in his absence. About fifty Cayuse had their lodges a mile away.

Two nights after the Grays said their final farewells, the autumn wind howled all evening with the scent of rain in the air. Narcissa was having a difficult time sleeping. The house moaned in the wind as if mourning for its master. The creaking of the floor was not from the weather but more sinister. This incident, three days after Marcus left, would have far-reaching consequences. In the first letter to Marcus, she described her experience as follows:

My Dear Husband,

I got dreadfully frightened last night. About midnight, I was awakened by someone trying to open my bedroom door. At first, I did not know what to make of it. I raised my head, listened for a while, and then lay down again. Soon the latch was raised, and the door opened a little. I sprang from the bed alarmed and closed the door again, but the ruffian pushed and pushed and tried to unlatch it. Finally, he overpowered me and pushed the door open. I yelled to Jack to help me, and the intruder threw off his blanket and ran for his life as Jack came running toward my bedroom.

The east dining-room door was open. I thought it was locked, but it appears that it was not. I fastened the door, lit a candle, and went to bed, trembling and cold, but could not rest until I had called Jack to bring his bed and sleep in the kitchen. Had the ruffian persisted, I do not know what I should have done.

I did not think of the war club, but I thought of the poker. Thanks to our Heavenly

Father, for He mercifully delivered me from the hand of a savage man. In talking to McKay and Tamsucky about it, I told them I came near beating him with the war club. They said it would have been good if I had done so and laid him flat so that they all might see who he was.

My love, where are you preparing to spend the holy Sabbath tonight? My heart has met yours at the mercy seat, and I trust blessings are in store for you tomorrow.

She referred to the war club as a souvenir. Their bedroom had a fireplace, so a poker was in the room. Although the intruder did not speak, they suspected that he was most likely Tamsucky, one of the two men who had assured Marcus they would protect his family and property while away, despite their previous disagreements. Tamsucky seemed genuinely concerned when he heard about the attack on Narcissa, and his promise to Marcus appears to contradict this behavior. However, as time passed, he was still suspected to be the intruder.

Mungo Mevway, the seventeen-year-old half-Indian, and half-Hawaiian who lived with them for four years, unexpectedly arrived at Waiilatpu after escorting the Eells and Walkers that night to Tshimakain. The following day when he saw Narcissa, she told him of her peril, and he rode full out to Fort Walla Walla. The Grays were still at the fort, and so was Thomas McKay, who had traveled with the Whitmans from the Rendezvous to Fort Vancouver. Mungo returned to Waiilatpu that day with letters from Gray and McKay, informing her that she must leave and that McKay would arrive shortly.

Many events that month took their toll on Narcissa, but the final blow of her frightful night caused her to collapse. She could not ride by horseback, so McKinlay sent a wagon and put a trundle bed in the back to carry her and her children to Fort Walla Walla. Her room was bitter cold without heat for a week, and the bedding was damp, both of which contributed to her illness. Two weeks later, at the invitation and insistence of Methodist missionaries at Waskopum (The Dalles), Narcissa and the girls went down the Columbia on a boat supplied by Hudson Bay Company. She made arrangements for David to stay at Fort Walla Walla with Mrs. McKinlay. A month after she left Waiilatpu, the invaluable gristmill burnt, along with two hundred bushels of wheat and corn. The fire destroyed the platform, the frame, the roof, part of the wheel, and some granaries. Even though McKinlay felt the fire started deliberately, it appeared that Tamsucky's fifteen-year-old son, Waiecat, set the fire accidentally. In a letter to Marcus dated February 7, 1843, Narcissa wrote:

> It is pretty difficult to ascertain whether it was the work of design or carelessness. Two boys, one being Tamsucky's son, and his friend--and we know them to be malicious--were fishing and threw fire down on the bank of the river that ignited the dry grass.
> Tamsucky says his heart is very hurt. He does not know what you will think of him when you come to hear of the burning of the mill after leaving him in charge of the property. He weeps like a child about it. He has beaten his son severely.

With Marcus gone from Waiilatpu, the Cayuse did not have his direct and steadfast counsel. Enter Dr. White, Baptiste Dorion, and fear.

Two Cultures Conflict

Istukus, called Stickus by the white men, had a good friend called Five Crows, also his cousin. His cousin was known by many names. His tribal name was Achekaia, but traders called him Five Crows or Five Ravens, and Rev. Spalding gave him the Christian name of Hezekiah. For ease, he will be referred to as Five Crows. So it was with many of their people--renamed for ease of the white man's tongue or given a Christian name.

They both became friends with many settlers and welcomed them into their land. Five Crows lived upstream from Stickus' village on the Umatilla River. His brother Tawatoe, named Young Chief by the traders, lived with him. They were half-brothers of Old Joseph, who was from Stickus's mother's band of the Nez Perce. Old Joseph was the father of Chief Joseph, who became famous when he was an older man.

Five Crows was the wealthiest man in the country, owning over one thousand horses, a few cattle, many enslaved people, and various sources of wealth. He was tall, considered handsome, and preferred the clothing of white men.

It was the custom of his brothers, the Nez Perce, to have more than one wife. Five Crows had five wives, and he knew that his friend Rev. Spalding disapproved of that custom of having more than one wife. It was the summer of 1841 when Five Crows met Maria, the daughter of the Hudson Bay official, Pierre Pambrun, at Fort Walla Walla. She was very young, but she was kind to the eyes. Five Crows wanted to be accepted by the missionaries and Maria, so he dismissed his five wives and presented himself to Maria and her father at Fort Walla Walla to claim her for a wife. Five Crows was a powerful man, and it was a great honor to be a chief's wife. Despite his affection and a great offer, Maria rejected him, which was a great insult to such a rich and powerful man. He promptly married one of his enslaved women, causing a scandal in his village.

After he met Dr. Whtiman's wife, he was captivated by her strawberry blonde hair, blue eyes, and strength of character, which many of the local tribes detested. "Maybe I will take a white woman for my wife someday," he told Stickus in confidence.

They could not understand the concept of having only one wife. When a woman lost a brave husband, either from enemies or by accident, another man village would bring her into his lodge and share his hearth. It was the custom to take care of their own. Another wife also lightens the burden of the other women. Wives were valuable resources and a sign of wealth. However, sometimes two wives can be too many. For example, a Nez Perce man once asked Rev. Spalding to baptize him into the church. This man had two wives, and the second one was very domineering. The Nez Perce asked Spalding, "Will it be necessary to give up my second wife to be baptized?"

"Absolutely," Spalding answered. "Polygamy is a sin. You will have to send your second wife away."

The Nez Perce was quiet and said, "You tell her."

Five Crows went to school at Lapwai, where he learned to speak English by Rev. Spalding. His interest in Christianity caused him to travel from Umatilla to Lapwai in the fall of 1841 and become a member of a class that Spalding was preparing for church membership. He attended classes there for two years. Out of twenty-one Nez Perce that Rev. Spalding christened, Five Crows was the only Cayuse allowed to become a member of the mission church. Stickus was a loyal friend to Dr. Whitman but was never permitted to join his church. Dr. Whitman's strict codes of religious ethics were never met by any other of Cayuse, either. When Dr. Whitman returned from the United States, he recalled being angry with Rev. Spalding for letting some of the Nez Perce men and Five Crows join his church. Meanwhile, the catholic priests were baptizing tribe members in large numbers. Tawatoe had joined the Catholic Church while his brother Five Crows became a Presbyterian, and that is when Rev. Spalding gave him a Christian name.

The Cayuse and Nez Perce people were confused and torn between their ancient way of life and the profound changes that came so rapidly. When Dr. Whitman left Waiilatpu to travel to his homeland, tongues wagged, and rumors brought fear to the local people. They held council with their chiefs and principal men. Baptiste Dorian came to the council meeting. The men passed the pipe six times, which was the custom to begin an important session, and then the people expressed their concerns: "Why has Dr. Whitman left so suddenly? Is he more interested in the white man's welfare than ours?" Chief Tiloukaikt asked.

Dorian answered, "I will tell you why. The traders at Fort Walla Walla told me he went to bring hundreds of Americans back. These people will trample across our homeland, thinking they have ownership of our country. They will build their lodges across our hunting trails. I have heard from the traders that a man called White is coming to our country to make war upon our people. He is coming to take away our land and enforce their laws on our people. I have been telling you many times that you must be paid for them taking your land."

Tom McKay was invited to this council meeting. He said, "If you do not protect the Americans, we will compel you to do so. The laws that Dr. White will bring to you are your fault. One of your people tried to attack Mrs. Whitman, and now she has left your village until her husband returns. You have stolen from them and ruined their fields of food they grew all spring, and you burned down their wheat mill."

Tamsucky defended this by saying, "I have cried tears over this. Dr. Whitman trusted me to care for his family and the property. My son Waiecat and his friend were reckless and caught the grass on fire. I have whipped him for his bad deed."

McKay answered, "This is one reason we are establishing a code of behavior with punishment for those who misbehave. I am relieved that the fire was an accident, and I honor your sorrow and regret. I will pass this information on to Mrs. Whitman, and she will be much relieved."

"We are all very sorry about Mrs. Whitman. It is too bad that she did not hit the intruder with her war club because we could have identified him and punished him in our way. Many of our people are sad that she and her children have left us because she did not feel safe," Tamsucky added.

Stickus tried to dress Dorion's wounds by saying, "You are acting like lost sheep with your shepherd gone. You know what a good friend Dr. Whitman has been to us. He is our *te-wat*, our healer. He has taught us to farm and grow food. He has opened his home for you to learn about his God, and you sing, and he tells you great stories of the man called Jesus."

Many men agreed, but Dorion continued to incite the younger, hot-blooded men after McKay left. At the same time, the elders remained calm and did not get worked up as Dorion tried to bring fear of the emigrants and imminent war to the people. "Well, if they are coming to make war with us, we will be prepared," spoke Tomahas.

Mount Saint Helens had begun to spew smoke and blow ashes, and lava rolled down her snow-capped face right after Mrs. Whitman left Waiilatpu. The Mountain God was angry. Was this an omen? Was Fire coming to their people?

Terrie Biggs

Dr. White, a "Notorious Blockhead"

Dr. Elijah White had been the first physician of the Willamette Mission. Sadly, both of his sons drowned in 1838. White had returned to the States for two years and was appointed an official Indian agent in the Oregon country by the Secretary of War. Before Marcus left on his return trip to the States, White returned to Waiilatpu with news that Oregon country was on a couple of agendas in Washington. A proposed settlement of the boundary in the Oregon country was drafted, which would go to Congress. A bill offered to give sections of land in Oregon to emigrants because they expected a massive migration the following spring.

Dr. White learned of three disturbing incidents: the attempted attack on Narcissa, the threatening of Henry's life during that time, and the fire that destroyed the grist mill, all occurring during Marcus's absence.

White's authority as a United States Indian Agent for Oregon country was questioned. Sir George Simpson, the Canadian governor of the Hudson's Bay Company, and the London Headquarters of the fur company forbid the men in the forts to assist or extend hospitality to White until they resolved boundary issues. Simpson considered White's appointment illegal according to the Joint Occupation Treaty of 1818 and felt that White had no authority over the Americans or the traders of the Pacific Northwest forts.

White, however, interpreted his assignment as a lawmaker and protector. He and Henry drafted articles of behavior and punishment related to the recent events that involved the local bands concluding with the attempted attack on Narcissa. Henry invited principal Nez Perce men to a meeting at Lapwai in December 1842 to present the articles while Marcus was still heading east, unaware of his wife's frightful night.

Henry asked Five Crows, the only Cayuse, to be present when they met with the Nez Perce. Among the twenty-two Nez Perce chiefs assembled at Lapwai was Hohots Illppilp, which means Red Grizzly Bear, also known as Bloody Chief, who was estimated to be at least ninety years old because he remembered meeting Lewis and Clark. Five Crows' half-brother Old Chief Joseph was there and alsoTimothy. Timothy was a great friend to Henry Spalding, as Stickus was to Marcus Whitman.

Many gave speeches, including those by White; Hudson Bay Official Archibald McKinley, chief trader at Fort Walla Walla; Tom McKay, a long-term Hudson Bay official; Cornelius Rogers; and Henry Spalding. Rogers had become fluent in the Nez Perce language, and his friendly personality made him popular with both the white people and the regional tribe members. McKay, Rogers, and Baptiste Dorion (Madame Dorian's son) served as interpreters. Except for Dr. White, all these men were held in high regard. Most Americans did not respect White, including traders and especially the tribes. In Narcissa's letter to her brother of April 14, 1843, she said, "Agent White is quite ignorant of Indian character and especially of the character of the Cayuse."

White presented eleven articles that he and Henry had drafted as follows:

Article I. Whoever willfully takes a life shall be hanged.

Article 2. Whoever [intentionally] burns a dwelling-house shall be hanged.

Article 3. Whoever [intentionally] burns an out-building shall be imprisoned for six months, receive fifty lashes, and pay all damages.

Article 4. Whoever carelessly burns a house or any property shall pay damages.

Article 5. If anyone enters a dwelling without permission of the occupant, the chiefs shall punish him as they think proper. Public rooms are an exception.

Article 6. If anyone steals, he shall pay back twofold, and if it be the value of a beaver skin or less, he shall receive twenty-five lashes; and if the value is over a beaver skin, he shall pay back twofold, and he shall receive fifty lashes.

Article 7. If anyone takes a horse and rides it without permission or takes any article and uses it without liberty, he shall pay for the use of it and receive from twenty to fifty lashes, as the chief shall direct.

Article 8. If anyone enters a field and injures the crops or throws down the fence so that cattle or horses go in and do damage, he shall pay all damages and receive twenty-five lashes for every offense.

Article 9. Only those who travel or live among the game may keep dogs; if a dog kills a lamb, calf, or any domestic animal, the owner shall pay the damage and kill the dog.

Article 10. If an Indian raises a gun or any weapon against a white man, it shall be reported to the chiefs, and they shall punish him. If a white person does the same to an Indian, it shall be reported to Dr. White, and he shall redress it.

Article 11. If any Indian breaks these laws, he shall be punished by his chiefs; if a white man breaks them, he shall be reported to the agent and be punished.

The last article established that the Indians and the whites were each to discipline themselves by their tribunal systems.

In an atmosphere of good fellowship, the Nez Perce chiefs agreed to accept the laws, which was the first time that any tribe in the region voluntarily agreed to accept the white man's law system. However, the experiment would fail from the very beginning. A great gulf separated the white man's concept of a sovereign state and tribal structure. The code of laws called for sanctions. Here was a glaring weakness, for no courts, police, or law enforcement agencies were among the Indians. Article 3 called for imprisonment, but there were no jails. Hanging was not an Indian method of punishment, and the fact that Articles 1 and 2 mentioned it shows that Dr. White wanted to warn the Indians that this might be the penalty that white men could inflict if circumstances warranted it. Article 11 gives the semblance of impartiality in claiming that the laws applied to the white man and the native people, which was impossible to fulfill, as Dr. White had no authority whatever over the American population of Oregon. The lash was the only sanction in the code that could be used because Indians had already accepted this form of punishment.

White's plan was to appoint a high chief of the tribes along the Umatilla River. He felt this plan would allow easier communication because the high chief would act as spokesmen and intermediaries for their tribes. He had no concept of their customs or specific roles that chiefs and principal men played in each band.

After the Nez Perce chiefs agreed to accept the code of laws, Dr. White requested that they select one of them as head or high chief. The Nez Perce had never had a leader who exercised authority over other chiefs because each had a specific role in tribal affairs. Dr. White and the other white men withdrew from the council, giving them two hours to appoint a high chief. The Nez Perce men were confused and asked to counsel with Cornelius Rogers and Thomas McKay, who served as interpreters. The decision took several hours, and the vote was between Apashwakaikt, also known as Meiway or Chief Looking Glass, and Chief Ellis. Ellis was a grandson of Bloody Chief and had the distinction of being a student at the Red River Mission School for four years, from 1830 to 1834. Ellis could speak English and was sympathetic to the missionaries, which made him the obvious choice of White and Henry. Ellis was the choice of the Nez Perce as a high chief.

Dr. White's party returned to Waiilatpu with Chief Ellis and four or five hundred Nez Perce to present the new laws to the Cayuse and Walla Walla tribes and select a high chief to represent both. Ellis was the interpreter in the council. One by one, the laws were read and explained. Yellow Serpent (Peu-peu-mox-mox) rose and said, "I have message to you. Where are these laws from? Are they from God or the earth? I think they are from the earth because, from what I know of white men, they do not honor these laws."

White explained, "All laws establishing a moral order in society came from God and are binding on all men."

Yellow Serpent felt relieved when White explained that the rules came from God, not man. "I punished my people according to the instructions we had received from others, and I am very glad to learn that it was so because many of my people were angry with me when I whipped them for crimes. My people told me that God would send me to hell for it. I am glad I am pleasing God."

Five Crows stood and addressed White and his party: "It does not become me to speak first. I am but a youth, as yet, when compared to many of these my fathers, but my feelings urge me to rise and say what I am about to utter in a few words. I am glad the chief has come. I have listened to what has been said. I have great hope that brighter days are before us because I see all the whites are united in this matter. We have much wanted something, and we hardly knew what it was. We have been groping for it in confusion and darkness. Here it is. Do we see it, and shall we accept?"

The laws were presented somewhat like the commandments given to Moses, which is how White perceived himself. Narcissa felt that White was ignorant of Indian character, especially the Cayuse. She thought they were the least peaceful and most challenging to get along with, and because they were rich, they were proud and arrogant. She knew the Cayuse would be very disturbed by these articles, see them as a threat, and said she expected trouble ahead. Gray was not as delicate with his impression of White when he called him a "notorious blockhead" and "a puffball of folly and ignorance."

The High Chief

**Sketch of Tawatoe or Young Chief
by Gustavus Sohon, 1855**

After about six days, many Cayuse and Walla Walla leaders finally agreed to accept the code of laws. However, Tawatoe refused the position of High Chief of their nation, but his brother and Stickus' good friend Five Crows took the position. A great feast followed the meeting. Dr. White paid for and butchered two oxen for the occasion. Local women were joyful when they were invited to join the feast, as women were not permitted to be a part of their council feasting.

Most of Stickus' brothers did not trust the white men and held back their consent because they thought this was a scheme to destroy them and take over their land. Adopting the laws of the white man began the tribes' surrender of their independence.

If Dr. Whitman had been there, Stickus believed that he would not have allowed these laws to be forced upon them.

Terrie Biggs

A Year's Absence

The Marcus Whitman Statue by Avard Fairbanks
depicting Whitman in buckskin clothing,
with a Bible and saddlebags

Marcus needed to visit Cincinnati, St. Louis, Washington, Boston, and relatives in New York from March to June to get back to his wife and family before winter set in. The primary purpose of his six-month journey was to appeal to the American Board of Foreign Missions to overturn their decision to close the stations at Waiilatpu and Lapwai. Henry wished him God speed and sent kind prayers to Marcus for the first time: their futures were at stake.

The safety and protection of the emigrants were under the authority of the former Secretary of War, John Spencer, who had appointed White as an Indian agent. Marcus was already acquainted with Spencer, so he visited him. He caused quite a stir in the capital. He made an astonishing figure dressed in his mountain clothes: buckskin pants, fur leggings, boot moccasins, and a buffalo overcoat with a hood that barely kept his extremities from freezing.

Spencer introduced him to James Porter, the current Secretary of War, and Daniel Webster, who was Secretary of State. He also arranged for Marcus to have a meeting with President Tyler, who was delighted to have the opportunity to talk with him about Oregon. Up to that time, no one had visited Washington who was as informed about Oregon as Marcus. His experience and knowledge of the land, the Indian tribes, the traveling conditions of the trail to Oregon, and the Americans living there were invaluable to the president.

Marcus had revolutionary and visionary propositions to offer the United States government that he refined while traveling. He presented his proposals to the men in Washington in written form and then sent them to Secretary Spencer for Congressional consideration after he returned to Waiilatpu. In essence, he proposed the need for protection and the welfare of the Oregon emigrants by suggesting a chain of agricultural posts or farming stations along the way.

Marcus explained, "The objective of the posts will be to set examples of the civilized industry to the several Indian tribes, to keep them in proper subjection to the laws of the United States, to facilitate the passage of troops and munitions of war into and out of the territory of Oregon, and the transportation of mail."

Section 5 of Marcus's proposal outlined the duty of the superintendents of the posts, which required them to cultivate up to 640 acres of land to raise produce, which the military and the passing emigrants could use. He said that if they raised food at these farming stations, it could be sold to the emigrants and "diminish the original burdens" of the travelers. This process would make the posts almost self-sustaining. He also proposed to equip each station with storehouses, blacksmiths, gunsmiths, and carpenter shops.

In contrast, a new Oregon bill proposed by Senator Linn that would establish a line of forts rather than a chain of agricultural posts won favor in Washington. Soldiers would run these forts rather than farmers and traders. These fortresses would keep Indians out, whereas farming stations would have helped the Indians and the Americans. Marcus's proposal was a concept of goodwill and helpfulness, but it was rejected.

Another section of his proposal was, at the time, revolutionary: faster mail service. He stated, "I need only add that contracts for this purpose will be readily taken at reasonable rates for transporting the mail across from Missouri to the mouth of the Columbia in forty days, with fresh horses at each of the contemplated posts." Marcus's extraordinary foresight brought about the original idea and methodology, which, seventeen years later, would become the Pony Express, which would begin in 1860 serving California; however, it did not extend to Oregon or the Pacific Northwest.

After a memorable three days in Washington, he passed through New York going to Boston. Dressed in his traveling garments, he went to the *New York Daily Tribune* and asked to see Horace Greeley. Taking one look at this mountain man, Greeley's secretary told Marcus that Greeley was not in and turned him away. Greeley caught a glimpse of him through his office window and ran out to stop him. Greeley's March 29, 1843, article in the *Daily Tribune* about Marcus gave a vivid description as follows:

> We were most agreeably surprised yesterday by a call from Doctor Whitman from Oregon, a member of the American Presbyterian Mission in that territory. A slight glance at him when he entered our office would convince anyone that he had seen all the hardships of life in the wilderness. He was dressed in an old fur cap that appears to have seen some ten years of service, faded, and nearly destitute of fur; a vest whose natural color had long since faded, and a shirt--we could not see that he had any--an overcoat, every thread of which could be easily seen, buckskin pants, etc.--the roughest man we have seen this many a day--too poor, in fact, to get an any better wardrobe. The doctor is one of those daring and good men who went to Oregon some seven years ago to teach the Indians religion, agriculture, letters, etc. A noble pioneer we judge him to be, a

man fitted to be a chief in rearing a moral empire among the wild men of the wilderness.

We are sorry to say that his first reception, on arriving in our city, was but slightly calculated to give him a favorable impression of the morals of his kinsmen. He fell into the hands of one of our vampire cabmen, who, in connection with the keeper of a tavern in West Street, three or four doors from the corner near the Battery, fleeced him out of two of the last dollars which the poor man had.

Greeley said, "Go west, young man, go west!" However, in his article about Marcus, he did not encourage western emigration, and when he heard of the 1843 migration, he called the people insane. Evidently, he never meant "go west" *all the way to Oregon!*

On March 30, Marcus entered the office of the American Board and was quite a surprise visitor to Secretary David Greene, who had no idea he was arriving. This meeting was their first after nine years of communicating solely by letter. He asked for the opportunity to appeal to the Prudential Committee to overturn their proposals to abandon the missions. He explained that conditions had changed due to the delay in getting mail. The three main complainants against Henry (Smith, Gray, and Rogers) were no longer at the mission. He and Henry had resolved to establish a cohesive and supportive attitude towards each other. Marcus showed them the strategic locations of the mission sites and argued to keep them operating. Greene realized that Marcus had not received his follow-up letter to the resolutions, which reversed their original decision.

    After his visit with Greene, Marcus felt that he had accomplished his mission and preserved his home and hard work, even though his trek east may not have been necessary.

Family Visits

With just three days left to visit his family, Marcus's mother asked, "My son, why didn't you come to see us before you went to Boston? We have suffered for your company for so many years, and you offer only three days for your mother."

"Business before pleasure, Mother, but I am here to visit you." His visit was hasty but appreciated so much by his mother. It would be his final goodbye to her.

Perrin Whitman, who would turn six the day after the Whitmans left for the Oregon Country, was the oldest son of Marcus's brother Samuel, a widower who had moved back to Rushville from St. Louis with his four children. During Marcus' visit with his brother, thirteen-year-old Perrin was captivated and filled with wonder by his uncle's adventuresome life. Marcus immediately bonded with the lad and persuaded his brother to let him take Perrin back to Waiilatpu with him, provided the boy agreed.

Perrin later recalled, "My father reluctantly consented after three days of pleading that the doctor should adopt me and take me with him if I was willing to go. My boyish instincts were aroused, and with the promise of a gun, a saddle, and a donkey, my consent was not delayed." Perrin would be a far more tremendous asset to the Whitmans and Indians than he could have ever imagined.

The pair left Cuba, New York, on April 24, 1843, where Narcissa's parents were staying. Marcus visited Jane, his favorite sister-in-law, who lived in Quincy, Illinois, with her brother Edward on the return trip. They were both still unmarried. He tried to persuade her to join them and teased her about the many eligible men back in Oregon. She would have been the only unmarried American woman, but she refused his offer and bade her favorite brother-in-law Godspeed.

Terrie Biggs

The Oregon Trail Established

The first mass migration of emigrants met near present-day Kansas City, Kansas, waiting for the prairie grass to grow enough to provide food for their livestock. Peter Burnett was among the excited emigrants and later became California's first governor. A roll was taken and listed the party as 295 males over sixteen who could bear arms. After all the stragglers joined, the estimate was 800 to 1000, making 120 wagons going west. On May 22, 1843, they were on their way, divided into two companies taking with them about 5,000 head of cattle, mules, and horses. Marcus and Perrin joined the caravan two weeks later.

Marcus warned the travelers about carelessly throwing away leftover food, as every scrap would be essential along the way. He never allowed them to stay two nights at one camp to provide new grass for the livestock. "Travel, travel, travel," was his constant advice. The wanton killing of the buffalo by thoughtless white men had reduced the magnificent herds that roamed in mighty numbers a few years prior. The pioneers could not count on buffalo for sustenance, and they would have to butcher their cattle as their journey progressed. The people relied on upon and respected his experienced advice. Marcus spent most of his time searching for a route for the wagons, as this was the first wagon migration to Oregon, and there were no ruts established. He plunged his horse into streams to find shallow places to cross without regard for the temperature of the water. Many nights, after working for the good of the caravan, he would attend to the sick. He was characterized as "always jovial, high-hearted, and happy, full of charity and courage, utterly destitute of cant, hypocrisy, shams, and weakness, and always terribly in earnest."

When the caravan reached Fort Hall, the Hudson Bay Company men could scarcely believe their eyes when they saw the immense stretch of the wagon line, the number of herds, and the squads of prancing horsemen. Captain Grant, the Hudson Bay official in charge of Fort Hall, greeted the travelers laughingly, "Have you come to conquer Oregon or devour it?"

Perrin overheard Captain Grant telling the people in the caravan that Dr. Whitman would starve them to death in the Snake River country. If they survived starvation, he warned them that they could never get their wagons over the Blue Mountains, so he urged them to go the rest of the journey by horseback as there were 500 women and children out of the thousand in the migration. Marcus, however, had a meeting with the weary travelers and swore upon his life that he would get them to the Columbia basin if they just stuck with him. One caravan member wrote in his diary, "Had we followed Grant's advice and abandoned the cattle and wagons at Fort Hall, much suffering would have ensued. Wagons and cattle were indispensable to men expecting to live by farming in a country destitute of such articles."

Marcus could not lead the caravan the entire way. Stickus remembered, "I met the wagon train in the Valley of the Grande Ronde after it had crossed the high desert, where people were refreshing themselves in the shade of the trees, and children were splashing and playing in the river. Unfortunately, I carried bad news in a letter for Dr. Whitman from Elkanah Walker, saying that both Henry and Eliza Spalding were critically ill with scarlet fever. My friend, whom my heart was made glad at his sighting, left in haste on horseback for Lapwai."

Stickus was then responsible for finding the route and successfully guided 120 wagons with their livestock and riders over the Blue Mountains safely into the Columbia basin. They went to The Dalles and over the Cascades to the Willamette Valley. At last, the wagon road to Oregon opened, establishing the Oregon Trail.

Marcus Returns Home

Narcissa's health had worsened during the year Marcus was gone. She had left Waiilatpu for six months after the attempted attack and had returned in the spring of 1843 to arrange a meeting with Dr. White, the Indian Agent, and the local tribe members. Shortly after her return, Dr. White strongly encouraged her to seek medical attention from Dr. Barclay at Fort Vancouver. She left two of her children, Mary Ann Bridger and David Malin, at Lapwai and took Helen Mar Meek with her to Fort Vancouver on June I, hoping they might meet up with Joe Meek, Helen's father, who was in the Willamette Valley. Dr. Barclay found an enlarged ovary and treated Narcissa with a medication that helped the symptoms, but unfortunately, she would find that the medicine would have nearly deadly side effects.

Two months later, Narcissa went to Oregon City and visited friends, including the Grays. Narcissa enjoyed her visits to the Pacific Northwest, having conversations and attending social gatherings with white settlers, and being able to converse in English. She was elated when she got word that her husband was traveling with the massive migration of emigrants headed to Oregon country. In the last week of September, she began a miserable, rainy trip upriver to The Dalles, where she expected to meet up with Marcus at Waskopum, but to her disappointment, he had been side-tracked.

Marcus arrived at Lapwai on September 25, 1843, and found the Spaldings recovering from the fever, so the next day he headed for Waiilatpu, eager to see his family. A friend from New York who arrived at Fort Walla Walla when Narcissa had first left Waiilatpu, William Geiger, answered Narcissa's request to oversee the mission while she and her husband were gone. Geiger had traveled to Lapwai to help the Spaldings when Marcus finally arrived home. Marcus found to his dismay, a party of emigrants from his caravan had ridden through Waiilatpu while Geiger was gone. They had broken into his house and left the door open to the Cayuse in the village. Marcus could not believe how irresponsible and reprehensible the men he had guided across the trail were.

The next day another message arrived requesting his help to deliver Mary Eells' second child at Tshimakain. He raced there and waited impatiently for six days for the baby boy to arrive. Finally, he started back the 140 miles to Waiilatpu, yearning to see his family. Narcissa's letter of her attacker and her flight from Waiilatpu had never reached him. David Malin had stayed most of the time with the Walkers, and Marcus met Walker on his way to take David home.

It was just over a year when Narcissa and Marcus finally reunited and headed back to their home. The exposure to the wind and rain on the river and the overland trip from Fort Walla Walla to Waiilatpu took their toll on Narcissa. She became sick and was bedridden for six weeks.

Unfortunately, the medicine Dr. Barclay gave her to cure a tumor on her ovary brought on problems with her aorta, which manifested themselves after her husband's arrival. She declined with bouts of high fever and developed an intestinal inflammation, an infection of the main artery below her heart.

She barely survived and described her illness as "a beating tumor which is liable to burst and end my life at any moment."

"There is no remedy for it," Marcus told her, nearly in tears kneeling by her bedside.

"I never expect my health to improve, and I never expect to continue long on the earth," she weakly replied.

However, by April, her health had slowly improved. During her illness, Marcus tended to her day and night. He helped with the care of the children and the arduous duties of maintaining their household and their farm. Life restored itself to her and their home.

Marcus had secured a pair of small millstones from one of the emigrants and put the mill back into operation immediately.

Perrin was the fourth child taken into Marcus and Narcissa's home and their hearts, but not their last. Soon they would have seven more.

Terrie Biggs

Catherine Sager Pringle,
The oldest surviving Sager child.

FIRE

"These whites are like a prairie fire, desecrating everything in their path."

The Sager Family & Emigrants
As told by Catherine Sager, Lorinda Bewley
and Chief Stickus

Introduction of the Sager Family
By Katie Pringle, Catherine Sager Pringle's daughter

My mother has a history. Catherine Sager Pringle is one of the pioneer women who survived the perils of a seemingly endless journey across the plains and through the Rockies in an oxcart. In 1844 she was little nine-year-old Catherine Sager playing around a log cabin with her two older brothers and three younger sisters. They were eagerly waiting to begin their journey to Oregon country.

Over the years, she has lectured in Oregon in its early days. Besides having contributed to the newspapers of the west, Mother furnished considerable data for the history of the Northwest Territory. When interviewed by a *Review* reporter, Mother said that her story was such a long one that, while it teemed with a thousand happy incidents, it was also full of painful memories. She could not do more than relate a few points that might be woven into a bit of history.

Clarke, my mother, and my father lived on a farm four miles from Salem, Oregon. They owned an entire section of land--640 acres. My parents named me after her, and I am called Kate.

My mother, aunt Elizabeth, and aunt Matilda told me many stories about their history. And what a history it was! The following is what I have learned from these three incredible women over the years, which I pieced together in my journal as they told me about their childhood experiences. Many fantasized versions of their lives stretched the truth and downright lied. Some delicate issues my mother could never speak about in public. I will be as sensitive as I can be to tender ears and careful not to dishonor my family, yet keep this story as she and her sisters remembered it, as told through her mother's eyes. I will fill in the details of her incredible young life as accurately as I know them.

We're on Our Way

By Catherine Sager

First, there was Mamma and Papa, and then Mother and Father. We knew the blessing of parents who loved us and cared for us. We also learned the heartache and horror of losing both sets of them and some of our beloved siblings.

I was raised with five other brothers and sisters, mainly in Platte County, Missouri. My papa, Henry, was an adventurer. He heard about Dr. Whitman, who had begun a mission in the Oregon country. Mother was rather sickly, and father said, "Naomi, it is for you I want to go. Nobody has the chills and fever the way you do every year in Oregon. Wouldn't you like to feel well?" Father had been to a town meeting the night before. He was busting at the seams wanting to go to Oregon. One man named Jake O'Brien jumped up, grabbed his fiddle, his wife played the spoons, and they began to sing a song about going to "Ory Gone," which mightily inspired Papa.

Well, that was that for Papa. Mamma gave him one of her looks because she knew the Sager men had itchy feet. Mamma ranted to Papa, "Your great grandfather in Switzerland felt he had to move to Germany. Your grandfather had to come across the ocean to this country. Your father could not bear to stay in his nice home in Virginia, so he moved to Ohio. And you just had to leave Ohio for Missouri, and now you want to go to Ory Gone!"

So, Papa sold our farm and his blacksmith shop in the fall, and there we were living just outside of St. Louis in a log home, waiting for spring to go to Oregon country. John was fourteen and claimed he was brave and not afraid of Indians. Francisco was twelve and liked to be called Frank. I was nine, and they called me Katie. Elizabeth was seven, Matilda was five, and our youngest was three-year-old Hanna Louisa. We called her by her middle name, Louisa.

"Why do we have to wait so long, Papa?" we would ask.

"We have cows and oxen, and the prairies must have time for grasses to grow to feed them along the way."

Mother hated to give up our farm. She did not want to go, already with six children and now with a seventh on the way.

"We're all stout-hearted, Naomi," he told her. "We can raise our children in God's country and be a part of history."

"What's stout-hearted, Papa," I asked.

"I'll tell you, Katie. It means brave and determined to finish what you begin." Papa was a stocky man of medium height, with thick, stubby brown hair and a short brown beard that Matilda loved to stroke as she sat on his lap. He had twinkly blue eyes and was always ready to laugh. He had big, gifted hands, which were equally capable of whether he was wielding his blacksmith tools or soothing one of us sick children.

We were raised in wide-open spaces with freedom of movement of ourselves and our feelings. Laughter and rollicking were part of our daily life. My brothers were always playing practical jokes on us girls. Barefooted much of the time and in loose clothing, we ran and whooped and hollered.

Papa set up a temporary blacksmith shop in an open shed near the house and had plenty of business making wagon wheels, blades for plows, and horseshoes. It seemed as if everyone was planning to go to Oregon in the spring.

With his arms around Mamma, giving her a big bear hug, Papa would often say, "You and my children are my greatest treasures in life." She'd pretend she was embarrassed and shoo him away, but she always smiled with such love at Papa.

Petite and pretty, Mamma had light brown hair neatly brushed and twisted into a knot at the top of her head. Her cheeks were pink, and her gray eyes sparkled. She gave us our schooling and was hopeful for a real school in Oregon country. We weren't much for churchgoing, but Mamma read us scriptures from her Bible every Sunday after supper.

Mamma said it was the happiest winter they had ever known, waiting to change our destiny in our little log house.

By April, everything was ready. Papa set the wagon by the house where it would be easy to load. Mamma neatly wrapped our rag carpet in clean canvas. Her new dishes, white China sprinkled with tiny pink rosebuds, were carefully packed in a small barrel with bran from the flour mill around them so that no plates would touch. She had to give up her loom, but Papa said she could take her cherry-wood chest. They used it to tote extra clothing on Mamma's linen sheets, pillowcases, and tablecloths.

In the back of the wagon, Papa laid a clean piece of canvas on the floor, and then he spread slabs of bacon and half a dozen hams on it. Next, he loaded the sacks of flour, cornmeal, sugar, beans, dried peas, and a few precious bags of dried apricots, peaches, pears, and raisins. The last things to go were the mattresses stuffed with straw, the feather beds, quilts, and blankets. There was barely enough room for the box that held Mamma's long-handled, three-legged skillet and her Dutch oven. Papa said we could fill the churn with milk in the morning and have butter by dinner from the rocking and swaying of the wagon drawn by our four oxen. He packed a water cask and a bushel basket holding our traveling dishes of tin and pewter, eating utensils, and dish towels. We had a small bundle of firewood for emergencies and a tent for him and the boys. Mamma and the girls used the mattress in the back of the wagon. There was a small area for the girls to play in. There were little notions all over, tied on strings and held in pockets in the canvas cover. Papa had a rifle, toolbox, water bucket, and tar bucket strung on the outside. The tailgate was on chains and could be opened for a table for Mamma to prepare meals.

We started for Oregon in good hearts and spirits in April 1844, in the second migration to the West. The first had gone in 1843. We crossed the river by ferry boats and proceeded with ox teams towards the interior. Mother was sickly from the start. The wagon made her seasick because she was with child. The rain had made the old canvas that covered the wagon smell terrible with mildew. The wagon master, Captain William Shaw, and his wife Sally were very kind and watched out for us. Sally soon became "Aunt" Sally and told us to walk to avoid seasickness. Mamma was too heavy to walk.

On warm evenings fiddles, drums, and mouth organs tuned up, setting feet to tapping. We danced and laughed. The fiddler's wife taught us this song:

OREGON BOUND
By Marv Ross
Well, a lightning bolt she hit the barn.
A flood came up and took our farm.
By the grace of God, we weren't harmed.

Some Trails Never End

But the river got our cow
And every year, we froze the ground,
While the price of corn kept going down.
So long, Ma, this farmer's Oregon Bound.
(Chorus)
I'm on my way to a higher ground
To a better world than I've ever found.
I've got my reasons for leaving this town, boys
So long, Ma, I'm Oregon bound

Now, in '37 they closed the banks
Said, "Sorry, boys, so long, and thanks,"
Price of gold fell off and sank
And it kept on a goin' down.
And the dollar that I made in May
Ain't worth a nickel come today.
Well, so long, boys,
This banker's Oregon bound.
(Chorus)
Oh, Amos here came home one day
Said, "Pack the bags. We're on our way."
Said, "Oregon is where we'll stay,"
And I couldn't change his mind.
So we sold the farm and smoked the pigs
Said good-bye, boys, and grabbed the kids.
So long, Ma, this family's Oregon bound.
(Chorus)
In New York town, they burned the church.
We stood our ground, but things got worse
So we pulled up stakes and began to search
For a place to settle down.
We looked to God to give a sign

> He guided us to the Kansas line.
> So long, boys, this preacher's Oregon Bound
> (Chorus)
> So long, Ma, I'm Oregon bound.

Near the end of May, Aunt Sally helped deliver our little babe, whom Mamma named Rosanna. We changed her name later to Henrietta Naomi, and you will understand why as our story unfolds.

Some Trails Never End

Seven Alone
By Catherine Sager

We endured hardships and hunger on our journey. Misfortune began when we got to Fort Laramie. I went to get out of the wagon, and my dress caught on the ax handle, and I fell. The fore wheels ran right over my leg and back. My leg slivered to pieces. Fortunately, it did not injure my back any. Papa would not allow anyone to call a doctor but set and tended it himself. When Dr. Degan, a Dutchman, came from another wagon group, he said in his thick accent, "I couldn't have done it better myself." I have got over it now, so I hardly limp at all, but the damp weather in Willamette Valley sometimes gives my bones an ache.

A few days after my accident, Papa and the boys took yellow fever. Dr. Degan worked day and night with poultices and hot drinks, and they began to recover.

The whole wagon train had been short of supplies, especially meat. We had passed into buffalo country, and it seemed a great miracle when a few of the enormous beasts were spotted that afternoon, and someone yelled excitedly, "Buffalo!" Papa could not stay in his bed, and despite Mamma's pleading, he lighted out after the buffalo to feed his hungry family. It was a sweltering day, and hours later, he returned dripping with sweat and exhausted and was burning up with fever. I was lying next to him, and I knew Papa was terribly sick again. Dr. Degan made every effort to comfort Papa, but he quickly grew weaker and shook with fever and chills.

Papa called Captain Shaw to his side, and I heard him say weakly, "Captain Shaw, I have heard about Dr. Whitman, the missionary."

Captain Shaw was very familiar with Dr. Whitman's mission. "Yes, many people stay there to replenish themselves and their stock over the winter."

"Please, Captain Shaw," Papa begged, "Take my family to Dr. Whitman. Naomi is very weak, and I am very worried about her health. Please, promise me you'll deliver them to the mission."

"Of course, I will, Henry. You rest now and know that your family will be in the care of the company until we get to the Whitmans."

I was still sick from my leg. Papa laid his hand on my head and said, "Poor child, what will become of you when your father dies?" And those were the last words he spoke to me.

All that night, Mamma kept cool cloths on his forehead, but to no avail. By morning Papa was gone, and I saw her pulling a sheet over our Papa's face.

"Oh, Henry, whatever shall we do now?" Mamma seemed in a daze. "If only we had stayed in Missouri."

We buried Papa on the banks of the Green River on August 26. The kind-hearted Dr. Degan volunteered to drive our wagon, and we wailed about having to leave Papa behind in the shallow grave.

Mamma's health was very feeble at the time of Father's death. The care of seven children--one a newborn baby, and me helpless and as much trouble as an infant, beside perplexities of traveling--soon broke her down. Mamma became delirious and took to her bed. She moaned and called for our dead Papa during these spells. It was heartbreaking to see her in this condition.

Poor Mamma did not have long to mourn. In twenty-six days, she followed our papa to her grave. She was conscious a few days before she died and bid us all goodbye, and she told us that we must be good children. She called Captain Shaw to her side and implored him to take us to Dr. Whitman's mission. Our mother became unconscious and remained so until she died and slipped away so easily that no one knew for hours that she died but thought she was sleeping. Buried without a coffin on the banks of Willow Creek, the kind-hearted company shed many tears for Mamma and us poor little orphans that stood around her grave. John and Frank put their arms around us girls, told us they loved us dearly, and swore to the Almighty that they would protect us always.

We were all taken care of by the kind people in the caravan, the pioneering spirit being what it was. No longer was there singing and dancing in camp at night. Everyone was too tired. Daily life had become a battle of grim endurance against time, weather, and weakness. One of our oxen died, and the others were very weak. Dr. Degan and Captain Shaw decided to cut down the wagon to pull it over the mountains. We heard hammers and saws as the men cut off the back half of our lovely big wagon. We had to leave behind most of our parents' precious possessions, including Mamma's cherry-wood chest, the beautiful rag carpet, and the barrel of dishes. I did my best to help Aunt Sally sort the items.

The wagon became a two-wheeled cart. Dr. Degan lashed the other two wheels to the cart. We cried to see the chest and our Mamma's belongings left on the trail. Aunt Sally sang this mournful song to express our sorrows:

WHAT WE LEFT BEHIND
By Marv Ross

A box full of ribbons,
A toy soldier's gun,
And the old chair of mama's
She rocked in the sun.
Oh, the cradle abandoned is still on my mind
I'm afraid I'm still missing what we left behind.

This table's too heavy,
This mirror's been cracked,
And the old chest of grandpa's will just hold us back.
Oh, this trail's lined with pieces of a long-ago time
I'm afraid I'm still missing what we left behind.

And I'm not afraid of lightning or the wolf at my door
And I'm not afraid of dying all alone anymore.
But when journeys are over, and there's fruit on the vine
I'm afraid I'll be missing what we left behind.

The kind doctor loaded us girls into the cart, and when Dr. Degan got in, he was too heavy, and it tipped backward, spilling everyone and everything to the ground. After checking that no one was hurt, John and Frank burst into laughter. The boys were always full of mischief and practical jokes, and it felt good to laugh again amid such sadness.

Mother & Father

By Catherine Sager

It took us six months to crest the Blue Mountains and see the valley below, a day's ride from the mission. We endured six months of riding and walking, eating dust, our bellies aching. Our torn and filthy clothing was worn through. Our shoes had no leather left on the soles, and there was no Papa to mend them, so now we girls were barefoot. Dirt and weather caked our skin. The whole company was hungry and exhausted. I remembered father's words about us being stout-hearted, but what a sorry sight we were! We seven poor orphans carried on to meet our destiny and greet this new land with both anticipations to fulfill Papa's dream and terror of what the future might hold.

Captain Shaw went ahead to find the Whitmans' house, leaving us in the care of the Dutchman, Dr. Degan. Captain found Mrs. Whitman at the mission, but as the doctor was absent, she said she would take charge of us girls, and Captain Shaw could take the boys to The Dalles. So it was that in the last days of October 1844, the good Captain and Dr. Degan delivered six of us pitiful little orphans to the mission at Waiilatpu. Our babe was still in the care of the company, being passed from woman to woman to nurse. Her health was so poor that for all we knew, she was already reunited with Mamma and Papa in heaven.

For weeks this place had been our talk by day and formed our dreams at night. The captain told the boys to help us girls find our bonnets. One or two were found. Now we waited outside while Captain Shaw went up to the house. He said to Mrs. Whitman, "Your children have come. Will you come out to see them?"

Mrs. Whitman came out of her house to greet her new family with a warm smile. She wore a dark calico dress with a gingham sunbonnet. Here was a perfect scene for the pen of an artist. Foremost stood the little cart with the oxen so exhausted they lay down. Sitting on the front of the cart was John, bitterly weeping. On the opposite side stood Frank, with his arms resting on the wheel, his head between his arms, sobbing aloud. On the near side stood us little girls, huddled together shivering in the cold, bareheaded, barefooted, and dressed in rags. We looked first at the boys and then at the house, and we began to cry, too. We cried because we were relieved that we finally arrived at the mission, and yet we were in fear of what our future held with this stranger. We cried because we could not bear to be separated, and finally, we cried because we grieved for Mamma and Papa. Dr. Degan and Captain Shaw stood nearby and watched the scene with suppressed emotion.

Mrs. Whitman came towards us slowly with warmth and sympathy in her eyes. She was the prettiest woman we had ever seen. The lady spoke kindly to us, but we were so frightened that we ran behind the cart and peeped shyly at her. She looked at the boys, and then she looked at us girls and said, "Poor children. No wonder you weep."

Seven-year-old Helen Mar Meek joined us in her pretty green dress, a white apron, and neat sunbonnet. What a contrast to our tattered rags! The lovely lady soothed us with her soft voice and came over to us, put her arm around me, scooped up Louisa into her arms, and led us into her house.

Our belongings were gathered up and carried inside. As we entered the house, Captain Shaw asked, "Do you have any children of your own?"

I could feel her tense as she glanced over to a grave at the foot of a hill and said, "The only child I ever gave birth to sleeps there." And then she continued, almost to herself, "It is such a great comfort to see the grave from my house."

We went inside, and Mary Ann Bridger, about nine years old, was washing dishes. Our tears of sorrow, fear, and despair turned into tears of gratitude and relief as our bellies were filled, our bodies were cleaned, and our clothes were freshened.

Debating and discussions took place between Captain Shaw and the Whitmans after Dr. Whitman returned home from nursing the sick. Adding seven children to their home was indeed a considerable endeavor and perhaps more than they might be able to handle. Mrs. Whitman wanted all the girls, and she was especially looking forward to the arrival of our babe.

They discussed what to do with my brothers. Dr. Whitman considered sending the boys to Tshimakain to be under the care of the Walkers and Eells. Captain Shaw, however, said, "It was Henry and Naomi's wish that the children be kept together."

Dr. Whitman said, "I am concerned about the American Board's reaction to me for adding such a family. They sent me to Oregon to minister to the Indians, and the Board might not allow money to support white children. Except for my nephew Perrin, three of our children are of mixed blood."

"Dr. Whitman," Captain Shaw argued, "you were sent here as a missionary, and whatever comes under that heading is your duty, whether natives or whites. Certainly, these children deserve missionary charity."

On November 6, 1844, Captain Shaw and Dr. Whitman signed a paper that stated that the seven of us were placed in charge of Dr. Whitman together with the property of our parents, Henry and Naomi Sager. That property consisted of three yokes of oxen, one wagon, one cow, one old steer, and several articles of clothing.

Captain Shaw told Dr. Whitman, "If the Walkers and Eells did not wish to take the boys, and you do not want the responsibility of keeping all seven children, then bring them all to me at Oregon City and Mrs. Shaw, and I will care for them." Then Captain Shaw mounted his horse and rode away.

We all cried tears of both sorrow and hope as our friend left. We recalled one of the songs called *Trail's End* that we heard on the trail when the journey ended, and the brave pioneers parted with their trail boss telling him, "Goodbye, my friend. Some trails never end." It was a song of triumph for reaching our destination and heartache in leaving our Mamma and Papa's dear friends and graves along that dusty trail.

The next day Dr. Whitman mounted his horse, rode out after Captain Shaw, and caught up with him just before they reached The Dalles. Dr. Whitman's horse was plum worn out chasing the captain, but he wasted no time firmly saying, "We want to keep the children, all seven. Please know that we will love and care for them as our own, and you do not need to worry about their welfare."

"May the Good Lord bless you and your wife, Dr. Whitman, for you have done a mighty fine thing for these children," He extended his hand and then continued on his way with a grateful heart.

When she arrived three days later, Rosanna, our five-month-old sickly babe, was no larger than a newborn, carried by a dirty older woman from the company. How the baby survived was a miracle. She was starving and barely alive. Mrs. Whitman gave her some milk and a bath in lukewarm water. She was starved and drank heartily but began vomiting. Mrs. Whitman put her in clean clothes and laid her in Alice's cradle. Every day Mrs. Whitman tended to her with such loving care, diluting the milk with water until she could hold it down. She was not troublesome, for she slept through the night until the early morning. Her habits of eating and sleeping were regular by the clock. She had such care and kindness that she grew rapidly.

We all agreed to change Rosanna's name in memory of our dear parents, Henry and Naomi. And so, Mrs. Whitman gave honor to our parents, calling her new baby Henrietta. From that time on, the Whitmans became "Mother and Father."

Dr. Whitman was a man of medium height with broad shoulders showing great strength and endurance. He had deep-set dark blue eyes, dark hair tinged with gray, rugged features, and was smooth-shaven except for a short beard under his chin, looking very much like early pictures of Abraham Lincoln. Mrs. Whitman was a tall, golden-haired woman who greeted us with open arms and a loving heart.

The Whitmans took us into their home and treated us as their own. We again had a mother and father. Mother told us that God had taken away her dear child so that they could open their home to all the orphan children. The Whitmans now had eleven children counting us seven. Helen Mar Meek was Elizabeth's age. Mary Ann Bridger and David Malin accepted us right away. Perrin was already fluent in the Nez Perce tongue. He was John's age, fourteen--a man's age on the frontier.

Terrie Biggs

Our New Life
By Catherine Sager

We were all prudently and adequately fed, well clothed, and attended school every winter. The Whitmans took excellent means to make us happy. Mother never permitted us to indulge in candies, sweet treats, pies, or cakes. She said it saved many a doctor bill, which we felt was a weak argument since our new father was a physician. She also never gave us medicine if she could help it. If we complained about headaches or were sick to our stomachs, she sent us to bed without supper or any meals. Sure enough, we rose the next morning feeling better and hungry.

Every day during the summer, before dinner, we were bathed in tubs until we could wash in the river. We had a bath once a week in the winter, at least.

We slept out of doors under the stars all summer, rode horses, swam in the river, and roamed over the hills picking flowers for Mother's collection of pressed wildflowers. John and Perrin were too old for school, so they helped Father with chores. Father was always jolly and kind and loved to romp with all of us children. He left the discipline up to Mother. Father would often turn his back and laugh when we got into mischief. Mother would point her finger at us instead of scolding us or reminding us of a chore. We jumped when she leveled her finger at us, and you would have thought her forefinger was a gun and was likely to go off. It must have tried her patience with eleven of us children. We always knew our place, and one place we were sure of was our place in her heart.

Frank and John held out, calling them Mother and Father for a while. Memories of Mamma and Papa were just too close for them. John came around, but Frank felt Mother was too strict with him and hated that finger when she pointed it at him. For the most part, the three older boys, John, Frank, and Perrin, were under Father's jurisdiction. They helped Father with the animals and did the heavy work in the fields and the grist mill. John was quiet, very responsible to the rest of the family, and quickly learned the Nez Perce language. Mother taught him how to write, and he recorded his experiences and thoughts every night in his diary. Mother spent her spare time writing, although her eyes gave her grief. Ultimately, we never saw a page of John's journal.

Frank's twelve-year-old memories of the ordeal on the trail left him rebellious and resistant to new parents: her pointing finger, Father's reasoning, their Bible classes, church, and washing chores, but the worst times for him were to come from our schoolmaster, Alanson Hinman, a devil of a man. He taught school during the winter months, with twenty-six of us enrolled, sixteen from emigrants, and ten from our family. Eliza Spalding was seven years old and lived with us while attending school. She had made the 120-mile trip accompanied only by an Indian woman. Twelve families wintered with us that year for a population of approximately seventy people.

"I ain't goin' ta school!" Frank announced to Mother, stomping his right foot on the frozen grass.

"There's no such word as 'ain't,' Francis."

"There's no such word as 'Francis' either. I am not going."

"Frank, you all ran free as the prairie wind, free with your actions and speech. We want a good future for you, and in doing so, it will take some discipline and, of course, education. Mr. Hinman…"

"Is a mean devil! He don't just discipline, he …." But Mother, who did not lay a hand on us, would not listen to Frank.

"No more said, Frank. You *will* attend school."

Mr. Hinman tried to crush Frank's spirit. He indeed bestowed upon my brother the cruelest whippings he ever received. Mother was very fond of this demon and did not know of the punishments he gave Frank. Finally, Mr. Perkins, who was staying at the mission for the winter, was sympathetic to their complaints about the beatings and encouraged Frank and John to leave with him and go to the Willamette Valley in the spring when the winter-bound emigrants left. John loved living there and never suffered from the wrath of Hinman, so he did not want to leave.

Spring brought fresh grasses and wildflowers. The mission was bustling with emigrants loading their wagons to continue. The Cayuse were also leaving for their spring fishing grounds. We were upstairs in our sleeping loft when Frank came over to my bunk and whispered, "Katie, I am leaving in the morning to go with the Perkins family to the Willamette Valley."

"No, Frank! You must stay with us. I cannot bear to lose another member of our family."

"I'm sorry, but I just can't stand the whippings and treatment from Mr. Hinman. Mrs. Whitman is always after me, pointing that accusin' finger at me. I swear, I can't stand no more of either of them."

John went down and told Mother that Frank was going to leave. He told me later that she began crying. Frank did not come down to the table the following day at breakfast. Helen went to fetch him.

Frank sent a message down with Helen, "Tell her I ain't comin' down. I'm leavin' this place for good."

Mother cried, left the table, went upstairs, and brought him down with her. He sat silently at the table. His lips were squinched so tight I thought his teeth would break. When he finished eating, he took his hat and started for the door without a word to any of us. Mother rose and went towards him. "Frank, you must not go. You must stay with me."

"I have to leave. I just can't stay any longer."

Mother motioned for John to bolt the door, but Frank ran out. I saw him mount a horse, and he kicked it. Mother, Elizabeth, and I cried about the loss of him. The rest of the children wailed. Mother mourned over his leaving and told me it was as though someone in the family had died. We felt the same. Our hearts were breaking.

Ironically father had left a week prior for the Willamette Valley to finalize our adoption into their family, accompanied by our teacher, Mr. Hinman, and a lady named Emma Hobson, leaving Perrin, John, and Frank in charge. While he was there, Father ran into Frank, but he did not encourage him to return. He wanted Frank to get it out of his system. Father had heard about Hinman's cruelty towards Frank and told him how sorry he was. I think Frank just needed some time.

Terrie Biggs

Legal Guardian
By Catherine Sager Pringle

Father called upon Captain Shaw and Judge Nesmith, who drew up an order which appointed him our guardian. He wanted to adopt us and give us his name, but Captain Shaw advised him against it. The value of Father's estate was $262.50, for which he had to post a bond. The court order dated June 3, 1845, read in part:

> Now on this day came Marcus Whitman, of this district, and represents as follows: That Henry Sager, died on or about the 30th day of August 1844, while on his journey immigrating to Oregon, and that one William Shaw did then take possession and charge of the goods, chattels, and effects of the said, Henry Sager, which were as follows: John C. Sager, Francisco Sager, Catherine Sager, Elizabeth Sager, Matilda Jane Sager, Hannah L. Sager, and Henrietta Sager, all, it is said, under the age of fourteen years, and furthermore, that the said William Shaw did, on the 6th day of November 1844, deliver to Marcus Whitman at his station, all the goods, chattels, and effects belonging to the estate of the

aforementioned, Henry Sager, deceased, together with the aforesaid children, all to remain with said Marcus Whitman until further arrangements could be made.

And now the said Marcus Whitman requests that a guardian may be appointed to said orphans by the court and that measures may be taken to secure the estate of Henry Sager, deceased, for the use and benefit of his heirs.

Whereupon the said Marcus Whitman gave bond for double the above sum and was appointed guardian of the above-named children.

The Whitmans always treated like their very own. Now it was official. They wanted to keep all of us! Father returned home and said that the boys should be preparing to go out on their own, so he gave John and Perrin a start in acquiring property, helping them buy cattle and horses to raise there. He told them he had no money to give but that the livestock, property, and education he provided would give them an excellent start in life. Father sent a letter and the horse to Frank and asked him to return to us.

One day that fall, our dearly missed brother rode in on his horse, looking very cautious about his reception. Mother ran to him, wrapped her arms around him, and said, "Oh, Frank, I am so glad you are home," Our mother cried again for his return. Eventually, Frank joined John in calling our new parents Mother and Father.

A stroke of good fortune came upon us when Frank got home. An onslaught of emigrants converged on us for the winter, and among them was Andrew Rogers. He was of good character, and Mother said he had strong Christian convictions.

Mr. Rogers was tall, fair, good-looking, smiling blue eyes, and always sported a happy face. In no time, he won our confidence and admiration. Mr. Rogers became our new schoolteacher in the absence of Mr. Hinman, whom we had nicknamed "Sinman." Mr. Rogers had a fine voice and a violin, so Mother turned our music and singing lessons over to him. We sang joyfully.

Mother arranged outings for us in the summer, usually on Saturdays. Sometimes we ate from a basket. Mother told John how strong he was, and he grinned and proudly carried her basket. Once, she even surprised us with an apple pie, for we rarely were allowed sweet treats. She carefully sliced it and placed each piece on the China plates she brought along. "Oh, Mother, please tell us the story of your dishes," we pleaded.

"Again?" she asked with a twinkle in her blue eyes. "Seems like I told you that history lesson last week."

We girls nodded our heads, "Yes. Tell us again."

"Well, in 1790, the United Kingdom heard about the story of two lovers in the land of China and honored them with this plate design."

"Tell us the story of the lovers, Mother."

"Please," she demanded.

"Oh, please," we girls answered. John and Frank rolled their eyes and went off to swim.

"Long ago, in the days when emperors ruled China, a Chinese high ranking official named Tso Ling lived in a magnificent pagoda under the branches of an apple tree on the right of the bridge, over which droops the famous willow tree. Graceful lines of a fence meandered in front of the tree. Tso Ling had a beautiful daughter, and he had promised her hand in marriage to an old, wealthy merchant. The girl, however, fell in love with Chang, a clerk who worked for her father. The lovers eloped across the sea to a cottage on an island. Her father pursued and caught the lovers and was about to have them killed when the gods transformed them into a pair of turtle doves. See, here on the top of the design?" Mother pointed, and we all nodded. "These doves are gazing into each other's eyes. These birds on the plates are the spirits of Chang and Kwang-se, a twin pair forever in love. So, the plate tells the legend of their love. And that, my children," and we all said in unison, "is the story of the pattern called Blue Willow."

We loved her stories. "How were you able to get these dishes here?" I asked. "There are no chips on them, like mamma's old dishes."

"We packed them in a barrel with sawdust. We knew if we used flour or cornmeal, we could eat it on the trail, and my dishes would be broken to smithereens."

Display at Whitman Mission representing her Blue Willow China

Mother would sit under the shade of a tree and laugh at our antics while we swam and rode horses or picked wildflowers. She taught us botany and had a grand collection of wildflowers that she saved and categorized. We had a small flower garden. Summers were filled with fun and frolic as we ran barefooted and bathed in the river every day. In winter, we wore moccasins. Mother sang like an angel and taught us lots of songs. Matilda loved to sing and had a sweeter voice than the rest of us girls.

Wash day was one chore we could not escape. At four o'clock in the morning, all hands were called into the kitchen by Mother. She produced tubs and all necessary supplies. With long aprons tied around them, the men and boys brought water and twisted the pounders while the women did the rubbing. With much joking, all went off in good humor, and by school time, которое was nine o'clock, the clothes were on the line. Mother had a "washin' receet" given to her before she left the States by a lady in Missouri, written by her grandmother. The lady thought that it was apparent that Mother was brought up in a refined home and hadn't done laborious work in New York. In the exact words of her Kentucky grandmother, it read:

> Bild fire in back yard to het kettle of rainwater.
> Set tubs so smoke won't blow in eyes if wind is pert.
> Shave one whole keg lie sope in bilin' water.
> Sort things--make three piles--one pile white, one pile cullord, one pile work britches, and rags.
> Stir flour in cold water to smooth, then thin down with biling' water.
> Rub dirty spots on board, scrub hard, then bile.
> Rub cullord but don't bile, just rench and starch.
> Take white thangs out of kettle with broom-stick handle, then rench, blew and starch.
> Spread tea towels on grass.
> Hang old rags on fence.

Pore rench water in flower bed.
Scrub porch with hot sopy water.
Turn tubs upside down.
Put on a clean dress, smooth hair with side comb,
brew up tea, set and rest and rock a spell, and
count your blessings.

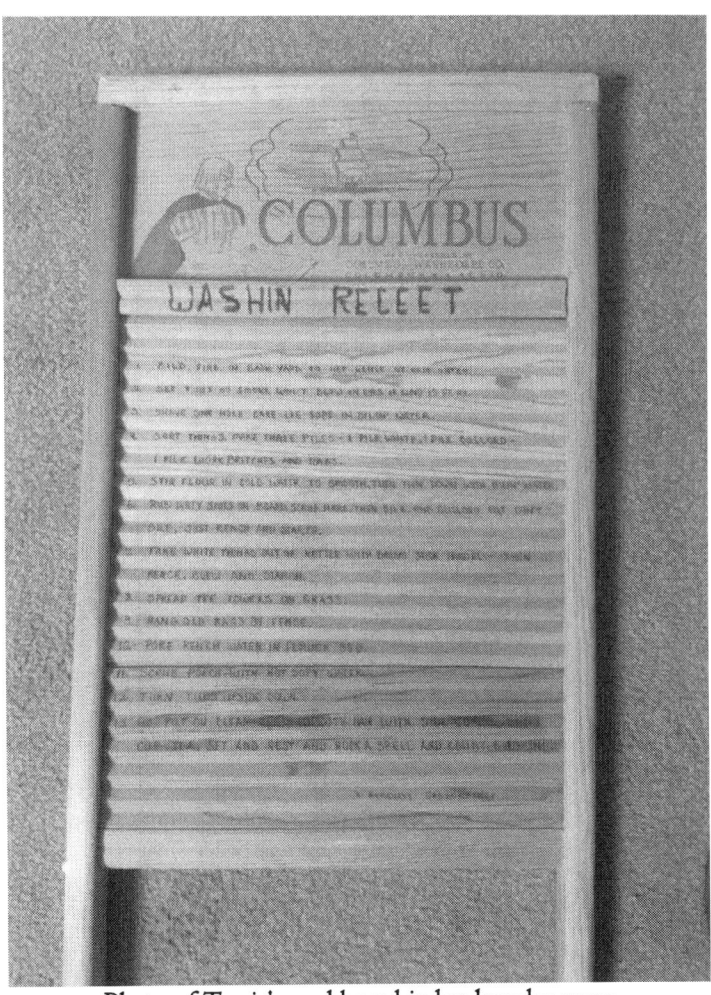

Photo of Terrie's washboard in her laundry room
With "Washin" instructions
passed down to her Tennessee Mother-in-law

Our religious training went like this: On Sunday morning, our parents reminded us that it was the Sabbath and warned us to keep quiet. We were encouraged to read. They held Sunday school at eleven o'clock and worship service for the American residents of Waiilatpu at three o'clock. Father or Mr. Rodgers, our teacher, usually read the sermon. Throughout the week, we had to memorize Bible verses. The prayer meetings were held on Thursday evenings during the winter for the adults.

Good Times

By Catherine Sager Pringle

Even though we had strict guidelines, we also had many good times. Guests filled our house, including scientists and military men, two explorers who became famous artists, the local men, helpers, and the parade of emigrants in the fall. Mother's custom was to show off her "family stairway" when she had company. She called all the children and placed them in line, standing according to height. After being formally introduced, we entertained the company by singing, accompanied by Mr. Rodger's violin. Mother and Father looked on during these exercises, their eyes sparkling with pleasure and pride.

Mother hired Mary Johnson to help with the chores in the house. She was about thirteen and had dark brown locks. One day Mary put on Mother's apron while working in the kitchen. Her back was to the door, and Father came in and pretended that he mistook her for his wife. He tiptoed up to Mary, threw his arms around her, and hugged her. She was very embarrassed. Father was as solemn as an owl and protested that he thought she was his wife. I could tell by the twinkle in his eyes he was playing a joke on her.

Another amusing incident took place one spring day in 1846 while we were picnicking near our house. The flowers were blooming, and the Chinook wind was mild. During our festivities, we were startled by the sudden appearance of a sizeable band of Nez Perce, who were going to the Great American desert to hunt buffalo. Father received them with all the hospitality of his nature, and he told them that he would give them a "big feast." Now, a big feast means a great deal to the Indians. A 30-gallon kettle was boiling, turning lard, water, and cornmeal into a mush, and then the large pot was placed in the Indian Room of the mission house as the visitors gathered around it. As a special honor, Father treated the Indians to tea with sugar. They produced large spoons made from horns and put more sugar in their tea than good breeding or taste would typically permit. We children were allowed to look on. The scene was amusing enough, but when the young Indians began to scrape and lap up the last remnants of food off of the floor, we rolled with laughter. We were immediately banished from the room for breach of etiquette until the room emptied. Mother never allowed us to show any disrespect toward the tribe members.

Tom Hill, a Delaware Indian traveling with the Nez Perce group, made an eloquent speech at the end of the day on the superiority of the educated races. He was wearing his finest clothing, including a fringed deerskin hunting shirt stained red, his britches fringed down the side, and moccasins with porcupine quills.

Life was sweet for us, and Mother said she had the best year of her life. Her health had restored, and even though she was strict--eleven children were a handful--she made it seem easy because we all felt loved. Could it be that life was just too sweet?

Ominous Signs
By Catherine Sager Pringle

We were enjoying our new life at Waiilatpu, while some of the Cayuse were never pleased with the presence of white folk. While Father was at work in his garden, an Indian named Tomahas rode up beside the fence and commanded Father to go to the mill and grind some corn for him. Father told him he would not order or bully him, that he must ask him in a proper tone. Tomahas was very demanding and told Father that he would go to the mill and grind his corn into meal. Father, annoyed, fixed the mill so it would not work and waited for Tomahas while holding an iron bar for protection. Tomahas ordered Father to put his weapon down.

"I will put my weapon down if you put your club down," Father said calmly.

They both agreed to disarm, but the vile man rushed at Father with his club as Father put his iron bar down. Father grabbed up the iron bar, and he warded off the blow.

Sharp words followed, and Tomahas demanded, "You must leave our land. You are not wanted here."

Father replied, "If it is the wish of the tribe, I will do so, but I am not inclined to pay any attention to the whimsical notions of one man." He paused and continued, "Now, I will grind your corn if you behave yourself."

Tomahas agreed condescendingly, and Father gave him his cornmeal. The affair finally settled, and the two shook hands. When Father returned to the house, he was exhausted in body and spirit and lay down on the couch, saying, "At this point, Mother, I will gladly leave if the Indians just say so. This animosity has tried me almost beyond endurance."

The hostility was not over when later at supper one night, after the younger children had retired, Father told us of another incident: Young Chief was very upset when word reached his village about two of his young men's deaths. He rode to our house one windy day in the late fall of 1845 and asked our friend Chief Stickus to accompany him because Stickus could help with translation. Father invited the two men into the kitchen and offered them some tea. Young Chief refused his drink. Mother left the room, giving Father an angry look for having to vacate her kitchen. Our brother Perrin stayed, for he was more fluent in the Nez Perce language than Father. Stickus and Young Chief used the Nez Perce tongue to talk with the white men, the trappers, the local tribes of the Walla Walla, and, of course, the Nez Perce, as the Cayuse tongue was considered more difficult.

"I am so glad to see you, Chief Tawatoe," Father said, addressing him in his Cayuse name rather than Young Chief. Stickus had told Father that it showed respect to address the men by tribal names rather than by white man's translation. "I want to talk with you about something important for your children. I would like to open a school for your children and..."

"We will not be sending our children to white man's school. This would be sending them to their death."

"I don't understand," Father said, perplexed.

"My nephew, Halket, was killed at the Red River Mission School. The white men there were responsible for his death."

"Yes, I have heard of this misfortune, but I have never heard of any evidence that he met his death violently or that it was at the hands of the Americans."

"No matter." Young Chief replied, "He was in white man's school. Another death of our people has occurred. Americans killed Elijah Hedding of the Walla Walla at Sutter's Fort in California country."

Stickus explained that Hedding and several Cayuse men and some Walla Walla and Spokane neighbors had gone to California to trade furs and horses for cattle. He had spent several years in the Methodist mission school on the Willamette named after a bishop. An argument began at the fort over horses and mules that the Americans accused the Cayuse men of stealing from a local band and claimed they had been stolen earlier from them, and they wanted their horses back. Stickus said, "That was not our way. We took them honorably. A white man who did not like our people shot Elijah in cold blood." Stickus told Father that his men returned home with a vengeance in their hearts and felt that it would be a fair exchange to kill a white man who held a high position. Dr. McLoughlin was the man they decided to kill, but they also thought they should kill Father. This threat had already come to Father's attention.

"Both of these fine men were killed, and both went to white man's schools. We will not allow our children to attend your school," Young Chief said, and before Father could respond, Young Chief continued, "We know you Americans want to take our land. We have now watched this endless parade of wagons pass through our land for two autumns. The Americans you brought with you outnumber our entire nations of Cayuse and Walla Walla. This year the number was even greater.

"We have been warned what has happened to other nations in the east. Our grounds are trampled on, and the sacred buffalo that fed many nations for hundreds of years are being slaughtered--killed as if they were only targets. Their hides and meat are left to rot. You have led these people into our land. You have fed them and given them shelter when our people are not invited into your lodge most of the time."

Father listened as Young Chief continued, "Your Americans bring sickness to our people. A friend of mine and two of his children died of your sickness a few days ago. The white man has brought poison to kill our people and steal our land. We will not eat with these murderers because they will poison the food to kill us. It is said that you are a bad *te-wat,* and you poison our people."

"I assure you, as God is my witness, no one has tried to poison anyone. You cannot hold me accountable for such base acts that someone told you. I go to help your people when I am asked. I understand your concern about those who have died. I am very much in fear for your people also. The Americans have brought sickness with them, from which they also have died. For many years my people had time to build a resistance to these diseases, so some of them recovered. Your people have never been exposed to these diseases before, and you have no way to fight it off."

"It is not expected that you would confess to poisoning us even if it were true," said Young Chief.

"I have poisoned no one," Father replied and then turned to Stickus and asked, "Did I not save you from death, Istukus?"

He nodded, yes.

Father appealed again to Young Chief, "No one wants to see your people die. I have tended to your people who were sick to save them. Such inflammatory language might remove all restraint from reckless men. I have no assurance but that your people might kill me at any time, which leaves me no choice but to leave this place."

"I do not want you to go right now," Young Chief said. "If you go, you must leave by your own decision. We will not force you to leave."

A drawing depicting Dr. Whitman attending the local people

After Young Chief left, Father was very upset and perplexed over his last statement. Father asked Stickus if he believed that he was poisoning our people. "No, I do not believe that. You saved my life, my friend. Tawatoe is a very powerful chief, but he is also a fair man, and that is why he will not force you to leave. He is, as am I, concerned for our people. Many hot-headed young men have come to him with stories. Just be cautious, my friend. I think that life here may not improve for you. He is friends with the Catholic priests who baptized him. He trusts them, and they would like to get our people to choose the priests to take over your work here."

"Thank you for the warning. You are a good friend. May I offer you some tea?" Stickus accepted and asked for a bit of sugar.

Life remained tense but calm until two years later, in August 1847. A settler at Waskopum in The Dalles had a dispute with an Indian called Equator, resulting in their deaths. Someone had stolen cattle from emigrants at The Dalles, and before long, there was trouble. When the fight was over, Superintendent Roberts, an official at Waskopum, performed the funeral ceremony over the two graves. He held a Bible in one and a pistol in the other.

The Dalles mission, Waskopum, was owned by the Methodists who offered it to the American Board. Mother said I needed relief from the care of Henrietta, so Mother and Father let me go with them to their annual mission meeting at Tshimakain, and they let me attend the meetings. The primary discussion was about purchasing Waskopum and who would live there. Mrs. Walker was not about to leave her home at Tshimakain. Mother and Father talked about possibly moving because some of the Cayuse men near our home conspired with the Catholic priests to replace us. A stroke of fate decided the occupancy of Waskopum. After we went home from the annual meeting, who should show up at Waiilatpu but Mr. "Sinman." He had a wife and child back in the Willamette Valley. Everyone was relieved when Mr. Hinman volunteered to move his family to Waskopum so that no one had to leave their homes and relocate. Our fear of him returning as our teacher was put to rest.

Perrin, who was about to turn eighteen the following March, would go there to help Mr. Hinman as an interpreter for the winter. However, the tribe at The Dalles spoke Walla Walla, so Perrin dove right into studying a new dialect. In August 1847, Hinman left with Father and Perrin. Hinman was going to get his family while Father and Perrin went to Oregon City to arrange the purchase of Waskopum. Father had a boat deliver Mr. Hinman and his family and their possessions to The Dalles, and it would take the Methodist occupants back downriver.

Father returned to Waiilatpu to prepare for the emigrants who would arrive that fall. Among them were Lorinda Bewley and her brother Crockett. Their lives would take an unexpected and fateful turn.

Terrie Biggs

Journey on the Oregon Trail
By Lorinda Bewley

In July of 1847, I turned 21, two months after my family began our journey to Oregon from Missouri. My parents were Catherine Ellis and John Bewley, who married in Tennessee in 1823. I was the second of twelve children and the eldest daughter. I was christened Esther Lorinda Bewley. In the early 1840s, my family left eastern Tennessee and moved to Indiana, then to Missouri. Two years later, we began our journey to Oregon with six of my brothers and sisters. Death was no stranger to our family, for three of my siblings had died before we began our journey. My cousin, Esther Bewley, of whom I was most fond and who was my age, lit a fire one cold evening in Tennessee and caught her dress on fire. Esther was only seven. After that, I preferred to be called Lorinda, so I would not be reminded of this tragedy to which I had been a witness.

Despite being plagued with poor health, I had the responsibility to care for my other brothers and sisters while we traveled. My Aunt Sophia, her husband Isaac, and their two young sons accompanied us on our trek west. Theresa Ellis Marquis (Mother's widowed sister) and her two young sons were also in our group. My father was the captain or trail boss.

For the first part of the journey, we had horses to ride and plenty to eat. We thought going to Oregon was nothing but fun. My father started with five horses, so we traveled most of the time on horseback.

Crossing the plains became tedious, especially for large families. When we got into Indian country, though, Indians began to run off our stock and would demand that we give them our provisions and clothes. They would come riding around our wagons with their faces and horses painted, brandishing their bows and arrows and tomahawks. We had a great fear of being killed. The company's men stood guard every night, and even then, the Indians would take a horse or a cow.

I found great comfort in my new friend on the trail, Isabella Wallace. She was seven years older than I and had two small daughters. Our families got on well together. Isabella seemed to hold me in high regard and described me as "brightly blonde, with laughing blue eyes and a cute snub nose." She called me a "smooth article," as I had attended a school for young ladies.

In contrast, I saw myself as small, frail, and poor health. Isabella was older but enjoyed the company of younger people. She tried to lighten the journey with a touch of romance.

"Lorinda, half of the young men in the train have started wearing their best neck scarves every day, have you noticed? Isabella told me that they are riding their horses around in a gallop, trying to gain your admiration," Isabella told me.

"I hadn't noticed, but I'll tell you a secret. I am very partial to Mr. Will Chapman. Will is from New York, and he has a fondness for exploration. Every night he eats at our fire like a member of our family. He tells me the most thrilling stories of his discoveries during the day as he ventures out. Father keeps advising him of the dangers of being on his own and straying away from camp."

Isabella said, "Well, your fondness of Will is no secret, my dear. Your eyes light up every time I see you look at him. I noticed, however, that Dan Young stops by and talks to you a couple of times a day. He is most impressed with himself. He has been sulking, and he mutters insults about Will around camp. He is very jealous of your attention toward Will."

"Yes, I am aware of his jealousy and moodiness, but Will is full of adventure and cheerfulness. I rode with him today, and when I returned, Father told me how Dan watched us until we were out of sight and viciously cracked his whip over his oxen's backs, damning the poor beasts."

"I would not be surprised if there were a brawl between the two. Will is tired of Dan's insults," Isabella cautioned.

There was little energy to spare for fisticuffs in the weeks that followed. After we passed Fort Laramie, a large party of Mormons with a vast and voracious collection of livestock, which included oxen, horses, cows, and chickens, had picked the area clean along the trail for the next 400 miles. Our company had to spread out in search of forage for the cattle. Our pace was slowed from an average of sixteen miles a day down to twelve miles a day.

The July heat mounted, and the grass was parched and dry. Dust filled our nostrils and eyes, caked our lips, and sifted into everything. The children began to break out with measles. Several people were incapacitated by malaria brought with them from the Missouri Valley. Other travelers, including myself, developed mountain fever, sometimes called the Missouri plague. Will Chapman rode alone those days because I was too ill to ride. Mountain fever, which is typhoid, comes from polluted water holes. The camps were dry, and the animals were as parched and exhausted as we. Men set off in all directions to search for water.

Will and Isabella's husband Victor rode to the ridge of a steep canyon. "I think I hear the sound of a trickle of water here," Victor yelled to Will. The canyon walls were almost perpendicular. Victor groped for toeholds and slid to the bottom, hanging onto bushes.

"There's water here, alright," Victor called up to Will. "It's just a trickle. We need some buckets and rope to haul it up," but he realized he would have difficulty climbing out of the steep canyon. "Will, I can't make it. My strength is gone."

"You've got to make it. Lorinda has the fever and keeps asking for water," Will urged.

Victor later said that Will's tone was imperative that it spurred him in a final effort. Will grabbed a handful of Victor's shirt, and Victor managed to heave himself up onto the lip of the canyon. They rigged a rope and hauled up several buckets of water. Will brought me water, gave some to the sick, and shared it frugally with the rest. Another party of men found a small muddy spring where the cattle, horses, and oxen could drink.

The older men of the company had been very concerned about Will's adventurous nature, taking off to explore alone. One day he set out at an angle to inspect a curious cleft at close range. He said he would catch up with the wagons miles ahead at the other side of Sweetwater, near Devil's Gate.

Will returned looking worn and exhausted and told us his harrowing story that night around the campfire. "At the mouth of Devil's Gate, the river poured over shelf-like formations of rock extending for quite a distance from either bank, leaving a deep channel in the middle where the water rushed through and under the rocks. I rolled up my clothes into a bundle and threw them onto the opposite bank. I waded onto the rock shelf and positioned myself for a broad jump. The rocks were slippery, and I landed in the swift, cold water of the channel. I barely caught a finger hold on the opposite ledge.

"The current was battering me, and I knew it was touch and go. If I lost my hold, I would be sucked into the channel and cut to pieces among the rocks." We all gasped while jealous Dan snorted under his breath.

"Very carefully and with full concentration, scarcely daring to move more than one finger at a time, I worked along the rock until I found a firm hand-hold to draw myself out. I was exhausted and shaken when I dressed on the far bank." His attentive audience sighed with relief, except Dan, who scowled.

"At the river's edge was a breast-high thicket of thorns and devil's club. I finally found a narrow thread of path, which I thought I could pass through. Then, I heard a curious dry rustling noise, and I froze. There was a line of huge snakes, heads up, coming along the little path, evidently bound for the river. Retreat was impossible, and I could not face the snakes. I put my head down and went crashing wildly into the thorns."

Dan Young went around afterward, muttering uncomplimentary remarks, referring to Will as "Windy" Chapman.

We were nearing the Promised Land, where man and wife could take 640 acres of fertile land: a land free from black slavery, chills, and fever, a place of freedom, with hospitality and brotherly love among all the settlers. The oxen were weary and straining at their yokes. Parts of wagons, belongings and dead oxen were strewn all along the way over the Oregon Trail. I picked up a toy soldier and wondered if the child who lost this was still alive. Women and children were walking to lighten the load, as the failing strength of the cattle and oxen was a constant worry. The grass was scarce, and we had no time to let the animals rest and graze. It was getting late in the year, and we feared a snowstorm when crossing the Blue Mountains.

By September, we were about three days from the Valley of the Grande Ronde when we gazed across the plain at the distant range of mountains, blue and mysterious in the approaching evening. Suddenly, a column of smoke into the still evening sky, and then another shot up into the still evening sky. We sent scouts in advance, and they came back swiftly.

"Indian signals! What do you make of it, Captain?"

"Sure looks bad. We can't turn back. Have to keep going. Pass the word along for the wagons to keep close together and see that your guns are loaded. We want to be ready for a surprise."

"The Indians out here are not on the warpath, are they, Captain?"

"Not the Cayuse or the Nez Perce, but we were warned to look out for the Snakes. I hear them fellers are a bad lot, always on the warpath, and we're gettin' into their country now. Could be their smoke signals."

We made every precaution to prevent a surprise attack, and to our relief, the long vigilant night passed quietly. On the third day, we reached the rim of the Valley of the Grande Ronde. We all gazed with delight at this most beautiful little valley in Oregon. The Grande Ronde River and several smaller streams looked like silver threads as they wound through the valley, their banks lined with poplar and alder trees furnished abundant shade for weary campers. We were told the Indians call it "The Valley of Peace." If an enemy comes into the valley, he is treated as a friend as long as he remains. This beautiful place is a favorite meeting place for the tribes of this region. Here they hold their councils, trade with each other, race their horses, and gamble, their favorite sport. The valley is an ideal hunting ground, and the mountains are full of wild game of all kinds.

We held our breath as a small band of Indians came riding toward us. One of them detached himself from the group and rode toward us with his hand raised in a friendly salute. He pulled his horse to an abrupt halt and, to our amazement, said in English, "I am Five Crows, Chief of the Cayuse. Dr. Whitman has sent us to meet you with a pack train of fresh vegetables, flour, and medicine. He heard there are sick among you."

Our hearts sang for joy, and our empty bellies yearned for that promise of nourishment. Even though I was suffering from chills and fever, I peeked out the back of the wagon. A man known as Chief Five Crows rode up to me. Obviously of high status, this man stared at me and sat perfectly still on his horse with what appeared like a blanket of snow painted on its rump. He was of medium height, well built with regular features, and dressed like a white man. His buckskin shirt was beautifully beaded. He was wearing a wide-brimmed hat over his short hair. Father helped me out of the wagon because I was too weak to stand. Five Crows unfurled a blanket from his horse and laid it down on the ground signaling for me to be placed upon it.

Then Five Crows mounted and kicked the horse's flank, departing in a flurry. He returned quickly with a piece of venison that he presented to Mother. "For the sick girl. My men bring you all the flour and potatoes you want."

That night we sat down to a veritable feast. We arose from it refreshed and with renewed strength and courage. Gone was the fear of being attacked, and we enjoyed the new feeling of security. We laughed for the first time in many weeks, and Mrs. Collins burst into song as she washed the dishes.

DOWN AT THE RIVER
By Marv Ross

Grab a friend, grab a pole
Come on down to the swimming hole.
Bring a dog, bring a rope
But don't bring Mamma 'cause she'll bring the soap
Bring the soap
Down at the river.
Bring the soap
Down at the river.
Some are lost, some are delivered
Take your place down at the river.

Some catch fish, some catch cold,
Some catch beaver and pan for gold.
Some catch hell, just ask Joe.
He found a turtle but lost a toe.
Yeh, he lost a toe
Down at the river.
He lost a toe
Down at the river.
Some are lost, some are delivered
Take your place down at the river.

Some wear hats of the latest style,
Some wear nothin' but a Kansas smile.
Some get caught, some get found
Some get a lickin', and they can't sit down.

Brother Roy lost his teeth
Dived in a river two feet deep.

Now he can't eat corn, he can't chew rind,
He talks kinda funny, but he whistles fine.
Yeh, he whistles fine
Down by the river.
Whistles fine
Down at the river.
Some are lost, some are delivered
Take your place down at the river.

Some folks splash, some have fun,
Some get sick from too much sun.
Some get clean, some composed
Some look funny when they hold their nose.
Some get kissed, some get spark,
Some get goose bumps in the dark.
Some get sober, and some get hit.
We all hate skeeters, but we all get bit.
Yeh, we all get bit
Down at the river.
We all get bit
Down at the river.
Some are lost, some are delivered
Take your place down at the river.

Some folks kick, some don't care,
Some blow bubbles and some lose air.
Some get saved, some can't swim,
Some find Jesus and jump right in.
Some folks splash, some folks scream,
Some spend miles swimmin' upstream.
Some just wade, others leave,
Some don't think 'til they're in too deep.

> In too deep
> Down at the river.
> In too deep
> Down at the river.
> Some are lost, some are delivered
> Take your place down at the river,

Five Crows, whose Christian name was Hezekiah and a principal chief and member of the Spaldings' church, sat with us around the fire that night as we danced and twirled to the music, curiously asking about our "war dance."

My father, Captain Bewley, chuckled and replied, "We dance for joy and amusement. Not war." Chief Five Crows explained that he learned his good English from spending winters at Rev. Spalding's school at Lapwai. He said that many of his people were eager to learn the white man's ways. They owned farms and raised vegetables and wheat. He told us that Rev. and Mrs. Spalding were like Mother and Father to the Nez Perce. The Spaldings had come across the plains to the Oregon country with Dr. and Mrs. Whitman when it was considered foreign land.

The wagon train broke up when we reached the Umatilla. Several wagons stopped at Waiilatpu, ours among them, arriving on October 10 and staying two weeks. Mrs. Whitman prevailed upon me to stay with her until next spring. She said that it was late in the season, and as my health was not very good, I consented to remain. My mother thought it would be for the best. My brother, Crocket, who was fifteen months older than I, decided to stay, also. Mrs. Whitman said she would be able to nurse me back to health. She suggested that perhaps I could be a caregiver to the younger children and a teacher to those who attended school.

Amos Sales, a young man, traveling with our family, also decided to stay. Dan Young and his family, consisting of his father Elam, his mother, and two brothers, James and John, had been hired by Dr. Whitman to work the sawmill at the foot of the Blue Mountains. Dan was delighted because I was staying on; however, I had promised myself to Will Chapman by this time. I told a very disappointed Dan that I would be going to Oregon City in the spring to be Will's bride.

Before my parents continued their journey, Father implored, "Now, doctor, take good care of my children."

"Yes, I will with the help of God," Dr. Whitman promised.

Lorinda & Crocket Stay at the Mission
By Lorinda Bewley

I said farewell to my family, knowing I would see them again in the spring. It looked first as if the Wallace family would winter there, too. Still, when Victor saw all the other wagons being loaded, he changed his mind abruptly and told Isabella to get her stuff together, and they left for Oregon City with the others. My dear friend Isabella and I were very sad when we separated. It was unlikely we would meet again, not knowing where our families would settle. But I was grateful for her company and good humor on the trail.

During my stay at Waiilatpu, I counted the number of people at the mission whom the Whitmans had to provide food, bedding, and various supplies. The amount of work each day was exhausting. They were responsible for the welfare of seventy-five people, of whom sixteen were men, nine women, and forty-five children under the age of eighteen. I started gaining my health and strength quickly with such kind and expert care and was able to help Mrs. Whitman with her small children. She asked me to be their schoolteacher for the winter.

The mission house was filled with activity and busy workers. Twenty-three from my wagon company, including Crocket and me, stayed there. The Whitmans had taken in eleven children, seven of whom had been orphaned on the trail. Eliza Spalding stayed there to attend school that winter, 120 miles away from her home at Lapwai. Also, two boys, John and

Stephen Manson, ages eight and thirteen, lived with the Whitmans. Mr. and Mrs. Osborn and their three children were going to winter there. Perrin Whitman was spending the winter at a place called Waskopum. I was looking forward to meeting him, as they said he was fluent in the language of the Nez Perce and could speak the Cayuse language. I wanted to learn some way to communicate with our neighbors. Mrs. Whitman would not allow her children to mingle with the native children, so I did not know how she would receive my interest in them.

 The emigrant house was just a stone's throw from the main house, accommodating thirty-one people. The blacksmith shop housed eight people. There was a small sawmill cabin brimming with eleven and a Cayuse lodge with two men who were of mixed blood: Nicholas Finley and Joe Lewis. Mr. Finley seemed to be fonder of the Indians than the white folk, and I did not like or trust Joe Lewis.

 My dear brother Crocket, fifteen, came down with Mountain Fever. I was so worried because so many emigrants had died of this ailment. On November 28, I also got very sick and burned up with a fever. I was delirious through the night. Dr. Whitman returned from Umatilla, attending to many sick and dying Cayuse. After he checked in on me, I heard Mrs. Whitman ask how I was doing.

 He replied, "She is in a peck of trouble."

 Mrs. Whitman said, "She has not received the care she needs. I have some water heating. I'll make her some broth and bath her."

 Sickness always made me feel a bit hopeless, and that night I could not stop whimpering. When the doctor asked me, I couldn't explain why, but I felt like something awful was about to happen. Dr. Whitman seemed very disturbed about some news he had received at Umatilla. Later that night, I heard Mrs. Whitman crying. It was so unlike her. Many of the children at the station were also sick with measles. Mrs. Whitman had been up all night tending to them. I guess she was plum worn out, and I could not help her.

Terrie Biggs

Knocking at Death's Door
Catherine Sager Pringle Continues her Story

    Chief Five Crows sent a messenger asking for Father to help with the sick and dying in his village. Father and Rev. Spalding had ridden thirty miles south on Saturday, November 27, 1847, to Cayuse and Umatilla lodges on the Umatilla River to save as many lives as they could among the Indians dying of measles by the dozens. The first Cayuse child had died in October, and the disease ravaged the local villages. I saw five or six buried each day. Rev. Spalding had arrived at Waiilatpu a week before their ride, and he helped Father build coffins.
    Before they left, Rev. Spalding told Mother, "It is most distressing to go into a lodge of some ten fires and count twenty or twenty-five sick with measles, others in the last stages of dysentery. We have no suitable means of alleviating their suffering, and only your husband to look after the needs of the ailing ones."
    Mother told him, "My heart is heavy with sadness for these poor natives and Mrs. Osborn, whose child died last night."
    Rev. Spalding replied, "We hope that this will show the Indians that the whites are just as susceptible to the ravages of the disease as they are."

"Yes, Brother Spalding," Mother offered. "We certainly are impacted. Last week, we closed the school down because so many children had measles and dysentery. Your Eliza seems to be one of the stronger children."

Father joined the conversation, and Mother said, "Marcus and Brother Spalding, while you tend to these poor souls, you must stop them from putting their sick in the sweat lodges."

"I know, my dear," Father answered. "I've warned them many times that sitting in the sweat lodge and being plunged into cold water when they are sick has not helped but has killed everyone I have witnessed."

Mother urged, "Do try, my love. You must persuade them to stop this dangerous practice."

"I'll make every effort, my dear."

Rev. Spalding said that he also would make a concerted effort to prevent the use of the sweat lodges while the disease was afflicting his neighbors.

Terrie Biggs

Father and the Catholics
By Catherine Sager Pringle

The coming of the Catholic missionaries in September of 1847 seemed to be a threat to Father. Many of the French-Canadian men were Catholics, but Father was friendly with them. I had never witnessed him upset about the Catholic influence until the Catholic missionaries arrived. Bishop Blanchet visited Fort Walla Walla, and Father was invited to meet him. When Father returned from the meeting, I heard him tell Mother, "I told them that I would not sell them provisions. I refused to help them unless they were starving!"

This incident was the only time I remember our gentle father seething with anger. Right after that visit, he did an odd thing. Bishop Blanchet devised a picture graph on paper about six feet long and eighteen inches wide, which the Catholics called a "ladder." The ladder presented to the Indian chiefs of the Northwest tribes was to teach them the history of Catholicism.

A ladder was given to Chief Tiloukaikt, and his son Edward proudly showed it to Father, who had just butchered a cow. Father smeared blood over the ladder and gave it back to the stunned Edward. I had never seen Father behave this way, and my impression was that he was warning Edward about what might happen if the Catholic priests were to live among the Cayuse.

Indeed, Edward interpreted Father's words as saying, "You see this blood? It is to show you that now because you have the priests among you, the country will be covered in blood! You will have nothing but blood!"

"Mother, why is Father so angry?" I asked.

"Well, Katie, there has been a lot of speculation about the Catholics wanting to take over our work here. Father heard that the bishop met with Chief Tiloukaikt and asked permission to get land for their mission site next to ours. There is a lot of tension right now. Father is just afraid for us."

"Afraid of what, Mother?" John asked.

"Afraid for our safety. Our Cayuse neighbors have never welcomed us here, unlike the Spaldings' Nez Perce. It may very well be time for us to leave."

I asked her, "Where will we go, Mother?"

"We have been considering moving to The Dalles in the spring," and I cringed, knowing our previous devil of a teacher, Mr. Hinman, was there. But nothing more was said of leaving our home.

When the bishop told Tiloukaikt that he would not pay for land adjacent to our Protestant mission at Waiilatpu, Tiloukaikt changed his mind about the Catholics settling there. Instead, in the last week of November 1847, Bishop Blanchett, Father Brouillet, and Deacon LeClaire arrived at the village of Umatilla--where Five Crows and his brother Young Chief lived--to establish the Mission of Saint Anne. Although Five Crows was more favorable to the Protestants, as a gesture of his preference for Catholics, Young Chief turned his cabin over to Bishop Blanchet and his two priests.

Father told Mother that he was sorry for his outburst with Edward over the Catholic ladder and that he would visit the priests and extend his hand in friendship and goodwill. The kind, hospitable father I knew was back.

Due to a stroke of fate, the Saint Anne mission was destined to exist for only a few weeks.

Council of Death

Joe Lewis arrived with the last emigrants that came to Waiilatpu. He was of mixed blood, born in Canada and educated in Maine, spoke fluent English, and brought practical skills as a mechanic, which he did not utilize. His fellow travelers disliked him, so they refused to let him continue with their company. Marcus and Narcissa took pity on him as Lewis was sick, and his clothing was nothing but rags. Marcus nursed him back to health, gave him garments to wear, and sent him on his way with a family continuing west. Lewis returned after three days, most likely discarded by the family due to his hateful manner. Nicholas Finley had a lodge located north of the mission house, and he allowed Lewis to move in with him.

Near the end of November 1847, Joe Lewis attended a council at Finley's lodge. Joe Lewis proved to be a viper. Although he had been there only a couple of weeks, his venomous bite was about to strike.

Finley opened the meeting by saying, "I have grave and disturbing news that should be shared among our brothers. Our people have been dying, some four or five a day. As you know, Chief Tiloukaikt has three children in his lodge dying, including his daughter. Listen, my brothers. Listen to Joe Lewis."

Lewis spewed, "When I first arrived, Dr. Whitman fooled me, pretending to be kind. I was lying down one night, not able to sleep. Rev. Spalding was whispering with the doctor and his wife, unaware that I was awake. Spalding asked the doctor why he did not kill the Indians faster. The doctor answered him by saying that they were dying fast enough. Doctor Whitman said he had been getting poison to kill the Cayuse and the Nez Perce. He said that young men would die off this winter and the old ones next spring."

There was an eruption of hollering, and many men jumped to their feet, raising their fists.

Chief Tiloukaikt asked them to be still and to sit down. In disbelief with a troubled brow, Tiloukaikt said, "The doctor and his wife grieved for our people who have died. He was sad and angry, and he explained to me that the Americans came with diseases that our people had never known. Day and night, he has been tending to our sick and dying with a heavy heart."

Tomahas spoke next, "Do you not recall that two of our men almost died from the doctor's poison when they ate his meat? He claimed that we should not have eaten that meat because they were poisoning the wolves. Now I see that he was trying to poison us all of this time."

"All your people will die unless you kill Dr. Whitman and Rev. Spalding," Lewis hissed.

Several of the younger men began to shake their fists and demand retaliation. The elders would have no part as they remembered how their band members had prospered since the mission was established. The elders knew of the growing number of white settlers. "You will bring great harm to our people by the white men if you kill these people."

Ignoring the elders, Tamsucky added, "He moved into our country with such boldness and took over our land, refusing to pay us." Most of the men nodded in agreement.

Clokamas spoke, "Do you also remember what Baptiste Dorian said? He told us that Dr. Whitman went back East to get men to fight us and take our land. These white men now come by the hundreds, burning a path through our hunting grounds, building more forts where we are not welcome to enter, ruining our land with their houses, and interfering with our customs. Then they force us to abide by *their* laws and say they will punish us if we do not obey them."

Ish-ish-kais-kais (Frank Escaloom) added more fuel to the proverbial fire. "Doctor Whitman has magical powers as a *te-wat*. I was at The Dalles when he passed through, and we greeted each other as friends. A white man had been killed, and the doctor refused to shake the hand of the man from the Walla Walla tribe who killed the white man. That night our Walla Walla brother died. Even though Dr. Whitman claimed he was innocent and that the man died because he choked on dried buffalo meat, this is proof of his powers as a *te-wat*. I know he caused his death. It is a mystery why he was not killed at the moment the doctor refused to shake his hand."

"He also tells us that we are not worthy of his church. He says we must give up our wives--women we have brought into our lodges whose husbands were killed. He calls this a sin," one of the men added, who experienced this firsthand.

Edward, Chief Tiloukaikt's son, added, "Our lodges have always been open to any visitors, yet his wife will not allow us beyond the kitchen."

"I am telling you again that the doctor is killing your people by poison," Lewis interjected. "You must kill them all right away before you have no one left alive in your village."

The final blow was struck, and the venom spewed. All these ideas fed the anger and frustration of some of the band members. Joe Lewis persuaded seven young men to plan an attack. Chief Tiloukaikt was very reluctant but finally agreed.

The Tension Mounts

Thoroughly soaked, Marcus and Rev. Spalding headed for Stickus' lodge downhill on slippery ground. Rev. Spalding's horse lost his footing and fell and rolled over him, causing severe pains to his head and one leg. They slept next to the fire in Stickus' warm lodge. Stickus conducted his family in devotions that Sunday morning and then fed his visitors a breakfast of potatoes, squash, fresh beef, and wheat bread.

Marcus boasted, "It is so gratifying to us that you have made such advancements. When we first came, your people were filthy and near starvation. Now, look at this wonderful feast we are enjoying grown by you and served in your warm, comfortable lodge."

Stickus had to intervene with foreboding news, which left Marcus anxious to get home in haste. Stickus had heard that Joe Lewis was whipping up the young men of the tribe into a frenzy and were planning to attack the mission. Later that day, while Marcus and Rev. Spalding visited Five Crows, Stickus' cousin, they crossed to the north bank on the river's south bank and called on the bishop and his two priests at Saint Anne Mission near Young Chief's house as he had promised Narcissa. Marcus stayed only a few minutes because he wanted to get home as soon as possible. However, he did invite Father Brouillet to visit his family when he passed by the mission to give them a chance to get better acquainted.

Terrie Biggs

Accused of Poisoning
By Catherine Sager Pringle

My brothers were sitting up with the sick children when Father returned home alone at about ten o'clock that evening. Rev. Spalding had remained at the Umatilla for two days recovering from his injuries before heading back to Waiilatpu. Father checked all the sick children and sent Frank and John to bed, and told them he would sit up with the children. The boys had their shoes off so they wouldn't wake anyone. Helen had been very ill before Father left; he felt her head, bent down, and gently kissed her forehead. He knew she would die soon.

I overheard Father wake Mother up. "Narcissa, I need to talk with you."

She had an exhausting day, nursing many sick children, including our babes Henrietta and Louisa. She yawned and stretched and put her arms around his neck. They were whispering, but I could hear him say, very wearily, that he and Rev. Spalding had visited Stickus. Father had told us stories of Stickus guiding wagon trains over the Blue Mountains year after year. He was a good friend.

I was in the room when father told Mother that Stickus had warned him that his life was in great danger and that he had pleaded with Father to take our family and leave the mission until things settled down. Stickus said that two mixed-blood men, Nicolas Finley and Joe Lewis, who was married to a Cayuse woman, held nightly councils at Finley's lodge on our mission grounds. They were trying to get Father killed for poisoning the local tribe members. Of course, Father immediately thought Joe's motive was for the Catholics to gain control of our mission.

Mother was furious, saying, "Poisoning them? Why you're dead on your feet from *doctoring* them. That scoundrel, Joe! He arrived here sick and on foot without a shirt on his back, and you gave him food and clothing and even offered him work." Mother cried softly. She was in fear for her children.

"Are they going to kill us?" I asked, so afraid that I began crying.

"Hush, child. You'll wake up the other children and frighten them. Everything's alright," Father said as he came over to my bed and soothed me with kind words until I fell asleep.

The following day was foggy and cold. Mother stayed in her room, and Elizabeth brought breakfast to her. Father told Mother, "The Indians are gathering around today. I suppose it's because we're slaughtering a beef. Frank killed it this morning and hung the carcass between the mill and blacksmith shop."

The local men always came for the leftover scraps of meat after butchering. About 11:00 a.m., several grieving villagers brought the bodies of three Cayuse children who died in the night to us for burial. Father accompanied them to the cemetery and was surprised that only a few villagers attended the funeral.

When Father returned to the house, he checked on Lorinda upstairs and found her crying.

"I don't know why I am weeping," Lorinda told Father. "I just feel evil is around us. I cannot shake it from my mind."

"You'd better go up and talk with her, Narcissa. She's distraught and scared," Father told Mother when he came downstairs. "I'm going to get her something to calm her down."

Terrie Biggs

The Attack

Sketch of the Mission
Left to right: the mill, emigrant house,
the blacksmith shop, and the Whitman's home
(the mission house)

It was about two o'clock in the afternoon on November 29, 1847. Some of the children had gone back to school on that Monday with a new teacher, Judge Saunders. John went into the kitchen where Mary Ann was washing dishes from the noon meal. John was winding a skein of brown twine, which would be used to make a new broom. Mrs. Osborn had come downstairs from her sickbed into the sitting room. Marcus was reading, and Narcissa was bathing Elizabeth and Catherine in a tub on the floor. Catherine began dressing, and Elizabeth was still in the bathing tub.

Narcissa went to the pantry off the kitchen to get milk for the sick children. The kitchen was full of Indians demanding the milk she was carrying.

"You must wait until I give some to my sick children," Narcissa said firmly.

Tomahas tried to force his way into the sitting room, but Narcissa shut the door and bolted it. Tomahas then demanded medicine as he pounded on the door, calling for the doctor. Marcus laid his book down and went to the door. When he unbolted it, Tomahas tried to force his way in, and Marcus stopped him.

"We need medicine," Tomahas demanded.

"I will come to the kitchen in a minute. Just wait there," Marcus told him. And he went to the medicine cabinet and got what was needed.

"Narcissa, bolt this door after me."

In the sitting room, the family members and Mrs. Osborn could hear loud and angry voices in the kitchen and, occasionally, Marcus's soft, mild voice in reply. Suddenly, a sharp explosion--a rifle shot--in the kitchen, and everyone in the next room jumped in fright. Narcissa's first impulse was to rush into the kitchen to see what had happened, but she quickly controlled herself. Her immediate concern was for the children. "Stop! No one goes outside. Stay here." She began dressing Elizabeth. "Mrs. Osborn, quick! Go to your room and lock the outside door."

Diorama of Marcus Whitman being killed as displayed at the Whitman Mission National Historic Site.

Mrs. Osborn called to her husband, and he used a flatiron to drive a nail over the latch.

Suddenly Mary Ann burst into the sitting room from the kitchen screaming. Narcissa grabbed her and shouted, "What happened in there? Did someone fire a gun?" as Mary Ann nodded. "Oh, my God! Did they shoot Marcus? Did they kill my husband?"

"Yes," Mary Ann howled.

"Oh my God, my husband is dead!" she wailed as she dropped to the floor with her hands covering her face.

After stopping shaking and sobbing, Mary Ann could finally tell what she witnessed as Narcissa rose to face Mary Ann: "The Indians, including Tiloukaikt and Tomahas, crowded into the kitchen. The doctor sat at the table facing Tiloukaikt, who had the doctor's full attention. Tomahas stepped behind the doctor, drew a tomahawk from under his blanket, and struck the doctor's head." Mary Ann was so distraught she had to stop for a moment. "When his head went forward, I saw Tomahas swing his tomahawk with such force to the back of the doctor's head that the doctor fell to the floor. Then, another Indian shot the doctor through the neck, to my horror.

"John grabbed a pistol and shot twice. I think he wounded two of them. Then someone shot John in the neck," and Catherine and Elizabeth were shocked and held each other as Mary Ann continued. "John stuffed part of the scarf he was wearing into his wound. The murderers ran out the south kitchen door when they heard yelling and gunshots outside, and I dove out the north door and came here," and then she collapsed in Narcissa's arms.

The few students attending school had just returned to the classroom from recess. The children noticed about eighteen or twenty Indians wrapped in blankets, watching the beef being dressed. The commotion in the kitchen must have been the signal to the other Cayuse to begin their attack. The students ran to the classroom window and saw the Indians dropping their blankets with their hands on their weapons hidden underneath, shouting and running wildly. Shots were fired. The schoolteacher, Judge Saunders, saw Mr. Kimball running to the mission house, his arm limp and bleeding.

"I must go to my family," Judge Saunders muttered as he left the classroom, but he was killed on the schoolroom steps.

As soon as it was quiet, Narcissa unbolted the door to the kitchen and found her husband lying semi-conscious in his blood. Tiloukaikt had mutilated his face so severely that she barely recognized him. Three women burst through the kitchen door from the emigrant house and helped her drag Marcus into the living room. Narcissa bolted the door and put a pillow under his head. Kneeling next to her husband, Narcissa took a towel and some ashes from the stove to stop his neck wound from bleeding.

"He's still alive," She reassured the children and then turned to Marcus, who could only utter one word at a time. "Do you know me, Marcus?"

"Yes."

"Are you badly hurt?"

"Yes."

"Can you speak to me?"

He shook his head no.

"Is your mind at peace?"

"Yes," and that was the last word his family heard from him.

"That wicked Joe. He has done all this!"

Joe Lewis came to the sitting room door several times with a gun.

"What do you want, Joe?" Narcissa asked him, but he ran out without answering.

After the first ball had been fired in the kitchen when Marcus was shot, the Cayuse men outside threw off their blankets and drew their concealed weapons. The first person killed outside was Mr. Marsh, operating the grist mill. The men who were butchering the beef were attacked. Jacob Hoffman put up a brave fight with an ax before being cut down. Nathan Kimball was working with Hoffman. Kimball's son, Nathan, Jr., watched from the schoolroom window as he saw an Indian shooting at his father, who was trying to escape. His father had on a white shirt, and Nathan could see that his father's arm was broken at the elbow, and the sleeve was red with blood. Kimball burst into the mission house and shouted, "The Indians are killing us. I don't know why the damned Indians want to kill me. I never did anything to them. Get me some water."

Elizabeth fully expected her mother to admonish him for swearing in the children's presence, but instead, she got water and began to clean his wound.

Narcissa was looking for Mr. Rodgers out the window of the east door. Mr. Rodgers had gone to the river to fetch water when he heard shots fired. Instead, he could have hidden and escaped and saved himself, but Narcissa saw him running desperately towards the house with several Indians on his heels. He was shot in the wrist and got a blow from a tomahawk behind his ear. He then crashed his elbow through the window of the east door before Narcissa could open the door for him.

Then Ish-ish-kais-kais, also known as Frank Escaloom, raised his gun and shot her in the right breast as she was standing at the door. She clasped her hand to her chest and fell backward, her only concern was for the children depending on her, and she poured out her soul in prayer for them, "Lord, save these little ones!" She was suffering from the wound, but she was still alive.

The women, including Narcissa, headed toward the attic, and Mr. Rodgers was pushing Catherine upstairs with Hannah in her arms. Catherine pleaded, "Wait! Who will take care of the other sick children? Let me take them up, too. Don't leave them here alone." Her two sisters, Louisa and Henrietta, along with Helen Mar Meek, were still downstairs. Although both were wounded, Mr. Kimball and Mr. Rodgers helped Catherine carry the sick children to the attic. There were thirteen people in the attic: five women, including Narcissa and Lorinda Bewley, two men, Helen and Mary Ann, and four of the Sager girls.

The Osborn family lived in the Indian room at the mission house. Mr. Osborn loosened the floorboards, and his wife, his three children, and himself hid under the floor in a three-foot space where they stayed undiscovered. The entire day they listened to the screams of women and children and the groans of the dying.

Meanwhile, Frank Sager was in the schoolroom and saw the Indians attacking people outside. He got all the children together and had them go to the loft, which required climbing on a table piled with books. His sister Matilda and Eliza Spalding were among them.

Matilda later said to Catherine, "Frank, our brave brother told us all to ask God to save us, and he kneeled and prayed for God to spare us."

Joe Stanfield ran into the schoolroom, looking for the three mixed-blood boys: the two Manson brothers and David Malin. Joe said that they would not be harmed because they were part Indian. He took them to Finley's lodge for safety. The next day Finley took the boys to Fort Walla Walla.

Joe Lewis then entered the schoolroom after the three boys were taken away. He was looking for Frank. Joe made all the children come down from the loft. They were taken outside and lined up to be shot. Eliza Spalding, who could understand their language, heard some of the Indians arguing against killing the children and covered her face with her apron so that she would not see them shoot her. There they stood in a long row, their would-be murderers leaning on their guns, waiting for the word from Chief Tiloukaikt to send them to eternity. Pity, however, moved his heart, for after observing their terror, he said, "Let us not kill them."

They were then taken to the Indian room in the mission house, where Frank saw his brother John lay mortally wounded on the kitchen floor. Trying to help John, Frank leaned over him and pulled at the scarf John had stuffed into his wound. Unfortunately, the blood began to pour out, and John died soon afterward.

"I know I'll follow him," Frank sobbed. That comment terrified his sisters. How could they lose *another* member of their family?

Eliza heard the Indians goading Joe Lewis, "If you are on our side, you must kill Frank Sager to prove it."

Joe Lewis grabbed Frank by the nose, jerked him forward, and called him a bad boy. The Osborn family under the floor heard Frank pleading for his life, "Oh, Joe, please don't shoot me."

Then the Osborns heard the shot. Frank fell at the entrance to the north door, mortally wounded.

Isaac Gilliland was sitting at the table at the emigrant's house when an Indian stepped inside and shot and wounded him. Mrs. Saunders, who was staying in the room next to Gilliland, ran to see what had happened. Frank Escaloom (Ish-ish-kais-kais) pointed his pistol at her, and she turned and ran to her room with the wounded Gilliland right behind her, but she slammed her door and locked Gilliland out. At first, she thought he was an attacker, and then he called to her to let him in. Once inside, he hid under the bed but soon came out and said, "It's no use to hide." Gilliland lay down and died about midnight.

Mrs. Saunders, even before she knew the fate of her husband or the rest of the mission residents, left the safety of her room at the emigrant house and went to Finley's lodge. The Manson boys and David Malin had just been delivered there. Several other Indian women were in the house. Some were Cayuse, some were Walla Walla, but they were friendly to Mrs. Saunders. About four hundred feet away from the lodge was the hill where three Indians were trampling Alice's grave. One of the Indians barreled toward the lodge to kill Mrs. Saunders, but Mrs.

Finley, a Cayuse, intercepted him and reasoned with him, and he rode off. Then Chief Tiloukaikt came forward, shaking his hatchet over his head. He threatened Mrs. Saunders with it, but again Mrs. Finley urged him to desist, and he also turned his horse around and left in a fury. Finally, Edward, the oldest son of Chief Tiloukaikt, approached rapidly, shaking his tomahawk in a rage over his head and that of Mrs. Saunders. She had sunk onto matting in front of the lodge, but the Cayuse women talked to him and shamed him. He, too, left on his horse.

Mrs. Saunders then went to John, the older Manson brother, kneeled and begged John to interpret for her to the chiefs, as she did not understand their language.

She said, "Tell the Chiefs that if the Doctor and men were bad, I did not know it. My heart is good, and I want to live. If they spare my life and the lives of the women and children, we will make caps, coats, and pantaloons for them."

John Manson told the chiefs what Mrs. Saunders had offered, and when he returned, Mrs. Saunders asked, "What did they say, John?"

"They are talking about it." After more discussion with the Chiefs, John told her that Tiloukaikt and the other chiefs agreed that none of the other women and children would be killed.

"Ask him if all the people in the mission house may move to the emigrant house."

Tiloukaikt nodded to her that it was acceptable. This plea took place about one hour after the attack began.

It had been quiet for about half an hour after the people went to the mission house attic. Henrietta and Louisa were lying down with Narcissa and were covered in her blood. Narcissa kept chanting, "My children. What will become of my children?"

Catherine remembered that her Papa had uttered almost those exact last words to her before he died. Could this be happening again--losing another mother and father?

They heard footsteps in the room below, and a voice called to them at the bottom of the stairs. Narcissa and Mr. Rodgers told the others to prepare for death. Lorinda found an old inoperative gun, and Mr. Rodgers pointed it down the stairs. Tamsucky called to Mr. Rodgers, who would not answer.

Narcissa said hopefully, "God maybe has raised us a friend. Please answer. Let's see what he wants."

Tamsucky told them that he had just arrived and knew nothing about the terrible events. "I want to help you and Mrs. Whitman."

"Mother," Catherine whispered, "Tamsucky was the one I saw kill Judge Saunders. Please be very careful. Do not trust him." They did not know that Tamsucky was also the one who had shot John.

Narcissa and Mr. Rodgers finally decided they should hear what he had to say, and Mr. Rodgers told him to come upstairs. Tamsucky reluctantly went upstairs and was intimidated by the gun barrel Mr. Rodgers wielded but shook hands with the adults. He seemed very sorry that Narcissa was hurt and sympathized with her until he won her confidence. He told her that the young men were planning on burning the mission house, and they should leave immediately and go to the emigrant house.

Mrs. Hall and Mrs. Hays left for the emigrant house after gathering arms full of clothing. Lorinda arose from her sickbed and went downstairs with Narcissa, Mr. Rodgers, and Elizabeth Sager.

"I need some air," Narcissa gasped. She was weak from the loss of blood and had to lie down at once. Mr. Rodgers helped her onto the settee while Lorinda covered Narcissa with a blanket and wrapped a sheet around herself for some warmth. Mr. Rodgers planned to take Narcissa, Lorinda, and Elizabeth to the emigrant house and return for the sick children. Mr. Kimball was too weak to leave due to his injuries, and since there was no one to carry the sick children, Catherine stayed with them and was going to wait for Mr. Rodgers to return.

Mr. Rodgers and Joe Lewis carried out the settee, passing by Marcus's mutilated body. Narcissa looked over and saw her husband, whose face had been cut to pieces, and she noticed that he was still breathing. They carried her from the sitting room through the kitchen and out the north door of the kitchen, stepping over Frank Sager lying in the doorway a few feet from his dead brother.

Lorinda was shocked to see the school children huddled in the corner of the Indian room of the mission house. When the settee was outside, Joe Lewis dropped the end he was holding. Many men were lined up with guns and immediately fired. Elizabeth saw the bullets hit her mother in the face. Mr. Rodgers was struck down, wailing, "Oh, my God!"

Lorinda saw them begin to cut Narcissa's face with their cowhide whips and roll her off the settee into the mud while yelling, "You're mean. You're mean."

A ball passed so close to Lorinda that it stung her fingers, and they were numb until the following day. As she ran with the other women to the emigrant house, Lorinda saw fifteen-year-old Frank bleeding and groaning. Elizabeth, a horrified witness to her second mother's death, ran upstairs to her sister Catherine. Elizabeth was not crying or shrieking-- filled with terror and shock--as Catherine gathered her in her arms. Elizabeth whispered, "Oh, Katie, I am so scared. What will become of us? Will we all be killed?" Catherine had no answer as she held her sister tight.

    Mr. Rodgers lingered for several hours, but Narcissa died instantly.

Terrie Biggs

Not Over Yet

By Catherine Sager Pringle

At the end of the first day, nine people were dead. It was inconceivable that I could be orphaned a second time at age thirteen. My heart was breaking after losing my brothers, mother, and father in one day. The dying was not over yet, though.

Mr. Kimball was in too much pain the first night to be any help to me with the four sick girls, the only ones left in the attic of the mission house. The other women had left when Mother was being carried to her death. The Indians seemed to be preparing to set fire to the house. We heard them ask for a fire, and they were splitting up kindling. We fully expected to perish in flames, but I felt it was more desirable than to be killed by savages. Night came on. The Indians seemed to have left the house after tearing it apart. Hardly daring to breathe, shaking with fear, I took all the children to one bed. Their clothes were saturated in Mother's blood where they had lain on the bed with her. I tried to soothe them, but they begged for water. They cried for hours, and one by one, they fell asleep, leaving Mr. Kimball and me still awake.

All night long, I heard the clock striking, and to this day, I still wince when a clock strikes. I would never have a striking clock in my home. I will never forget that awful night, not knowing what a new day might bring.

The next morning Mr. Kimball wanted to go out for water. He asked me to rip up a sheet off the bed to wrap his arm. I told him, "Mother would not like to have the sheets torn up."

Sadly he replied, "Child, don't you know your mother is dead and will never have any use for the sheets?"

I tore a sheet into strips with a broken heart and wrapped his injured arm. Then he asked me to put two blankets around him to keep him warm in case he fainted outside. I put his hat on his head, and he picked up an empty pail for water. Concealing himself as best he could, he hid in the bushes until sundown, waiting for the Indians to leave the riverbank so he could get water. Mr. Kimball never came back. I found out later that on his way back to the house while climbing over a fence, he was shot by Frank Escaloom and died immediately.

Finally, that morning, some villagers brought us a small water vessel and a loaf of bread. They refused to go back for more water, and I could not bear to hear the sick girls' piteous wails for water. I found my shoes and went to the river with a pail. One of the men sitting on the fence pointed his gun at me. I was terribly frightened but walked on. A man sitting next to him knocked the gun up, and it went off in the air, saving my life. I had to pass by the dead bodies of my parents and brothers downstairs. When I returned to the attic with the pail of water, I broke down and wept. Then I brought the girls downstairs, and Joe Stanfield appeared at the pantry and demanded, "Stop that crying. They are all dead, and this will do them no good. If the Indians see you crying, they will be angry."

Many Cayuse women were in the sitting room and wept for us. They loaded us with the clothing they had gathered. Joe

Stanfield told me to take the children to the emigrant house. I carried Louisa, and Elizabeth brought Henrietta. The four of us left with Mary Ann, but we had to leave Helen, Joe Meek's daughter, who was near death. I assured her that I would come right back for her. Soon after, Mrs. Saunders went back with me to the mission house, where we found Helen sitting in bed, screaming at the top of her lungs, surrounded by Indians. She thought I had deserted her.

A Few Escape

Everyone ended up in the emigrant house except for the Canfield family, who had make-shift accommodations in the sawmill. The Osborn family, who had hidden under the floorboards in the Indian Room of the mission house, had listened in terror while Narcissa, Mr. Rodgers, and Frank were killed. They slipped out of the house late that night, making the twenty-five-mile treacherous journey to Fort Walla Walla on foot.

Mr. Hall also managed to escape, following the river to Fort Walla Walla. He gave McBean, a trader at the fort, an inaccurate report, as Mr. Hall had only known Father and Mr. Marsh had been killed. In the meantime, Nicolas Finley was escorting the three mixed-blood boys to the fort. Mrs. Saunders wrote a note to McBean listing eleven people she thought had been killed, including Osborn and Canfield, who had escaped.

That afternoon James Young, the brother of Daniel who had been sweet on Lorinda on the trail, was killed while passing a Cayuse camp about a mile from Waiilatpu. He was driving a team of oxen hitched to a wagon loaded with lumber he brought down from the sawmill at the foot of the Blues. The Cayuse even killed his oxen.

McBean sent an interpreter named Bushman to Waiilatpu, but he left after a few minutes, terrified, and returned the twenty-five miles to Fort Walla Walla the same night. McBean also dispatched a letter to Peter Skene Ogden of the Hudson Bay Company at Fort Vancouver, which arrived there on December 6. Ogden was a renowned negotiator because he was familiar with the culture and behavior of the tribes.

Mr. Hall was sure his wife and five children had been killed at Waiilatpu, so he left the fort's safety for The Dalles by canoe, fearing that the Indians were after him. His boat capsized while attempting to navigate the rapids, and his body was never found. He was officially considered one of the victims of the events at Waiilatpu.

Canfield and his family were staying in the blacksmith shop. He was wounded when he ran to the shop and managed to conceal himself and his family. That night the brave Canfield left for a 120-mile trip on foot to warn the Spaldings. He felt that his family would be safe because he heard that the women and children would not be harmed.

After traveling for a day or two, Canfield fell in with a Nez Perce and his son driving cattle. They accompanied Canfield to Lapwai, arriving four-and-a-half days later.

"Has Mr. Spalding arrived yet?" he asked Elisa Spalding.

"No, but we expect him every day."

"I have heavy tidings. They are all murdered at the doctor's mission."

Eliza was silent for a moment. Then she rose to her feet and replied, "I was not prepared for this, but go on, sir, let me hear the worst."

"Dr. and Mrs. Whitman were murdered, and your husband, without doubt, shared the fate of all the men who, I fear, were all butchered."

The next day a relieved Eliza got word that her husband had been warned of the attack before he arrived at Waiilatpu, and he was alive. She was worried sick to hear that her daughter was a captive at Waiilatpu, but she was told that her daughter was still alive.

Henry Eludes Death

Father Brouillet, the Catholic Priest at Umatilla, had ridden into Chief Tiloukaikt's camp on November 30, where he learned of the killings and offered assistance to the six women and thirty children at the emigrant house. While in their sickbeds, two men were still alive, missed in the attack: Amos Sales and Crocket Bewley, Lorinda's brother.

Father Brouillet and Joe Stanfield loaded the dead bodies into a wagon drawn by oxen while a grief-stricken procession of women and children accompanied them. Something frightened the beasts, and they ran, dumping the bodies on the ground. It was a dreadful experience as the corpses were reloaded and taken to the burial site. Two Walla Walla men and Chief Beardy, who regularly attended the services on the Sabbath and who opposed the violence, helped Joe Stanfield dig the mass grave in the mission cemetery. It was three feet deep and wide enough for all to lay side-by-side. Narcissa was the first to be lowered into the grave. As the bodies were taken off the wagon, the women and children wept for each lost friend or loved one.

Brouillet performed a Roman Catholic burial service in Latin, which no one could understand, but no one objected because there were no words to express the sorrow and losses anyway.

Father Brouillet heard that Spalding was an intended target of the twelve or fourteen Cayuse insurgents, so he left to intercept Henry, who was traveling from Umatilla to Waiilatpu after he had recovered from his injury. Henry's delay in arriving there spared his life.

Before he left Waiilatpu to intercept Spalding, Catherine Sager told Brouillet that Perrin Whitman was the rebels' prime target at The Dalles. She admitted that the teacher she despised--Mr. Hinman--and his family were also there with Perrin. Then Catherine prayed to Brouillet, "May God protect them all and forgive me for loathing Mr. Hinman."

Edward, Chief Tiloukaikt's son and Brouillet's interpreter, accompanied the priest. Luckily Edward fired his pistol to light his pipe and neglected to reload it. At that point, Brouillet realized that Edward was gunning for Henry. A few minutes later, Henry galloped toward them and halted his steed alongside them. He took Brouillet's hand and asked, "Have you been to the Doctor's?" Henry had no idea of the events which had taken place at the mission.

"Yes."

"What news?" Henry asked.

"Sad news," said Brouillet.

"Is anyone dead?"

"Yes, Rev. Spalding."

"Who is dead?" Henry asked, holding his breath, knowing his daughter was there and many of the children were dying of measles. "Is it one of the children? Is my daughter well?"

Before he answered his questions, Brouillet spoke to his interpreter in French, asking him to plead with Edward to spare Henry's life. After hesitating, Edward said that he could not decide to save Henry. However, he would ask the other men, and Edward turned his horse and headed to his village.

When Brouillet told Henry of the dreadful news at the mission, he said, "Oh, my God, they have killed the doctor! They will certainly kill me if I go there."

"Yes, I fear that was Edward's intent in bringing me to you," Father Brouillet replied. "War parties were sent to Lapwai and The Dalles to kill all Americans."

Brouillet implored, "You must flee at once. A party of Cayuse will surely come after you when Edward returns to his camp and tells them he has seen you."

The interpreter advised Henry to go to The Dalles, the opposite direction of his home. They would be looking for him on the trail to Lapwai. The priest gave him some food. However, his family's safety at Lapwai outweighed his fear for himself, so Henry, exhausted and miserable, rode through the night, pushing his horse beyond endurance toward his family. He hid himself the next day and continued at night. About midnight, he heard horses approaching. Somehow he went undetected. Friday morning, he stopped to rest, but he neglected to hobble his horse, and it ran away. He was ninety miles from home and on foot in December. His shoes were too tight, so he left them behind with his rain-soaked blanket. He continued to hide during the day, and he walked about thirty miles each of the next two days. In one of Henry's letters written in January 1848, he expressed his ordeal:

> My feet suffered from the frozen ground. I avoided the places where there were camps and forded the streams far from the trail in case the Cayuse might be waylaying. I hid on the Sabbath, and hunger, pain in my feet, and weakness were

great. I needed sleep but could get none because I was so cold. From the moment I stopped traveling in the morning until I started at night, I shook to the core of my body with cold.

Rev. Spalding came upon Timothy's camp, but his trusted friend was at Waiilatpu, trying to bring young Eliza home. As he passed through, Henry overheard a man in the lodge saying a blessing, thanking the Great Spirit that no one was killed at Lapwai. "Oh, what an angel of mercy to the human family is hope!" Henry thought.

Luckily, he found canoes when he needed to cross the Snake and the Clearwater Rivers. With hunger gnawing at him, and his feet swollen and bleeding, he had to conceal himself again when he came within range of his house. His mission house was being looted. A Nez Perce woman found him, reassured him his family was safe, fed him, and lovingly tended to his feet. Later he described himself during his ordeal as, "More dead than alive from starvation, want of sleep, freezing, horribly swollen and mangled feet, yet somehow I miraculously escaped."

The reverend was reunited with his wife Eliza at the lodge of his friend Craig where they remained safe and well-cared for until the end of December, but he worried about their little girl.

In April of 1848, Henry wrote a very long and detailed letter to Narcissa's mother and father, informing them of her death and giving an account of the events:

> My dear mother and father in Christ,
>
> It has become my painful duty to inform you of the death of your daughter, Narcissa, and her worthy and appreciated husband, your honored son-in-law, Dr. Whitman. My dear sister

> Narcissa, with whom I have grown up as a child of the same family, with whom I have worked so long and so intimately in the work of teaching the Indians, and my friend Dr. Whitman, with whom I have for so many years kneeled in prayer, taking sweet counsel, have been murdered, and their bones scattered upon the plains…

He gave a graphic and accurate account of the ordeal, continuing with:

> And now, shall I attempt to soothe your bleeding hearts? It would be like one drowning man stretching out his hand to hold up another. I am in the deepest waters of misery that my dear brother and sister Whitman are no more…"

The letter revealed a kind heart and compassion for the Prentice family, and beneath it all, it showed that Rev. Spalding had always loved Narcissa.

Life in Captivity
By Catherine Sager Pringle

Many good people came forward to plea for the killing to stop. Nez Perce Timothy and Eagle intervened on our behalf, and Chief Beardy and our good friend Stickus. Chief Tiloukaikt was warned by the Hudson Bay Company officials that there must be no more killing. Only a small group of the Cayuse tribe had taken part in the attack. Most were either unaware of the conspiracy or refused to join. Many Cayuse were shocked at the violence committed by their tribe. Several of their women cried over us and gave us many things.

I will never forget Mrs. Saunders' bravery and how she cared for us. She was the one who bravely went to the Finleys' house while her husband lay dead. She was the one who cared for us children when she found we were still alive the second day. She was the one who met with Father Brouillet and gave him food, and organized making shrouds for the bodies out of Mother's sheets and muslin. However, she could not prevent certain violations from occurring; Stanfield, who dug graves and helped with the burials, continued to loot our house.

From the onslaught of the killings, Chief Beardy, who had faithfully attended Father's services, was our greatest ally. The following day after the initial attack, the rebellious men assembled and vowed to kill the women and children. Because Mrs. Saunders could not speak the Nez Perce language, she lifted Eliza Spalding on a table to act as an interpreter to plea for their lives and those of the survivors. Chief Beardy went to Eliza, patted her on the head, and said, "No, we won't kill you."

When Mrs. Saunders had gone to the Finley lodge, she saw an Indian at our house. He rode toward her, and she saw that it was Beardy; he was weeping and told her that he would do everything to stop the killing. Whether it was her intercession or the speech of Chief Beardy that turned the tide, I know not, but Chief Tiloukaikt faced the men who did the killing and said, "It is enough. No more blood will be shed. The doctor is dead. The men are all dead. These women and children have not hurt us, and they must not be harmed." At the time, Tiloukaikt was unaware that some men had escaped death.

We were captives, over forty of us. Lorinda was relieved and grateful to find her brother overlooked on his sickbed. Crockett was in a room with Amos Sales, both very ill with typhoid but unharmed.

After I was awakened to eat, I checked on Louisa to see how she was doing. She was lying there with her hands thrown over her head, and she seemed to be in a sound slumber. Placing my hand on her face, I found it icy cold. I lay my ear to her mouth, but her breath was gone.

"Louisa is dead," I said, sobbing. It was on December 5. She had passed away so peacefully that the time of her death was unknown, just like Mamma, our first mother.

That day Dan Young came from the sawmill to find out why his brother had not returned. Mrs. Saunders gave him the dreadful news that his brother had been killed and warned him to say he was an Englishman and not an American and to ask permission from Chief Tiloukaikt to return to the sawmill. The chief admonished Dan for traveling on Sunday, a carryover from the strict observance of the Sabbath that father and Rev. Spalding had taught.

No Indian had been shown how to operate the gristmill. Dan's father was a miller, so the chief sent an armed Cayuse escort with Dan to the gristmill and guaranteed his family's safe return to Waiilatpu in exchange for operating the mill. Before he left, Mrs. Saunders reassured Dan that Lorinda was alive.

That same week Timothy and Eagle, the Nez Perce men from Rev. Spalding's mission, arrived to take little Eliza back home. Eliza wept for joy at the sight of her dear friend Timothy.

"Don't cry," Timothy soothed her in his arms. "You will see your mother soon."

The captors, though, refused to let Eliza go. Timothy and Eagle then planned to kidnap her in the night, but the Cayuse, suspecting this, said that if they did so, they would be pursued, and Eliza would be killed. With sad and weary hearts, Timothy and Eagle returned to Lapwai without Eliza. She had been the first child to be born in the present-day state of Idaho to white American parents, and her parents were terrified that she might follow Alice's fate and die.

On December 8, Helen, Joe Meek's daughter, died. Rebecca Hays, who became a widow on the trail, lost her infant son the next day, leaving her one boy.

Chief Tiloukaikt, along with many Cayuse men and women, regretted the killings. Three of his men--his son Edward (who had been given his Christian name by Narcissa in honor of her brother), Wai-e-cat (Tamsucky's son who had accidentally burned the gristmill), and Clokamas--were out of the sorrowful chief's control. On December 8, my sister Elizabeth was witness to their continued wrath. Shaking and crying, she told me what she had witnessed. "Edward came in and found two men still alive. He took a bedpost and fixed it up as a war club. Eliza and I and some of the other children were in the room. Crocket Bewley and Amos Sales were lying in bed. Edward raised his war club and hit Crockett on the head while two other Cayuse watched. We were terrified and ran out of the room, screaming. Edward said, 'Come on back, you must stay in the room till we are finished.'

"They forced us to go back into the room while they beat Amos Sales and Crocket all over their heads. When they had battered their heads until they were dead, the vile men dragged them out into the yard. It was such a horrifying scene, one I will never forget." The next day Joe Stanfield took the bodies away and buried them.

These were the last two killed, making a total of thirteen. Sometime later, we heard that Mr. Hall, the first to reach Fort Walla Walla with the news of the attack, had drowned. His wife and children were devastated by the news. Forty-seven of us were held captive, including five men, eight women, and thirty-four children, none of us knowing what lay ahead.

The men who kept us captive supplied us with an abundance of food, both meat and vegetables. We were allowed to have all the sugar found in our house. We continued to milk cows, collect wood, and bring in water. Calico and muslin were brought from Mother's storeroom so that the women could keep their promise: Mrs. Saunders made and sewed clothing for the Cayuse men. Some women knitted socks. At first, we cooked meals for our captors, but they would not eat until we had first tasted them, afraid that we had poisoned the food. The Indians crowded into all the rooms at the emigrant house during the day until late at night. Mrs. Saunders asked Chief Beardy to stay with us until after the young men returned to their lodges, sometimes as late as one or two in the early morning.

Another violation was what the men did to three of the young women. Edward, Chief Tiloukaikts' son, had tried to buy the beautiful brunette Mary Smith when she was on her way to Waiilatpu with her family. Of course, the Smith family was appalled as they did not understand that this was the custom of the Indians to offer gifts to a girl's family for her, and to the Cayuse, it was an act of honor. The men were interested in Susan Kimball, a young lady whose father had been killed. They were both asked to be wives voluntarily, but they refused. However, when the young women were threatened to be taken by force, they consented because they had witnessed Tamsucky raping Lorinda Bewley and did want to experience the same brutal violation.

The chief told them they had made a wise decision and called on the young men that wanted white wives to come forward. Two men came forward: Clark (Edward's brother and son of Tiloukaikt) and the other was Frank Escaloom, both influential and affluent and both able to speak some English. The girls were told to choose between these young men. Mary Smith chose Clark and Susan chose Frank. Clark changed his mind, and Edward quickly stepped up to claim Mary as his wife.

Mary was a brave girl. She appeared to accept that Edward had taken her as his wife, and in his presence, she was cheerful, but in secret, she wept. Never was a young bridegroom prouder of his wife than Edward. He strutted about with that consequential air so familiar with the Cayuse. He would ask, "Where is my wife?" which caused great amusement by everyone who heard him.

Joe Stanfield, who had eyes for Mrs. Hays for some time, told her that unless she consented to be his wife, the rest of the women and children would be killed. The night that he insisted on going to bed with her, she put her four-year-old boy between them. Finally, in exasperation, he told her, "Go to hell," and did not bother her again.

Five Crows Took Me for His Wife

By Lorinda Bewley

Sketch of Five Crows on left
By Gustavus Sohon, 1855

Artist unknown on right

Another image of when he was older

Tamsucky raped me before my brother's very eyes and in the shocking presence of many of the captives. Crocket dared not raise a hand even if he had the strength. Afterward, the women surrounded me outside on the ground and brought me into the house. They did not know what to do as this was beyond their experience. I heard Crockett's screams as he and Mr. Sales were being murdered the next day. I hid under my bed and sobbed in indescribable grief. They had been beaten on their heads with a bedpost and thrown outside in the bitter cold. The Indians told me they would kill me if I went near my brother. My brother suffered all night and died the following day.

An express rider arrived from Fort Walla Walla three hours after Crockett died, saying if the Cayuse killed any more men, the Hudson Bay Company would join the Americans to punish them. Sorrowfully, he did not get there in time to save my brother's life. The day Crockett died, the Umatilla chief, Five Crows, sent two men on horseback to take me to his lodge to be his wife. Eliza Spalding recognized one horse as her father's, and the poor darling thought her father was dead.

I recalled the look that Five Crows gave me in the Valley of the Grande Ronde when he met our party just one month earlier. My friend Isabella had teased me, "Lorinda, I believe this man is sweet on you," and I blushed red as a beet.

I was still very ill from the fever and resisted, but I was frightened. The men threw a buffalo robe over me, wound me up with a rope, and tied me astride a horse to deliver me to Five Crow's lodge. It was twenty miles, and night overtook us on the way. There, alone with two strangers who I thought would be savages, I felt that my situation was utterly desolate. One of the men called Big Belly told me he was a Christian, and with many tears, he expressed in broken English his grief at what had been done at the mission. He provided for me with much care and kept a fire burning on that snowy, freezing night. At bedtime, he knelt, prayed, and wept. I could hear my own name *Tit-mai*, Little Woman, repeated in his prayers. From that day forward, I called him "Great Heart." His tribal name was Chief Camaspelo, and he would prove himself my valuable ally.

The next day on reaching Umatilla, he pleaded so eloquently for me that Five Crows allowed me to go to the priests' house for two days. It was occupied by Bishop Blanchet, Father Brouillet, two priests, and three Frenchmen. I thought that Five Crows brought me there to protect me from the other hostiles at Waiilatpu, but most of the nights, Five Crows forced me to go to his lodge and be subject to his desires during the night. I escaped violation for the first four nights. The first night Five Crows came for me, I refused to go with him. He went away angry, and the bishop told me, "You had better go, Miss Bewley, as he might harm all of us."

I could hardly grasp what this "man of God" was saying to me. He did not care that I was being raped. He turned his back on me and went into the sitting room.

I begged and cried to the bishop to protect me, either at his house or to be sent to Fort Walla Walla. I told the bishop, "I will do any work by night and day for you if you will protect me."

The bishop sent an Indian with me who took me to Five Crows' lodge. I was relieved yet confused when Five Crows showed me the door and told me I should leave and take my clothes, which I did.

Three nights after this, Five Crows came for me again. The bishop ordered me to go. My answer was, "I would rather die." He still insisted that my going to Five Crows was the best thing I could do for *their* sakes. I was in the bishop's room with the three priests present. I found I could get no help and left.

Five Crows seized me by the arm and jerked me away, dragging me to his lodge to spend the night in his bed. I returned to the bishop's house early in the morning, only to be violently taken away again the next night.

On my return, one morning, one of the young priests asked me, with a good deal of glee, "How do you like your companion?"

What an absurd question! Did he not have eyes, ears, or soul? I cried most of that day, for I had no protector.

One day Father Brouillet called me outside and told me, "If you go to the lodge anymore, you must not come back to my house."

"What should I do?" I asked him, totally frustrated.

He said, "You must insist or beg of the Indian to let you stop going to his house. If he does not let you, you must stay at his lodge, and you may not come back here."

The next day at the house, I did not feel well, and toward night I went to bed, determined that I would die there before being taken away. Five Crows came, and when I refused to go, he hauled me from my bed, threw my bonnet and shawl at me, and ordered me to go with him. I would not, and when he was not looking at me, I threw my bonnet and shawl under the table, and Five Crows could not find them. I sat down, determined not to go, and he pushed me nearly into the fire. The Frenchman living there was in the room with me. The bishop and priests were pacing back and forth in their quarters. When Five Crows was smoking, I went to bed again, and when he was through smoking, he dragged me from my bed with more violence than the first time.

I told the Frenchman, "Go into the bishop's room and ask him what I should do."

He told me, "The bishop said it was best that you go with him."

"But Father Brouillet said that I must not return to this house again if I went," I gasped in desperation.

"The priests dare not keep women about their house. It could be scandalous for them," the Frenchman replied.

The Captive
1891 Oil painting by Eanger Irving Couse

For them? Were they deaf and blind? I still would not go. Five Crows then pulled me away so brutally, without my bonnet or shawl, that my hands were skinned from holding on to the table. I made myself as disagreeable as I could to him, but still, every third night, he took me, and I was returned to the house without protest from the bishop. Five Crows must have threatened them if they did not let me go back.

Terrie Biggs

Council at Saint Anne's

All the Cayuse chiefs along the Columbia River became afraid. Fourteen young men committed these crimes at Waiilatpu, for which the whole Cayuse nation would be blamed. The chiefs and their people felt they would be subject to a fearful retaliation by the Americans. Chief Camaspelo [Big Belly or Great Heart to Lorinda] told Bishop Blanchet he disapproved of the killings, as did many chiefs. Messengers were sent to the chiefs and sub-chiefs asking for them to assemble at Saint Anne's Mission at Umatilla on December 20 to hold council. Stickus lived across the river and attended the meeting, Tiloukaikt, Tawatoe, Five Crows, Camaspelo, and many sub-chiefs. It lasted an entire day.

Chief Tiloukaikt spoke for two hours, giving Cayuse history and the impact the invaders had on their way of life. His son Edward also took his turn and emphasized the loss of life Cayuse suffered because of the white man's diseases. Edward gave a touching picture of the afflicted families who buried their mothers, fathers, sisters, and brothers, including his younger siblings, the day before the attack. Some of their people were the only survivors of their entire families. He told them that Joe Lewis had described that Dr. Whitman plotted to poison the Cayuse in the village to take their land and horses. Edward said to them that before Mr. Rodgers died, he admitted to Joe Lewis, it was true, but Stickus knew this was Joe speaking with a forked tongue. He had refused to be a part of his and Finley's nightly council sessions, and that is why he warned his friend, Dr. Whitman, about pending danger.

Edward explained how Americans had murdered two of their people--Elijah Hedding, the son of Peu-peu-mox-mox, in California and the other a student in the American school. Six Cayuse had died of measles the day before the attack, and three more died the morning of the attack.

Edward said, "A life for a life. That is our custom," Joe Lewis and Nicolas Finley had convinced the younger hot-headed members of the Waiilatpu band they were being poisoned. They, in turn, drew in Chief Tiloukaikt to get his permission. Tiloukaikt was also Stickus' friend and knew his heart was heavy with sorrow and fear of reprisal. The Cayuse knew they must now negotiate as a nation, not as individuals.

Peter Skene Ogden, the Negotiator

A grim photo for a jolly man

Three days later, all the chiefs met at Fort Walla Walla to negotiate the release of the captives with Peter Skene Ogden, a highly respected Hudson Bay Company official. Five Crows refused to give up Lorinda and would not attend.

Opening the council meeting, Ogden said, "We have been among you for thirty years without the shedding of blood. We are traders and of a different nation from the Americans, but don't forget, we supply you with ammunition, but it was never for the purpose of killing Americans, who are of the same color, speak the same language, and worship the same God as we do, and whose cruel fate causes our hearts to bleed. Why are you chiefs if you cannot control your men?

"Dr. Whitman was not guilty of poisoning your people. How could he be responsible for so many deaths in widely scattered places? Your people have been dying of measles, a white man's disease, and the doctor mercifully tended to your sick and helped you bury them when they died. His heart was saddened by your tragic losses, as is mine.

"I am not here as a representative of the Americans. I am here as an official of the Hudson Bay Company. I left Fort Vancouver before any Americans in the Willamette Valley had been notified of the killings. The Company has nothing to do with your quarrel. I will see what can be done for you on my return if you wish it, but I do not promise to prevent war. Deliver your prisoners to me, and I will pay you a ransom, and that is all I can promise."

There was no one more qualified than Ogden to negotiate for the hostages. He had the power to stop all trading between the company and the tribes. He arrived at Fort Walla Walla without soldiers, only sixteen boatmen ready to transport the people to safety who were held captive at the mission.

The ransom was set at fifty blankets, fifty shirts, ten guns, ten six-foot strands of tobacco, ten handkerchiefs, black powder, and one hundred balls. Many young men objected, including

Edward and Frank Escaloom, because they did not want to give up their American wives.

Ogden allowed the dispatch to reach Henry for six days, imploring him to lose no time in joining him at Fort Walla Walla. The Spaldings abandoned nine buildings constructed during their years at Lapwai, which consisted of their cabin, a schoolhouse, a meeting house, a print shop, storage facilities, and a gristmill. Twenty acres had been cultivated for growing vegetables and wheat, and they had also planted two hundred fruit trees. They had to leave bushels of corn, flour, peas, potatoes, books and primers, and their livestock. The estimated value was over $10,000, accumulated with hard work and no salary from the Board. On December 28, 1847, they left it all behind and traveled with four other adults and three children, escorted by forty armed Nez Perce neighbors, ensuring their safe journey to Fort Walla Walla.

For three days and three nights, Ogden didn't sleep a wink. Slowly and cautiously, he raised the price he offered for Lorinda until the chiefs determined that Five Crows must give her up. It cost more to redeem her than the rest of the captives combined. It was reported that Ogden's hair turned white during this ordeal.

Christmas Pie

By Catherine Sager Pringle

We celebrated Christmas in an Indian village. An incident was tragically humorous that day, which made me laugh. But I think of things that I cried over, mostly a Christmas without Mother, Father, Frank, John, and Louisa.

The guards were wandering savages in whose charge nobody was safe. Many times, we thought our final hour had come. They ordered us around like slaves and kept us busy cooking and sewing for them. We hailed the coming of Beardy as a providential event.

When the holiday dawned, the elder folk resolved to make the children as happy as the means at hand would allow. Mrs. Saunders had brought some white flour and dried peaches across the plains, and someone brought them to us at the emigrant house. White flour was a luxury, as were peaches. Mrs. Saunders made bread on Christmas morning and also made peach pies. Chief Beardy had been so kind to us that we invited him to our Christmas dinner. It seemed we had ever so many pies, and Beardy thought he tasted nothing so good in all his life. He sat in one corner of the kitchen, cramming piece after piece of the peach pie into his mouth. We gave him all the pie he wanted, even if some of us went hungry because Beardy was a friend whose fidelity we depended on for our lives.

And so, we had our Christmas festival and sang and thanked heaven that we were still alive. After dinner and about an hour after Beardy left for the night, we were frightened by a series of cries saying, "Kill them! Tomahawk them!"

A band of angry men started to attack the house! We saw them from the windows. Our time had come. Some of us began to pray, some were in shock with terror, and some wailed. The day that opened with fair promises was about to close in despair.

To our amazement and horror, the Indian band was led by Chief Beardy himself, the man we counted on as a friend to protect us in just such emergencies. He was calling for the death of all the white women. However, fortune favored us at this critical juncture, for just as the hostile men entered the house, messengers arrived from Fort Walla Walla. The messengers included Katherine, the wife of a Hudson Bay employee who knew Beardy well. They approached him and inquired the reason for his wild ravings.

"Me poisoned," cried Beardy, "Me killed. White squaw poison me. Me always white man's friend, now me enemy. White squaw must die."

Not knowing about the pains that lie in wait after gorging himself on peach pies, he had rushed to the conclusion that the pies had been poisoned when he vomited up peaches. Katherine explained to Beardy that he had suffered from the effects of excessive indulgence in American pie. It took a long time for Katherine and the messengers to convince Beardy that the women were innocent of any intention to cause him pain. Katherine and the messengers talked Beardy into a reasonable frame of mind, and he called off his men. Peace once more prevailed.

"Why, in heaven's name, Katie, would the man have thought he was being poisoned?" Mrs. Saunders asked me.

I began a long explanation. "Probably for a couple of reasons, Mrs. Saunders. Before my sisters and brothers came here, a rumor started that Father had tainted some meat with poison to eliminate coyotes and wolves preying on the sheep and other animals. Some dogs belonging to the Cayuse who live here died after eating the bait. Father, though, knew what danger would have put his life in, and he told us he never did such a deed, but John Young said he knew two men had poisoned bait for the wolves and claimed Father told them to do it.

"Another time, Mr. Gray put some 'bad medicine' in watermelons to discourage the tribal people from stealing them. Again, Father got blamed for Gray's stupidity. The night before we were attacked, I overheard Father whispering to Mother that that devil, Joe Lewis, had been telling all the Cayuse that they were dying because Father was poisoning them."

"My word!" she exclaimed. "It's a miracle that we weren't all killed for 'pie poisoning.' It's frightening to have the truth twisted so easily."

We were all happy that night, glad that Mrs. Saunders' pie had not been the cause of the wholesale slaughter of white families, and our hearts and spirits were filled with hope from the news from the Fort on that unforgettable Christmas day.

The messengers who explained the bellyache to Beardy had brought joyous news, the best Christmas gift for which we could have wished. Tiloukaikt told Mrs. Saunders that all of us could leave for Fort Walla Walla on Wednesday, December 29.

Terrie Biggs

I am Free
By Lorinda Bewley

I'll never forget the morning of December 28. While I was at Five Crow's lodge, Great Heart [Camaspelo] rode up leading a horse and handed me a note from Mr. Ogden, stating the joyful news that he had succeeded in securing my release. He said that I had nothing to fear and that Great Heart would accompany me as fast as possible to Waiilatpu.

I could hardly believe what I had read. I fell to my knees and thanked my heavenly Father for His great mercy to me. Five Crows prepared tea and good breakfast for me. Great Heart told me that preparing a meal himself was the highest compliment a chief could give. Five Crows put a blanket and buffalo robe upon the saddle to make it comfortable for me to ride and sleep at night. Tenderly he wrapped a thick shawl around me, helped me on my horse, and gave me food for my journey.

He said goodbye kindly, with much feeling, and I thought I detected a tear in his eye. It took years for me to understand that, in his culture, he had taken me as his bride and that he had formed an attachment to me--in his way, maybe he even loved me. I was told later that he grieved for years at losing his "wife with the golden hair."

As we left on horseback, with Great Heart leading my horse, he suddenly took a closer grip on the halter and exclaimed, "Bad Indians come."

A war party of two hundred galloped toward us and formed a circle around us. Great Heart began to plead and argue and protest. After some time, one man dashed forward, snatched the halter from Great Heart's hand, and led me around and around the circle at a fast gallop, almost unseating me.

At last, he returned me to the center, and Great Heart regained possession of the halter. Finally, the grim circle parted, and Great Heart laid the whip on his horse. We continued at this gait for two or three miles until my horse stumbled, fell, rolled over, stunning me, and sprained my wrist. Great Heart was afraid I was dead, but I told him I was alright. He put me on his horse, saying, "He no stumble again."

We made camp the first night. The winter days were short, and just at dark on the second evening, the twinkling lights of Waiilatpu came into sight. Oh, how great it did look to me!

Terrie Biggs

Journey from Captivity
By Catherine Sager Pringle

We had the pleasure of receiving Lorinda early in the evening. We were so relieved and happy to see her. The following day, we began our twenty-five-mile journey from captivity to Fort Walla Walla in five wagons, some drawn by horses and some by oxen. The oxen-driven wagons were very slow, and we didn't think we could get to the fort in one day. Our friend Chief Stickus rode with us. As we stopped at noon for dinner, Chief Beardy and Chief Tiloukaikt caught up with us, galloping their horses. Tiloukaikt was waving his whip and shouting, "*Hon-tets, hon-tets,*" which meant hurry. "Bad Indians coming! No camp. Get to fort."

Chief Beardy joined our caravan, and he and Stickus pushed the oxen to their limit in the cold winter downpour. Lorinda was riding in Young's wagon with Dan and his family and was the last to reach the fort. Peter Ogden ran out of the gates to greet us. As soon as we met this large jovial man, we Sager girls called him "uncle" from that day forward.

"Is Lorinda here?" he asked anxiously.

"Yes, she is here," John Young answered as Dan helped Lorinda out of the wagon.

Uncle Pete took her in his arms and said, "Thank God, you are safe at last. I feared they would never give you up."

Thus ended one whole month of captivity, although it seemed much longer. We were safe in the fort but still holding our breaths. The "bad Indians" that we had been warned about arrived a couple of hours later and began to rant and rave outside and kept up a fearful commotion all night. Inside the fort, the Indians stormed about and seemed to be working themselves up--perhaps to kill us. The fort was poorly staffed, and Mr. McBean, the fort commander, was fearful because he had not witnessed this type of behavior before. Uncle Pete kept the women and children in locked rooms with guards. It was another frightful night for us all. Lorinda was terrified that she would be retaken. By morning the riled-up Indians had calmed down, and so did our nerves.

We rested there for two days until Rev. and Mrs. Spalding arrived and were reunited with their brave daughter Eliza. Such a touching sight! Little Eliza was quite different from the little girl her mother had left only one month earlier. She was thin as a skeleton. Canfield, who had escaped to Lapwai to warn the Spaldings, was with them and also reunited with his family. They were the only two families still intact. The Osborn family, who escaped the night of the attack to the fort's safety, accompanied us to the American settlements in the Willamette Valley. Waiilatpu was no longer a haven for us and the emigrants.

Everyone was loaded into three large batteaux (rowboats) and started down the river. I looked back at the shore. McBean was waving alongside David Malin, who had been our brother for three years and one month. David was told that he would not fare well as a mixed-blood child among the Americans in the Willamette Valley. He stood there sobbing and broken-hearted as the only remaining family he knew sailed away without him. Elizabeth, Matilda, Henrietta, and I--the last members of our Sager family of nine--wept for poor little David. We never knew what became of him.

We adored "Uncle" Pete. His common-sense knowledge of the Indian culture had saved our lives. We loved climbing onto his broad, portly lap at the fort, and we four Sager girls rode with him in his bateau. A man with an inexhaustible fund of good humor laughed heartily, talked loudly, and joked with us. He told us about his voyages up and down the river. He had such funny stories about his children, and we laughed and howled for the first time in what seemed a lifetime. The men of the Pacific forts loved him, and he was highly respected and admired by the natives.

"I have made the round trip up the river in the winter to Walla Walla and back many times, but this is the first-round trip I have ever made without one drop of rain," Uncle Pete said solemnly to us after we were safe. It was a kind Providence that we were not rained on, for many of the party were in poor health and some very ill. Sadly, Osborn's four-year-old son died from exposure during our voyage to freedom. Later we heard that eleven-year-old Mary Ann Bridger died the following March. These two children were considered casualties of the attack.

Portages were a part of the journey down the mighty Columbia River, and while making one, Lorinda got more terrible news about her family. Her father and her aunt Sophia Bewley had both died in mid-December while camped near the Sandy River on their way to Oregon City. The shock of hearing about Crockett's death and the capture of Lorinda was too much for her father, and he died, literally broken-hearted. Lorinda's aunt had been ill. She lost her nephew, her brother, and was unsure of Lorinda's fate, which overwhelmed her. She died a day after her brother.

As we neared the dock at Fort Vancouver, Uncle Pete's home, the boatmen broke forth and sang the "Canadian Boat Song" with a zest that showed their joy at safely reaching home.

> Fair these broad meads--these hoary woods are grand;
> But we are exiles from our fathers' land.
> Listen to me, as when ye heard our father
> Sing long ago the song of other shores--
> Listen to me, and then in chorus gather
> All your deep voices, as ye pull your oars.
> From the lone shieling of the misty island
> Mountains divide us, and waste of seas--
> Yet still, the blood is strong, the heart is Highland,
> And we in dreams behold the Hebrides.
> We ne'er shall tread the fancy-haunted valley,
> Where 'tween the dark hills creeps the small clear stream,
> In arms around the patriarch banner rally,
> Nor see the moon on royal tombstones gleam.
> When the bold kindred, in the time long vanis'hd,
> Conquer'd the soil and fortified the keep--
> No seer foretold the children would be banish'd,
> That a degenerate lord might boast his sheep.
> Come foreign rage--let Discord burst in slaughter!
> O then for clansmen true, and stern claymore
> The hearts that would have given their blood like water,
> Beat heavily beyond the Atlantic roar.

Terrie Biggs

(Meaning of unusual words: sheiling means highland cottage; claymore is a Highland broadsword)

Alone Again
By Catherine Sager Pringle

We were given a warm and comforting reception at Fort Vancouver on the Willamette River, staying at James Douglas's home. He was in charge of the fort along with Uncle Pete. A week later, when we arrived in Portland, we were overwhelmed. Governor Abernathy and hundreds of people lined the western side of the river, and a company of volunteers under the command of Colonel Gilliam was camped on the eastern banks. As we pulled in toward the wharf, many men fired their rifles in salute. The gunfire terrified us, and we dove for the bottom of the boat. Captain Shaw, who delivered us Sager children to the mission, and Colonel Gilliam, who commanded the wagon train we had traveled, ran to us. The captain said comfortingly, "It's alright, my dear children. The guns were fired to honor you." Then three cheers went up for us. Our hero, Uncle Pete, took his bows graciously and winked at us, knowing this welcome was primarily meant for the captives.

How incredible to see both Colonel Gilliam and Captain Shaw from our wagon train! So much had happened since last we saw them. Lorinda left us at Portland to go to her mother in the company of Will Chapman, whom she had pledged to marry while crossing the plains. She indeed did marry him, and they raised a family and spent fifty years together until she died in Sheridan, Oregon, in 1899.

The Spaldings, Mr. Stanley, and we girls were taken to Oregon City. Governor Abernathy and his kind wife invited us and the Spaldings to be guests in their home for a few days. We were sad to part from the Spalding family because we were so close to little Eliza. We had been through so much together. The Spaldings headed for the Tualatin Plaines to live near friends, and then later, I heard that they moved again to southwest Oregon.

During our captivity, Governor Abernathy had formed a company of riflemen called the Oregon Volunteers. Uncle Pete held them back to avoid an attack, which might have frightened the men holding us into killing us all. After our release, volunteers pursued the men who had attacked and killed our friends and family at the mission. The volunteers included Will Chapman, Lorinda's betrothed, Captain Shaw, Colonel Gilliam, and Baptiste Dorion. Dorion was Madame Dorion's son who had stirred up the Cayuse a few years earlier, telling them that Dr. Whitman was bringing in Americans to make war upon them, and Charles and Thomas McKay, both of mixed blood.

Thrust upon the mercy of new guardians, we four were separated and taken into different homes, totally alone without each other's company. Elizabeth lived with three different families, the last being very harsh on her because she yearned to see me. I was able to visit her only once in four years. When I married Clark Pringle, his kind heart allowed me to bring Elizabeth and Henrietta to stay with us. Matilda lived with Mr.

Giger at the Tualatin plains and married at age fifteen to Mr. Hazlette, who was twice her age.

We had heard that Five Crows had been shot by Tom McKay's brother, shattering a bone in his arm, in one of the battles with The Volunteers. He went to his Nez Perce family, who nursed him back to health. Once back home at Umatilla, he never again participated in Indian affairs.

The traitor, Joe Lewis, took all the money and personal belongings of value that he could find at our house after the killings. He feared his life was in danger, mainly from the Cayuse at the village, who suspected him of treachery and disloyalty. Somehow, he coaxed Tiloukaikt's sons, Edward and Clark, and another Cayuse man involved with the captivity to follow him to the land of the Mormons. While they were sleeping near Fort Hall, Joe Lewis slit the brothers' throats and kept all the valuables. They were found dead in their blankets by a Hudson Bay Company man who came upon them on his annual trip for supplies. The third man escaped and later gave the grizzly details to authorities. He had known Clark and Edward, easily identified them, returned, and gave the grim news of their deaths to the Cayuse at Waiilatpu. It was a massive blow to Tiloukaikt, who had lost all of his children, either from disease or murder. Finally, Joe Lewis was killed in 1862 in an attempted stagecoach holdup in Flathead country, and I say good riddance to the scoundrel.

In 1897, fifty years after the attack, we remaining Sager women returned to Walla Walla, which had become a thriving town. Eight of the seventeen survivors still living, including Elizabeth, Matilda, and me, reunited there. The house was packed for evening ceremonies at the Opera House of Walla Walla for a monument dedication. The next day we traveled with a large crowd by train to Waiilatpu to honor those who had fallen. Henrietta had gone to California and became an actress. We heard a terrible rumor that she was murdered in Red Bluff, California, by a scoundrel who shot and tried to kill her husband. We have never had proof of her death, but we never heard another word from her since her last letter in the 1860s from San Francisco.

Catherine, Elizabeth, and Matilda,
three of the Sager sisters at the 50th anniversary
at Walla Walla in 1847.

The good people of Walla Walla formed a memorial association. They raised $2500 for a granite statute and a slab of Vermont marble to cover the graves atop the hill that we had climbed many times in our childhood at Waiilatpu. It was the hill where our mother's little angel Alice lies and where mass graves entombing our Whitman parents, Frank, John, our babe Hannah Louisa, and all the others.

The stones for the memorial did not arrive on time, but the ceremonies proceeded. I was called upon to speak, which was uncomfortable for me. I related our love and heartache for those taken in such a cruel manner. We had joyous times with our Whitman family, who had taken us all into their arms and hearts, and for that, we are forever grateful. Not a day goes by that I fail to remember my lost brothers, sister, and the Whitmans.

May they all rest in peace.

The memorial site at the Whitman Mission National Historic Site, near Walla Walla, Washington

Terrie Biggs

Unconfirmed Photo of Stickus

RETURN TO EARTH

War & the Militia

As in all countries, the nation of Cayuse, along with their Nez Perce, Umatilla, and Walla Walla neighbors, consisted of individuals with their values, prejudices, personalities, likes, and dislikes. One cannot judge a nation by the individual nor the individual by a nation. Many of their people were tolerant (mostly the elders), and a few young men quickly reacted without considering the consequences. Chief Tiloukaikt was sickened and tormented that he let a few rebellious youths influence him in the killings at Waiilatpu. The neighboring tribes felt, on the whole, Cayuse were reckless, loved to make war, and lived to dominate. But some of the people, like Camaspelo, Beardy, and Stickus, were tolerant of the Americans and had close friends among them.

Over the next two years, there were several skirmishes with the Oregon Volunteers, who joined with Hudson Bay Company people. One clash in March 1848 began as Gray Eagle, a shaman, and Five Crows, the supreme chief of the Cayuse, rushed headlong towards the troops. Gray Eagle shot a dog belonging to an American volunteer rifleman. He was shot and killed by Thomas McKay of the Hudson Bay Company after Gray Eagle had threatened to kill McKay. Charles McKay, brother of Thomas, shot Five Crows in the arm. Five Crows went to his Nez Perce half-brother, [i] Old Chief Joseph, to recover.[3]

Most indigenous people had traded with the Canadians of the Hudson Bay Company forts in the past: some Canadians were Scots, and some were French. Until the murderers of the Whitmans were turned over, the Americans and the Hudson Bay Company people refused to issue them ammunition. The traders called those who wanted to kill the Americans and those who would not surrender "hostiles." Many people separated from their accused brothers, including Nez Perce chiefs Peu-peu-mox-mox, Otter Skin, Camaspelo, and Tawatoe. Tawatoe's stand drove a wedge between him and his brother, Five Crows. As the supreme chief of the Cayuse, Five Crows was considered the leader of those who were involved in the attack.

Walla Walla Chief Peu-peu-mox-mox by artist Paul Kane

---

[3] Old Chief Joseph was the father of the famous Chief Joseph who, in 1877, lead the Nez Perce tribe 1170 miles after being forced to abandon their land in the Wallowa Valley of present-day Oregon. In one of his notable speeches, he uttered, "I will fight no more forever."

Soon after Five Crows was wounded, Stickus rode with two of his tribal members and a Nez Perce man to meet with a delegation of white men. He went forward carrying the American flag and approached Colonel Gilliam. He offered to take Joe Lewis in exchange for the men responsible for the killings at Waiilatpu.

Henry Lee, the superintendent of Indian Affairs, demanded that the murderers be punished and that stolen property be returned. They would have to pay for any property not returned. Every dwelling at the Waiilatpu mission site had been burned except the grist mill. The delegation returned to their people at Waiilatpu and the Umatilla to let them know about the troops and that they demanded the return of Dr. Whitman's property. A couple of days later, Stickus delivered forty head of cattle and sheep, a few horses, fifty-six dollars in cash, and two thousand dollars worth of property. He also had persuaded Joe Lewis to go with him, but he was diverted by some other Cayuse and fled. Turning over the accused men would be a long and challenging process.

In August of 1848, the Oregon Territory was established and served by Governor Lane. A regiment of troops called the Mounted Riflemen came from the United States over the Oregon Trail; they consisted of six hundred men and a few women and children on their way to Oregon City in 1849. This massive force of horses, mules, wagons and troops was frightening to the tribes as they marched across their land. Now reduced by half, their spirits were weakened, and their prestige among the Columbia River tribes was lost. Hudson Bay Company men no longer would sell them guns and ammunition. They said it was to prevent the men on the run from getting weapons and ammunition to fight. However, the locals needed them to hunt to feed their people and for defense. They had become dependent on their farms, and now they were forced to roam again for food.

Stickus joined Tawatoe, sixty Cayuse, twenty Nez Perce led by Timothy, a Walla Walla chief, and five of his men to bring Tiloukaikt to the American officials. Chief Tiloukaikt kept on the move with his stock of cattle, horses, lodges, women, children, and elders. Two years had passed since the killings. He was weary and weakened. The men were warned that if they failed in bringing the suspected men to the officials, the militia would be deployed and make war on their people. Too many of their people were already in the spirit world. Tiloukaikt had already lost ten of his men and all his sons. Eventually, Tamsucky and Shumkain, both considered the two principal murderers, were killed by a Nez Perce attempting to turn them over to the authorities.

Tiloukaikt and his band were close to starvation while hiding in the snowy Blue Mountains. Tawatoe captured all his livestock and successfully pleaded for Tiloukaikt to surrender himself and his men. Tawatoe, in good faith, said to Tiloukaikt, "The white men in the Willamette want to ask you what you know about the killings. If you go there, you may have immunity from punishment."

The military forces were superior to the Cayuse, and many more innocent people would be killed if war were declared on the entire Cayuse tribe. Faced with starvation and annihilation of their people, Tiloukaikt had no choice but to surrender himself and four others to Tawatoe: the brothers Ish-ish-kais-kais (Frank Escaloom) and Tomahas, Clokamas, and Kai-ma-sump-kin. However, the act of surrender was considered an admission of guilt for killing the people at the mission.

Hanged by the Neck

With many warriors of the Cayuse tribe, Tawatoe and Stickus escorted the five men to The Dalles, where Governor Lane met them along the way, took them to Oregon City, and turned them over to Joe Meek. Joe Meek had been appointed U. S. Marshall and was responsible for the men. Tawatoe and Stickus had been summoned to "testify," along with Chief Camaspelo and five other Cayuse, so they continued by horseback to Oregon City. Tawatoe offered fifty horses as payment to the defense counsels. To their horror, there was no immunity provided to the men they handed over, for they were all shackled like dogs, put in a small building, guarded by twenty soldiers, and held for trial.

Tawatoe was no longer young, neither in spirit nor in years. He had witnessed too many changes that his people had suffered. Tawatoe sat proudly and erect in the hotel saloon used for the trial. A rail which they called a "bar," was set across the middle of the room. It separated the crowd from the court people.

The Cayuse had no experience with the white man's tribunal system. Many people came to watch, and many men were on the judge's side of the bar. A man named Frank Holland described what their people were accused of doing. "Said Indians....did commit the crime of willful murder in and upon the body of said Marcus Whitman, against the peace and dignity of the United States aforesaid, and contrary to the form of the Statute in such case made and provided." So many confusing words.

Years earlier, chiefs had agreed to Agent White's code of eleven written articles, and he had explained that the word "statutes" meant laws. They had agreed to Article One, which stated, "Whoever willfully takes life shall be hanged." They did not know what this punishment called "hanged" meant. The last article read, "If any Indian breaks these laws, he shall be punished by his chiefs; if a white man breaks them, he shall be reported to the agent and be punished."

They did not expect their people to be tied in chains and dragged to a white man's court. The men thought the five men would be able to tell their story, and *their* chiefs would punish them, as written in the laws we ignorantly agreed to. They still did not know which "statutes" had been violated. Someone mentioned the Little Blue Book and the Big Blue Book and said that they were laws in Iowa, which was in what the Americans called their "states." Iowa was part of America, and the Oregon government had adopted Iowa's laws. This blue book said, "Murder shall consist of the unlawful killing of a human being with malice aforethought. The punishment of any person convicted of the crime shall be death."

Holbrook called a prosecutor--who was the man accusing their people--practiced out of one Blue Book and Judge Pratt out of the other. It was very strange to them. Their men on trial and those in the room could not understand their words because most local people did not speak English. This council went on for days, and their interpreters could not keep up, so they stopped trying as it became too confusing. Chief Tiloukaikt and the other four men did not understand what was said. The men knew they were accused of killing Dr. Whitman; however, the others killed at the missionary settlement on Cayuse land were never mentioned.

The fourth day, Judge Pratt coughed to clear his throat and read a judgment and sentence to the court, "You, Tiloukaikt, Tomahas, Clokomas, Ish-ish-kais-kais [Frank Escaloom], and Kia-ma-sump-kin having been duly convicted by the finding and verdict of the jury, of the crime of willful murder as alleged in the indictment are; therefore, each adjudged to suffer death by hanging, and you and each of you are ordered and adjudged to be taken from hence to a place of security and confinement and there kept until Monday the 3rd day of June, A.D. 1850, and on that day at the hour of two o'clock in the afternoon, be taken by the Marshal of the District of Oregon, to the gallows or place of execution to be erected in Oregon City, and thereby be hanged by the neck, until you are dead. And may God in His Infinite Grace have mercy on your souls."

The prisoners waited for the interpreters to explain what was happening. They did not understand what gallows and hanging by the neck meant. They understood whiplashing. They understood cutting. They understood spearing. Since white men brought firearms, they also understood shooting. Their men were filled with horror when the interpreters explained the means of their deaths. Being choked by the neck was not an honorable way to die, and they could not meet their Great Spirit by such a shameful death.

In interviews of the men on the way to the gallows taken by two soldiers on June 2 and 3, 1850, none of the men thought they would be arrested and put on trial. Tiloukaikt proclaimed, "When I left my people, Tawatoe told me to come down and talk with the big white chief and tell him who killed Dr. Whitman and others."

Kia-ma-sump-kin, who had been given James's name, explained, "My chief sent me to declare who the guilty persons were; the white chief would then shake hands with me, Tawatoe would come after me, and we would have a good heart."

Clokamas stated, "Our chief told us to come down and tell who the murderers were."

Tomahas, who reportedly was observed to have killed Dr. Whitman and Crocket Bewley, echoed the same sentiment, "Our chief told us to come and see the white chief and tell him what had happened, and teach us to live in peace with the white men when we return home."

When asked why he allowed himself to be taken prisoner, Tiloukaikt stood tall and proudly replied, "Did not you missionaries tell us that Christ died to save his people? So die we to save our people."

Photo of Chief Tiloukaikt and painting of Tomahas
By artist Paul Kane in 1847

The delegation of men was told later that perhaps two thousand white men and women came to watch their brothers die in this dishonorable fashion. Many brought firearms in fear of us, but they did not come to cause trouble. On the day of the hanging, the people returned home weary and horrified, feeling doomed. They do not know where they were buried, but their bodies returned to their Earth Mother in the end.

They knew that the last of their dignity, honor, prestige and thousands of years of culture was gone forever. Chief Tiloukaikt lives in their history as a hero who sacrificed himself to save his nation from annihilation, leaving just over one hundred of their once proud and mighty Cayuse nation to carry on their heritage.

Life's Circle

"Grandfather, why did the white men call you Stickus? What does that mean?"

"Unlike my name Istukus, Stickus has no meaning, but it seemed easier on their tongues."

"Tell me a story, Grandfather. Tell me again how our people first found horses. That always makes me laugh."

"Yes, that is a good story. We were on foot, and our hunting grounds were quite limited. Our enemies, the Shoshones, a weak and unworthy people, were camped on the Malheur River. A war party of our brave and noble Cayuse and our neighbors, the Umatilla, were ready to attack the Shoshones. Our scouts peered over the bluffs with such cleverness and cunning, like Coyote.

"Oh, Great Spirit, our enemies are riding on elk!"

The end?
Some trails never end.

REFERENCES
Significant People

Beardy, Chief - Tenino tribe; tried to dissuade the Indians from the killings and was a friend during captivity.

Bewley, Lorinda & Crocket — brother and sister who stayed the winter with the Whitmans.

Bridger, Jim, and Mary Ann — famous mountain man and his daughter put in the care of the Whitmans.

Camaspelo, Chief (Big Belly or Great Heart by Lorinda) - Cayuse chief on the headwaters of the Umatilla who brought Lorinda to and from Five Crows lodge.

Catholic Priests at St. Anne Mission - Bishop Blanchet and Father Brouillet

Clark — Son of Tiloukaikt, killed by Joe Lewis

Edward — Son of Tiloukaikt, also killed by Joe Lewis

Eells, Rev. Cushing & Myra — came with the first reinforcements to the mission, assigned to Tshimakian with the Walkers near present-day Colville, Idaho.

Feathercap (Wap-tash-tak-mahl), father of Tamsucky.

Five Crows (Five Ravens, Achekaia) - Cayuse chief on the Umatilla. He was appointed to the high chieftaincy when his brother did not accept after White's laws were accepted. Christened by Spalding. Had Lorinda taken to his camp after the killings at Waiilatpu.

Gray, Joe – half Iroquois who helped to instigate the attack.

Gray, Rev. William & Mary – William traveled with Whitman party to Oregon. Helped build the Emigrant House. Caused trouble for Whitman and Spalding.

Greene, Rev. David - Secretary for the American Board of Commission for Foreign Missions.

Hinman, Alanson – brutal schoolteacher at the mission.

Jack (also referred to as John) – Hawaiian who worked with the Whitmans for many years.

Lewis, Joe - mixed blood who said Whitman was poisoning the Cayuse.

Maki, Joseph & Maria – Hawaiian missionaries at Waiilatpu.

McBean, William –succeeded McKinlay as chief trader at Ft. Walla Walla.

McKay, Thomas - long-term Hudson's Bay Company employee, interpreter for White, government agent. His daughter Margaret lived with the Whitmans to attend school.

McKinlay, Archibald - retired as manager of Ft. Walla Walla.

McLeod, John – Hudson Bay leader who escorted Whitman's across plains.

Meek, Joe – mountain man who rode with Whitmans on their journey. He left his daughter Helen Mar with Whitmans and was appointed as U.S. Marshall guarding the Cayuse who surrendered.

Ogden, Peter Skene - Chief factor at Ft. Vancouver and negotiated for the release of the hostages at Waiilatpu and Lorinda Bewley at Umatilla.

Parker - Rev. Samuel - explored for a mission for the American Board. Sent by the Board to solicit funds and recruit missionaries for the projected missions.

Pambrun, Pierre - chief trader and Ft. Walla Walla. Died after a fall from his horse.

Peu-peu-mox-mox – Also Yellow Serpent.

Prentiss Family - mother and father: Judge Stephen & Mrs.; siblings in birth order: Stephen, Harvey, Narcissa, Jonas, Jane, Mary Ann, Harriett, Edward, and Clarissa.

Rogers, Cornelius - interpreter; worked at Waiilatpu.

Rogers, Andrew –schoolteacher at the mission.

Ross, Alexander - Built Ft. Walla Walla with Donald McKenzie.

Sager Family - mother and father: Henry & Naomi; children in birth order – John, Frank (Francis), Catherine, Elizabeth, Matilda, Hannah Louisa (who was called Louisa), and Henrietta.

Saunders, Mary – Captive whose husband was killed. She helped the children and was considered brave by the Sager children.

Shaw, Captain – wagon master during the Bewley's' journey on the trail.

Stickus (Istukus) - Half Cayuse and Nez Perce. Narrator of "Earth" and a good friend to Whitmans.

Spalding Family – Henry, his wife Eliza & daughter Eliza. Accompanied the Whitmans overland and built a mission at Lapwai.

Tackensuatis or Rotten Belly – Nez Perce Chief who escorted the Spaldings to Lapwai.

Tamsucky or Feathercap (Tomsucky, Tum-suc-kie) – lived at Waiilatpu. His son, called Waie-Cat, may have been responsible for the grist mill burning. Blamed for the attempted attack on Narcissa. Played a part in the killings. Raped Lorinda

Tawatoe – Also called Young Chief, brother of Five Crows.

Tiloukaikt (Teloukaitk Telequoit) - Chief at Waiilatpu. Succeeded Chief Uptippe. Sons were Edward & Clark.

Tomahas (Tomah Hash, Tamahas, Tau-mau-lish, To-ma-kas) lived at Waiilatpu, considered the one who killed Dr. Whitman.

Umtippe - Cayuse chief at Waiilatpu when Whitmans arrived. Found Alice Clarissa in the river.

Walker, Rev. Elkanah & Mary — came with first reinforcements to the mission. They were assigned to Tshimakain with the Eells near present day Colville, Idaho.

White, Elijah — assigned as government agent for the Indians. He presented the first American-written laws to the Nez Perce and Cayuse.

Whitman, Perrin - nephew of Marcus Whitman, referred to as an adopted son by Narcissa. He came with his uncle in the first massive Oregon migration at age fourteen. Later Perrin married Samuel Parker's daughter, and they lived in Idaho, where he was an interpreter at Indian schools and a respected businessman.

Whitman Family - Marcus & Narcissa; natural child Alice Clarissa. Children raised as their own:
1840 Helen Mar Meek, daughter of Joe Meek
1841 Mary Ann Bridger, daughter of Jim Bridger
1842 David Cortez renamed David Malin
1843 the seven Sager children & Perrin Whitman

Young Chief (Tawatoe or Tauitau) - Brother of Five Crows at Umatilla.

Young, Daniel – traveled in the caravan with Lorinda Bewley across the trail and stayed at the mission with his family who operated the sawmill.

Some Trails Never End

Significant Places
(Also, see map on page 1)

Fort Vancouver – the headquarters of the Hudson's Bay Company at present-day Vancouver, Washington, north of Portland, Oregon.

Kamiah – the Smith's station in Nez Perce territory, east of Lapwai, in present-day Lewis County, Idaho, bordering Idaho, County

Lapwai – near present-day Lewiston, where the Spaldings established their mission in Nez Perce territory

Umatilla (as referred to in this book) – home of Five Crows and his brother Tawatoe, where St. Anne's mission was established for a short time. Located 25 miles south of Waiilatpu on the Umatilla River.

Waskopum – near present-day The Dalles, Oregon, was a Methodist mission.

Waiilatpu – about nine miles from present-day Walla Walla, Washington, where the Whitmans established their mission and a Cayuse band lived part of the year.

Terrie Biggs

Tshimakain – Walkers & Eells station among the Spokane tribe in present-day south-central Washington in Yakima County near Colville.

People at the Mission When Attacked

Captives 47, 74 total people at the time of the incident, plus Stanfield

14 Killed, including the drowning of Hall - 11 men, 1 woman, 2 children
3 Died in captivity--all children
6 Escaped--2 men, 1 woman, 3 children
5 Released--3 mixed-blood boys, 2 mixed-blood adult males
47 Captives, including Stanfield--5 men, 8 women, 34 children

Killed

Marcus and Narcissa
John & Francis Sager
Jacob Hoffman
Isaac Gilliland, tailor
Judge Saunders
Nathan Kimball - 2nd day
William Marsh - grinding wheat at the mill

Died after initial incident in order of deaths

James Young (brother of Daniel) - 2nd day delivered lumber to mission from a nearby sawmill.

Andrew Rogers - At the river, getting a pail of water when the shooting began. He was shot through the wrist and tomahawked behind the ear.

Crockett Bewley A week later: (Lorinda's brother)

Amos Sales - a young man traveling with the Bewleys and stayed at the mission.

Peter Hall - escaped but may have drowned while crossing the Columbia at the Upper Falls is listed as the fourteenth victim.

Died of measles From Dec. 5th to 10th

Hanna Louisa Sager, age 6, December 5

Helen Mar Meek, age 10, daughter of Joe Meek, died on the 8th

Napoleon Hays, an infant died on the 9th.

Tried and Hung

Clokamas
Ish-ish-kais-kais (Frank Escaloom)
Kai-ma-sumpkin
Tiloukaikt
Tomahas - reportedly killed Marcus Whitman and Crocket Bewley

Timeline

1802 – September 4, Marcus Whitman born

1806 – March 14, Narcissa Prentiss born

1835 – February, Narcissa met Marcus at Prentiss house

1836 – February 18, Marcus and Narcissa were married
February 19, newlyweds left Rushville, NY
March 3, departed for Oregon
December 10, Narcissa arrived at Waiilatpu
after 295 days, and 2500 miles

1837 – March 14, Alice Clarissa was born

1838 - July 11, Narcissa received her first mail from home
August, Reinforcements arrived at Waiilatpu

1842 – October 3, Marcus left for the states
October 6, attempted attack on Narcissa

1843 – March 21, Marcus arrived in Washington, D.C.
May 22, Marcus and Perrin join the first wagon
Migration to Oregon
September 25, Marcus arrived at Lapwai to help the
Spaldings
November 4, Marcus reunited with Narcissa at Fort
Walla Walla to bring his family home.

1844 – April, the Sager family start for Oregon
October, the Sager children are delivered to Narcissa

1845 – June, Marcus became the Sager children's legal guardian

1847 – November 29, the attack at the mission
December 29, the captives were released

1850 – June 3, the "convicted" Cayuse are hanged

Bibliography & Reference Sources

Drury, Clifford M., *Marcus and Narcissa Whitman and the Opening of Old Oregon, Volumes I & II,* Northwest Interpretive Association, 1994

Frazier, Neta Lohnes, *Stout-Hearted Seven, The True Adventure of the Sager Children Orphaned on the Oregon Trail in 1844,* Northwest Interpretive Association, 1984

Helm, Myra Sager, *Lorinda Bewley and the Whitman Massacre,* Pacific Northwest Interpretive Association, 1984

How Can One buy the Air? Chief Seattle's Vision, Native Voices, the Book Publishing Company, 1992

Hunt Bonnie Jo & Lawrence J. Hunt, *Cayuse Country,* by Bonnie Jo, Mad Bear Press 1999

Hunt, Philip Mulkey, *Lorinda Bewley – Pioneer Woman, Victim of Violence,* Published by the Lorinda Project, An Oregon Nonprofit Organization, Portland, Oregon

Jesset, Thomas E., *The Indian Side of the Whitman Massacre,* Ye Galleon Press 1973

Landeen, Dan & Pinkham, Alan, *Salmon and His People, Fish & Fishing in Nez Perce Culture,* Confluence Press, 1999

Lansing, Robert B, *Juggernaut: The Whitman Massacre Trial, 1850,* Ninth Judicial Historical Society, 1993

The Letters of Narcissa Whitman, 1836-1847, Ye Galleon Press, 1986

Marshall, Joseph M., III, *The Journey of Crazy Horse: A Lakota History,* Viking, 2004

Peltier, Jerome, *Madam Dorion*, Ye Balleon Press (no date)

Ruby, Robert & John Brown, *The Cayuse Indian, Imperial Tribesmen of Old Oregon*, Pacific Northwest National Parks & Forest Association, 1992

Sager, Catherine, Elizabeth & Matilda, *The Whitman Massacre of 1847*

Stern, Theodore, *Cayuse, Umatilla, and Walla Walla*

Stories That Make the World, Real Literature of the Indian People of the Inland Northwest, as told by Lawrence Aripa, Tom Yellowtail, and Other Elders, compiled by Ken Nerburnh, Ph.D. & Louise Mangelkoch, M.A., The Classic Wisdom Collection, 1991

Thompson, Erwin N., *Shallow Grave at Waiilatpu*. The Sager's West

Victor, Frances Fuller, *The River of the West, The Adventures of Joe Meek, Volume One, The Mountain Years*, Mountain Press Publishing Company, 1983

Internet & Miscellaneous Sources

Adventures of the First Settlers on the Oregon or Columbia River, reprint of the original edition, London 1849, www.rosen.xmission.com

Excerpts and copies from Catherine Sager Pringle's scrapbook at the Whitman College archives, Walla Walla, Washington

Manuscripts from Tamastslikt Cultural Institute archives, Pendleton, Oregon

Mountain Men, broadcast on the History Channel

Stonee's Lore, Legends, and Teachings, www.ilhawaii.net

Traditional Scottish Songs, Canadian Boat Song www.rampantscottland.com

Washington Irving's Astoria, on-line at www.rosen.xmission.com

The Whitman Killings, November 29, 1847, Whitman Mission National Historic Site, www.nps.gov/whim/history

Women of the Fur Trade 1774-1821, www.northwestjourne.ca

About the author

Yes, an earlier glamor shot

For a CD of music in the book from "Voices from the Oregon Trail" by The Trail Band, visit http://www.trailband.com. Terrie Biggs has been writing creative non-fiction for years. She lives in La Grande, Oregon, with her husband, Dan. Their four children are adults. She has a lifetime passion for kitchen design and owns her own business, Kitchens by Terrie. Her books are also in the Amazon Kindle store.

Check her out at
http://www.novelsbyterrie.com
or visit her "Terrie Biggs" page on Amazon
See progress and updates on Novels by Terrie Facebook page

Please take the time to do a review on Amazon because you can inspire hundreds of readers. I encourage comments or corrections.
Email: novelsbyterrie@gmail.com

Other Books by Terrie

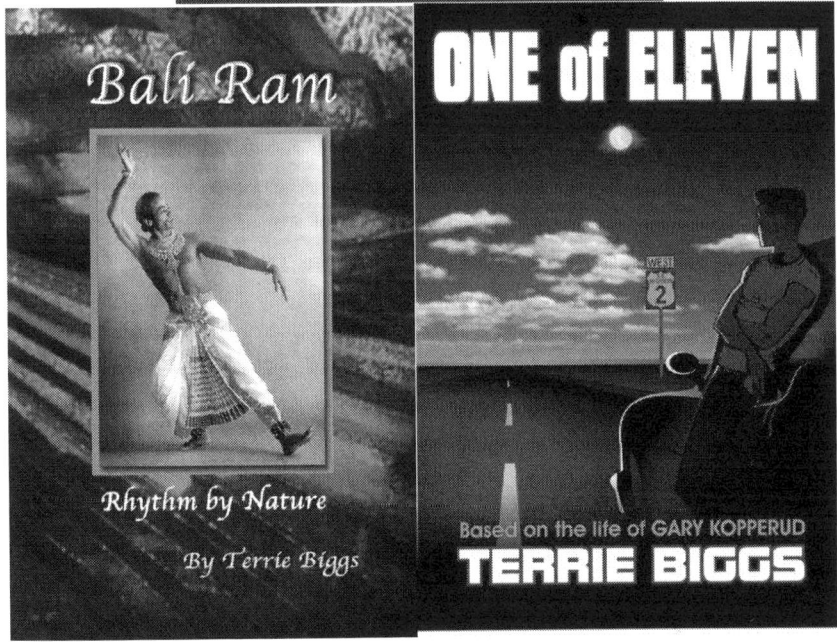

Terrie Biggs

Made in the USA
Middletown, DE
07 June 2023

32196635R00210